LOVE

MAKES A FAMILY

LOVE
MAKES A FAMILY

Portraits of Lesbian, Gay, Bisexual,
and Transgender Parents and Their Families

Photographs by Gigi Kaeser & Edited by Peggy Gillespie
Foreword by Minnie Bruce Pratt
Introduction by Kath Weston
Afterword by April Martin

UNIVERSITY OF MASSACHUSETTS PRESS AMHERST

Publication of this book was made possible by a grant from the Tsunami Foundation

This book is based in part on the exhibit entitled *Love Makes a Family: Living in Lesbian and Gay Families*, exhibit text © 1995 by Peggy Gillespie and Pam Brown, exhibit photographs © 1995 Gigi Kaeser

Designed by Coni Porter, Fitzwilliam, NH
Photographs printed by Geoffrey Bluh
Typeset in Sabon
Printed and bound by C & C Offset Printing Co. Ltd.

Library of Congress Cataloging-in-Publication Data
Kaeser, Gigi.
    Love makes a family : portraits of lesbian, gay, bisexual, and transgender parents and their families / photographs by Gigi Kaeser ; edited by Peggy Gillespie ; foreword by Minnie Bruce Pratt ; introduction by Kath Weston ; afterword by April Martin.
        p.   cm.
    Includes bibliographical references.
    ISBN 1-55849-160-0 (cloth : alk. paper). — ISBN 1-55849-161-9 (pbk. : alk. paper)
    1. Gay fathers—Interviews.   2. Gay fathers—Portraits.
3. Lesbian mothers—Interviews.   4. Lesbian mothers—Portraits.
5. Bisexual parents—Interviews.   6. Bisexual parents—Portraits.
7. Transsexual parents—Interviews.   8. Transsexual parents—Portraits.   9. Children of gay parents—Interviews.   10. Children of gay parents—Portraits.   I. Title.
HQ76.13.K34   1999
306.874—dc21   98-30266

British Library Cataloguing in Publication data are available.

To Jean Beard, extraordinary friend and exceptional colleague

— *PEGGY GILLESPIE*

To my husband, Jim Maraniss, and our children, Ben, Lucia, and Elliott

— *GIGI KAESER*

CONTENTS

Family Album

Minnie Bruce Pratt

I have a thin stack of photographs from my fiftieth birthday party. This morning I've drawn them from a crumpled white envelope to look at them for the first time since that evening. I've delayed looking—the weight the pictures carry is heavy.

That night there were flowers, candles, jazz, blues, and salsa, party favors that uncurled like snakes, and a huge sugary cake. My two beautiful grown sons and I and my beloved Leslie gathered with friends in an echoing room. There I usually sat at long tables in political meetings, shoulder to shoulder with others, listening, talking, our hands busy stuffing envelopes for the next demonstration. But that night the room was transformed with balloons, streamers, banners—and photographs everywhere. Leslie had set up tall cardboard stands with pictures documenting my "fifty years of love and struggle."

At the center were pictures of me and my sons. Each of them as a newborn—in these I am only a pair of hands, an edge of face and hair. Them at seven and eight, sitting knee to knee on top of my VW bug—I am standing by the open car door, one hand turning nervously against the other. I'm about to drive the children back to their father, who wrested custody of them from me. He has had me declared an unfit mother, because I am a lesbian.

In all the pictures of us together we are smiling. There are no snapshots of the moments of terrible pain—the images that flash through memory over and over, like a home movie of agony. *In my rearview mirror I see them behind me as I drive away from their new home. They are crying,* *running a little after me, then standing still, their hands falling defeated beside them.*

Perhaps every family album has these private pictures, the stories we try to guess at from a few hidden whispers and the grief-struck eyes above someone's smiling mouth.

That night there were other pictures of me. As teacher —in academic robes at commencement; with my pecan pie at a supper I organized for students in my class on lesbian culture. As writer—with other women in an editorial collective as we lean over page proofs, standing alone to read from one of my books; at an anti-right-wing demonstration where one of my erotic poems has been turned into a placard. With friends at an anniversary of the March on Washington for Civil Rights. And being arrested, with some of the same friends, and hundreds of others, in civil disobedience at the Supreme Court, protesting the decision that our love is a "crime against nature."

That night the photographs showed a humane, creative, justice-loving life that the current law of the land would keep separate from "the children"—my children, all children. But the pictures of the three of us together are still at the center of my years.

This is the family album of one of the many of us who have been told we are not fit to have a family, told that we can stay in the family only if we are quiet and invisible, told not to "flaunt" our life, not to make a scene. This is the family album of one of the many of us who have said, "The old definition of family is too small for us and our children.

Not for us the *familias* based in laws of property, where *family* means the unfree members of the household, the women, the children, the servants, and the slaves."

One June day, in his teenage years, my oldest called to talk about a video he'd just seen on public television, a documentary about gay families. I said to him, "You know, I've never asked how you've felt about my being a lesbian, how you think it's affected you." And he said, "Your being a lesbian didn't affect me. What hurt me was not being able to have you with me."

My story is but one of many, that of a woman who mothered her children almost in isolation for years. Who struggled to hold them as a family even though the law decreed that they could not even enter her home if she shared it with another adult. Who strove to teach them connection to the forbidden others in her life, those who might give them a new kind of family, a different kind of world, where no people would lose their family because of hatred against how they love or the color of their skin, because of their despised femaleness or their poverty.

Today I turn to the photographs of my party after a more recent conversation with my children about *family*. Do they think of themselves now as my sons? In my relationship with Leslie, as our sons? Do they see themselves within a larger extended family like that gathered in my festive birthday room?

I look at the pictures for clues to begin another of the conversations, lifelong, that I hold with my children about who we are together, in a world where powerful malign forces work to break us apart.

I unfold the creased envelope. The pictures from that birthday night show the four of us standing awkwardly together. One son smiles but looks down; the other frowns, turned inward. My smile is tense, Leslie's face is drawn and tired from a recent illness.

Yet beyond that snapshot are moments when we are smiling. The four of us piling into a car later that night, crammed in with presents, cards, chrysanthemums, and cake, laughing giddily that we are like a clown car in the circus, like a party ready to burst out when a door opens, everything in hand that we need for another feast.

I hold the pictures that show we are here together. We have fought to claim our lives with each other despite years that we have been physically, forcibly, separated. Despite years of no words to explain to others what we are to each other. How—despite what law, custom, religion may say— we are heart of each others' hearts.

Peggy Gillespie

A family is a bunch of people, or not so many, who love each other.

— *LIZA MACKENZIE STYLES, AGE 7*

Family means two different things to me.

One is the family of my birth. . . . I've also built a completely separate family,

which includes my lover, Alix, our son, Wolf, our Daddy donor, Dan, Wolf's godmother, Claudia, and GrandMary.

We've constructed a family . . . of people who have become related by dint of having a child together. . . .

At this point, Wolf's real proud that he's got Mama and Mama.

— *DOROTHY ALLISON*

The activism and increasing visibility of lesbian, gay, bisexual, and transgender (LGBT) people has led to a full-fledged gay civil rights movement during the past two decades. In just the past few years, many well-known gay people have appeared in the media spotlight. Actress Ellen DeGeneres came out in the most public way possible, melding her television sitcom character's life with her own emergence from the closet amid great hoopla and controversy. Pop superstar Melissa Etheridge appeared on the cover of *Time* magazine as a proud prospective lesbian mother during her partner's pregnancy. Kevin Jennings, executive director of the Gay, Lesbian, and Straight Educators, Network (GLSEN), who has worked to make schools safer for LGBT teachers, students, and families, was named to *Newsweek's* list of one hundred people to watch as America prepares to enter the next millennium. Many workplaces and towns nationwide decided to offer domestic partnership benefits to same-sex couples, such as health insurance, that traditionally have been reserved for married heterosexuals. In a landmark case in 1997, a New Jersey Superior Court judge ruled that a gay couple, Jon and Michael Galluccio, could coadopt their foster son. This made New Jersey the first state in the nation to determine that homosexual partners are as qualified to be parents as married heterosexuals.

In that same year, Senator Bob Kerrey of Nebraska spoke out in favor of same-sex marriage, arguing, "Marriage is not under attack from rising numbers of homosexual Americans who are making commitments to each other. Marriage is under attack in that moment when a man or woman is tempted to forget their commitment to love 'until death do us part.' Divorce—not same-sex marriage—is the No. 1 enemy of marriage." And ten-year-old Sol Kelley-Jones, the daughter of two lesbian mothers, was given the Young Activist Award by the ACLU for speaking out against homophobia during legislative hearings in Wisconsin.

Despite significant advances in gay rights, the proliferation of anti-gay amendments and referendums, stemming from a combination of fundamentalist religious fervor and right-wing conservative politics, makes it clear that there still is a great deal of work to be accomplished. On February 8, 1998, the *New York Times Sunday Magazine* published an article by Alan Wolfe, a Boston University professor, entitled "The Homosexual Exception: A New Study Shows that Suburban Americans Are Surprisingly Tolerant—of Everyone but Gay Men and Lesbians." According to Wolfe:

> If there is one commandment to which Americans pay homage, it is the one formulated by a 34-year-old stay-at-home mother from Sand Springs, Oklahoma: "Thou shalt not judge."
>
> All of which makes the negative judgments of so many respondents [in our study] on homo-sexuality so striking. Four times as many people we spoke with condemned homosexuals as were willing to offer them positive acceptance. Some simply refused to discuss the subject, as if the mere mention of the word would violate their religious beliefs. Others responded with nervous laughter or an obvious desire to change the topic as quickly as possible. Still others, ever

> reluctant to use a word that implies a judgment about someone else's behavior, had no trouble finding these words, all of which cropped up in my interviews when the subject of homosexuality was raised: "abnormal," "immoral," "sinful," "unacceptable," "sick," "unhealthy," "untrustworthy," "mentally ill," "wrong," "perverted" and "mentally deficient." In all likelihood, Americans are less homophobic than they were before the gay rights revolution, but middle-class Americans have not come to the conclusion that homosexuality represents an alternative that is the moral equal of any other.

Echoing these unsettling sentiments, the people of Maine recently voted by a small margin to repeal the gay rights law in their state, thus legalizing discrimination against gays once again. In a 50-49 vote, the U.S. Senate rejected a bill outlawing job discrimination against gays. In 1993, a juvenile court judge in Virginia awarded custody of lesbian mother Sharon Bottoms's son, Tyler, to Bottoms's mother, who claimed that Bottoms was unfit to raise her son because of her sexual orientation. The state appeals court reversed the decision in 1994, but a divided Virginia Supreme Court reinstated it, ruling that growing up in a gay household could subject Tyler to "social condemnation." In March 1998, a circuit judge extended Ms. Bottoms's visitation rights with Tyler by a few days, but continued a ban on contact between the boy and his mother's lover. Similarly, a judge in Florida shifted custody from a child's lesbian mother to her ex-husband, who had been previously jailed for the murder of his first wife. The judge declared that the child ought to be raised in a "non-lesbian world."

During the past few years, the Hawaii Supreme Court has been wrestling with the pros and cons of legalizing same-sex marriage. The court could rule any day, but the Hawaii legislature is trying to pass a law specifying that marriage is between one man and one woman in order to prevent the enforcement of a pro-gay marriage decision by the court. Anticipating that Hawaii might approve same-sex marriages, the U.S. Congress passed the Defense of Marriage Act in 1996 which denies federal recognition of same-sex marriages. The act easily won in the Senate by a vote of 85-14 and in the House of Representatives by a vote of 342-67. While campaigning for reelection in 1996, President Clinton said he had long opposed governmental recognition of same-sex marriages. Publicly proclaiming his deeply held belief in the sanctity of traditional heterosexual marriage, he speedily signed the Defense of Marriage Act into law on September 20, 1996.

The general public as well as many of our most powerful political leaders holds tenaciously to the idea that LGBT people do not deserve legal protection from job and housing discrimination. A majority of Americans still believe that gays should not be allowed to defend our country's ideals of democracy and equality in the military. Hate crimes and acts of violence against gays are on the rise, the most recent being the brutal murder of Matthew Shepard, a student at the University of Wyoming. The high incidence of suicides by gay youth tragically reflects this atmosphere of intolerance and fear.

Epithets such as "dyke," "faggot," and "you're so gay" are often the insults of choice among school-age children. Although school personnel usually respond swiftly to the use of racial slurs, anti-gay language is often routinely ignored and even tolerated in many schools and other public settings. Institutionalized homophobia also prevents many children of gays and lesbians from sharing personal information about their family structure with their friends. Fearing ridicule of their parents' sexual orientation, many students with LGBT parents are also afraid of being called gay themselves.

Interviews with students confirm these observations. Teenager Eric DeMarco Benjamin spoke about his painful encounters with prejudice and homophobia:

Growing up with lesbian moms wasn't easy. Some kids teased me and tried to beat me up. They thought that I was gay just because my parents are. . . . Still, sometimes, I don't tell people about my family. It's hard to bring girlfriends home because I don't know how they will react. Despite this, I'm really proud of my family. . . . I hope that someday gay people will have as many rights as everyone else.

Sixteen-year-old Rayna White, an African American daughter of a lesbian mother, pointed to the similarity between the current laws banning gay marriage and the anti-miscegenation laws that were overturned in 1967 by the Supreme Court. Rayna told us:

My grandpa majored in biology in college, but he wasn't allowed to teach at a high school because he was black. Not long ago, I spoke on a panel at a high school with my mom. This guy in the audience told my mom that he wouldn't want her to teach his kids because she is a lesbian. It reminded me so much of what happened to my grandpa. I think homophobia is like any other "ism." It's the racism of today. Like racism, you learn it from the people you grow up with, from your parents, from television, from society.

Ashley Watson, the ten-year-old daughter of a gay father, said that she wished her peers would be better educated about gay people and not hold to stereotypes and misinformation. "Kids in my old school teased me," Ashley said, "because they didn't know the full definition of 'gay.' I don't really blame them, but I hope someday that kids will understand what 'gay' really means."

Children with concerns like those of Ashley, Rayna, and Eric stirred our interest in LGBT families and the struggles they face in our society. In 1993, Gigi Kaeser and I created a photo-text exhibit entitled "Of Many Colors: Portraits of Multiracial Families." Gigi photographed and I interviewed forty multiracial families, all of whom shared with us the impact of racism on their lives. Some of the families in this exhibit were headed by gay or lesbian parents. We heard stories from these parents about their children who not only faced challenges related to their family's racial background, but who also had to deal with homophobia on a regular basis.

In order to help make schools and communities safer for lesbian, gay, bisexual, and transgender individuals and their families and to educate the public about the diversity of family life in America, Gigi and I decided to create a second photo-text exhibit that would focus entirely on families with LGBT members—mothers and fathers, grandparents, and teenagers. We applied for a grant from the Massachusetts Cultural Council and began to work on this project, soon adding a third person, Pam Brown, to the project staff. We entitled this new photo-text exhibit, "Love Makes a Family: Living in Lesbian and Gay Families."

The process of creating the exhibit involved several steps. First, we contacted local friends who were willing to be in the exhibit and followed their leads to find other families. Then we advertised in lesbian and gay newspapers and newsletters in New England and the New York area. After selecting a group of families as racially, economically, ethnically, and structurally diverse as possible, we began the process of photographing and interviewing them. Family members were usually interviewed together so that individual members could hear each other's responses and could converse back and forth. When children or teenagers were interviewed, however, these interviews were often conducted in private so the kids would feel freer to talk. With very young or shy children, we asked the parents to pose a few simple questions to their children and write down or tape the answers.

After completing the interviews, two versions of the text were created: one was age-appropriate for elementary school students and the other was edited with older students and adults in mind. The edited text was then sent back to the families for their approval. Changes, additions, or deletions by family members were welcomed in order to preserve the authentic voice of each participant and to make sure the facts were correct. Many families made no changes, others changed just a few words or corrected information, and a few made more extensive changes.

In 1993, the Massachusetts Governor's Commission on Gay and Lesbian Youth reported: "For many gay and lesbian students, school is not a place of learning, but a place where they feel profoundly isolated, sometimes even suicidal; a place where they are abused and terrorized by violence for being different." As a result of this report, which noted that one-third of all teen suicides are committed by gay youth, Massachusetts passed a law mandating that schools be made safe for all youth regardless of sexual orientation. The commission developed a set of Safe School guidelines to protect gay youth and the children of gays and lesbians from harassment and abuse. In May 1995, "Love Makes a Family: Living in Lesbian and Gay Families" made its public debut at the Peabody Elementary School, a public school in Cambridge, Massachusetts. Peabody School principal Ellen Varella hoped that presenting the exhibit would be an initial step in meeting the state's newly created Safe School guidelines. In spite of some controversy, the exhibit was successfully displayed at the Peabody School where it was filmed by Debra Chasnoff and Helen Cohen for *It's Elementary*, their award-winning documentary about teaching gay issues in elementary schools. After that, it began touring the nation.

In the winter of 1996, the discussion of whether four elementary schools in Amherst, Massachusetts, would show "Love Makes a Family: Living in Lesbian and Gay Families" grew into a highly rancorous public debate. These four schools had already shown our first exhibit, "Of Many Colors," without any controversy whatsoever. When each of the school principals finally decided to display "Love Makes a Family," the debate escalated into a nationally publicized court case. Five local families sued the superintendent of schools and the principals in an attempt to prevent the exhibit from being shown, on the grounds that it would "sexually harass" their young children. A Federal Court judge quickly dismissed their attempted injunction, citing the First Amendment in defense of free speech. The exhibit was hung for two weeks in each school without incident.

In response to viewing "Love Makes a Family: Living in Lesbian and Gay Families" in his school, one Amherst child was overheard saying, "What's the big deal? They're just families." A fifth-grader wrote in a guestbook, "I really liked how you showed that people in gay, lesbian, and bisexual families are no different than anyone else." A fourth-grader wrote, "I didn't know much about being gay or lesbian until I read some of the exhibits. It is interesting that so many people love others of the same sex. I'm glad there are people willing to take a chance in this world." My favorite comment was by a feisty sixth-grader who wrote a challenge to the adults in his school and community: "The way you feel is the way you feel. No one can change that. All people were created equal. Remember?"

In June 1996, Gigi Kaeser and I founded a nonprofit organization, Family Diversity Projects, Inc. (FDP). Our work since then has included the creation of two new exhibits: "In Our Family: Portraits of All Kinds of Families" and "Nothing to Hide: Mental Illness in the Family." Family Diversity Projects distributes multiple copies of these exhibits as well as "Of Many Colors: Portraits of Multiracial Families" and "Love Makes a Family: Lesbian, Gay, Bisexual, and Transgender People and Their Families" to schools, colleges, mental health centers, public libraries, museums, workplaces, houses of worship, conferences, pride festivals, and community centers nationally and inter-

nationally from Alaska to Florida to Germany. Everywhere the exhibits have appeared under the auspices of FDP, people have written to us asking that we put together books on these topics. In 1997, the University of Massachusetts Press published our book *Of Many Colors* about multiracial families, and then decided to publish this book as well.

Love Makes a Family: Portraits of Lesbian, Gay, Bisexual, and Transgender Parents and Their Families differs from the original exhibit in significant ways. The exhibit includes gay teenagers and their parents; however, Gigi and I chose to limit this volume to LGBT parents and their children. Six of the families from the exhibit are not included in the book, and eighteen families from across the United States have been added. Gigi photographed and I interviewed these additional families in order to incorporate a broader range of family structures and geographic and racial diversity than was represented in the original exhibit. I have reedited all of the original exhibit text for style and content, and once again, the families were offered the opportunity to review their revised text. I also reinterviewed several families to reflect their current situations. I have compiled an up-to-date resource guide and bibliography. Essays by three authors known for their writings about the issues of LGBT parenting are included in this book to offer readers additional perspectives.

The families you will meet in this book were not selected using scientific methods, nor are they intended to represent all LGBT families. Far from it. They are simply brave people willing to tell their stories to the world. Most of these families are relatively happy, stable, and loving. Not unlike heterosexual families, they face day-to-day difficulties and struggles. For all the controversy they engender, these families are living ordinary lives. As Doug Robinson, a gay father of two young sons, put it, "Our family life is a very traditional American family life—early morning getting up, eating breakfast, getting dressed, making sure everyone has matching socks, getting the boys off to school, and then going to work. At night, it's homework and getting ready for bed."

Having interviewed more than forty families headed by LGBT parents, I would like to extend an invitation. I'd like political leaders, anti-gay activists, and ordinary citizens who wouldn't describe themselves as homophobic but still believe that growing up in a gay household is not the healthiest environment for children to take the time to meet just one of the families in this book and look at them in a "different way," as young Ashley Watson hopes you might do. Go into their home, listen to their voices, look into their faces as they look at each other and out at you, meet their relatives and pets, and see for yourself what is at the core of their family values. If one family doesn't convince you, please turn the page and meet another family. I don't think you can deny that what you are seeing, hearing, and sensing in these family portraits is love. It may sound corny, but it's true. Love does make a family.

I agree with *Detroit Free Press* columnist Deb Price:

"Regardless of the route children take into this world, they do need one particular kind of family once they arrive: a loving one." Love alone, however, does not mitigate the complex issues facing LGBT-parented families. The adverse impact of homophobia is what distinguishes these families from heterosexual families. *Love Makes a Family: Portraits of Lesbian, Gay, Bisexual, and Transgender Parents and Their Families* is a testimony to the strength, courage, and dignity of all LGBT parents who strive to create a safer world for their children in a society that makes their families invisible at best and illegal and criminal at worst. This book is meant to honor these families, and Gigi and I hope that it will be of some help to them in their continuing struggle for legal recognition and equality.

October 1998
Amherst, Massachusetts

ACKNOWLEDGMENTS

Above all, we want to express our gratitude to each and every member of the families in this book. It took extraordinary courage and commitment to "come out" in such a public way, and we want to acknowledge your bravery and your willingness to stand up for all LGBT-parented families. Thank you for being such shining examples of real "family values."

We gratefully acknowledge the generosity and unwavering support of the Tsunami Foundation, which made the publication of this book possible. We hope that its goal to "make a difference" will be realized in this book.

For extensive editorial help, we especially want to thank Jean J. Beard, who, with endless patience, astonishing energy, creativity, relentless determination to find just the "right word," and a peregrine falcon's eye for detail, made major contributions to the final text of this book.

Our special thanks to Geoff Bluh for printing the photographs and for good advice all along.

Leslie Hoffman, a consultant on equity issues and formerly the Western Massachusetts Safe Schools Coordinator for the State Department of Education often speaks on behalf of Family Diversity Projects. She has offered us her wisdom and enthusiastic support, and we are grateful for her help and friendship. We also wish to thank Diane Fernald and Drew Epstein for their legal expertise and advice. Pat and Peter Schneider of Amherst Writers and Artists deserve thanks, too, for their long-term encouragement and fiscal sponsorship. For her overall help with Family Diversity Projects, we wish to thank Rose Evans, whose multiple skills and willingness to do anything gave us time to focus on this book. In addition, Rose helped organize and put together the resource guide section in this book. Our appreciation goes to Lauren Bristol who did a thorough job proofreading and helping to reedit the exhibit text for this book. We appreciate our grant writer, Sharon Varditira of Meridian Consulting in Amherst, Massachusetts. She has used her talent to put our plans and hopes into words that have enabled Family Diversity Projects to get the grants we need to continue our work. And we wish to thank our new administrative assistant/writer, Rebekah Boyd, for her invaluable time and effort on our behalf, including her excellent editorial help as well as her help in researching and further updating the information in the resource guide and in organizing our office, no small task.

Greg Jones, a skilled and energetic arts producer, helped us raise needed funds by producing a benefit performance for our nonprofit organization, Family Diversity Projects, Inc. Choreographer/dancer Bill T. Jones and dancers Roz LeBlanc and Maya Saffrin from Bill T. Jones/ Arnie Zane Dance Company donated their time and immense talent to create this memorable benefit. We can't thank them enough for their caring and generosity.

The support of Family Diversity Projects Advisory Board continues to be invaluable. Jacqueline Bearce (Affirmative Action coordinator, Amherst Public Schools), Ellen Hofheimer Bettmann (director of Research and Development, Anti-Defamation League's A WORLD OF

DIFFERENCE Institute), Warren Blumenfeld (author and scholar), Virginia Casper (co-director, Early Intervention Program, Bank Street College of Education), Debra Chasnoff (director of the film *It's Elementary*), Kate Clinton (comedian and author), Helen Cohen (producer of the film *It's Elementary*), Ray Drew (executive director, Family Pride Coalition), Tim Fisher (former executive director, GLPCI), Mary Ann Grimm (Amherst Safe Schools Task Force member), Karen Harbeck (attorney and author), Anna and Molly Heller (COLAGE), Linda Heller (president, Family Pride Coalition), Kevin Jennings (executive director, GLSEN), Arthur Lipkin (author and educator), Stefan Lynch (former executive director, COLAGE), April Martin (author), Leslea Newman (author), Felicia Park-Rogers (executive director, COLAGE), Bonnie Tinker (executive director, Love Makes a Family, Inc.); and our youth Advisory Board members, Ekene Nwokoye, Liza MacKenzie Styles, and Ashley Watson.

We want to thank Bruce Wilcox and the staff of the University of Massachusetts Press for their skillful efforts on behalf of this book. We appreciate their professionalism, attention to detail, and interest in social justice.

For the creation of the exhibit "Love Makes a Family: Living in Lesbian and Gay Families," we acknowledge Pam Brown. She worked with us in interviewing many of the families in the original exhibit, editing the texts for the exhibit, writing some grant proposals, and helping to bring the exhibit into schools. We want to thank Beth Bellavance-Grace for her talented printing of some of the photographs in the original exhibit.

We also thank all the individuals and organizations who have helped and continue to help bring the exhibit into the public eye all over the world. Though you are far too numerous to mention individually, you know who you are. We do wish to call attention to Al Ferreira of Project 10 East; Mary Bonauto of GLAD (Gay and Lesbian Advocates and Defenders), who represented the exhibit in the lawsuit; John Guimond, who designs our promotional materials; Ann Whitall, our newest consultant; the members of the Amherst Gay and Lesbian Parents Group; the members of Valuable Families of Northampton, Massachusetts; Karen Bellavance-Grace, co-owner of Pride and Joy in Northampton; Amy Jacobson; Moko, a constant and dear friend; Richard Michelson and the staff of R. Michelson Galleries, especially Michael Ledgere; Kinko's of Northampton and Collective Copies in Amherst. Our special thanks go to the generous funders who made the creation and distribution of the exhibit possible: the Astraea National Lesbian Action Foundation; the Funding Exchange; the Out Fund; the Massachusetts Cultural Council—a State Agency; the Amherst and Northampton Arts Lottery councils; the Chicago Resource Center; and the Leo Wasserman Foundation. We also wish to acknowledge our most recent donor, the Gill Foundation, for its enthusiastic support for Family Diversity Project's ongoing work.

Peggy Gillespie and Gigi Kaeser,
Co-directors, Family Diversity Projects, Inc.

Peggy Gillespie wishes to thank her family members, Gregory Gillespie for his unwavering support of her work and her daughter, Jay, for her understanding and terrific suggestions. She wishes to thank her close friend Nan Niederlander for her enthusiasm and caring heart. She also wants to thank Caryn Markson for her wisdom and clarity. Peggy wants to acknowledge above all, Gigi Kaeser, for her clarity, sense of humor, honesty, and backbone throughout this unusual journey.

Gigi Kaeser thanks Peggy Gillespie for steering the ship and Jean Beard for providing a much-needed ballast.

LOVE
MAKES A FAMILY

Capturing More Than the Moment: Lesbian/Gay Families in the Making

INTRODUCTION

Kath Weston

"The thing is, I'm getting tired of taking my lover's pictures out of the album and editing all my slide shows." Simple words offered to explain one man's decision to come out to his parents. The removal of a photograph: a simple measure taken to protect relationships from disruption and change. Embedded in such simple measures are the intricate maneuvers required to shield any committed relationship from view. In this case, the man decided upon another deceptively simple act. He let the pictures stay. "Who's that?" his visiting parents asked, and photographs inevitably gave way to words. Their son might never have told them, "I'm gay," but he needed to say, "This is David. My partner, David. There's our friend Yvonne—she's over here all the time, just like family. And standing next to David is his daughter. She's five. Looks just like him, doesn't she? She calls him Dad; she calls me Papa."

Nothing works quite like a family album to sort out relationships, certify desire, and anchor meaning to reminiscence. As the pages turn, the questions mount, and stories generally follow. One way to read the photographs and interviews included here in *Love Makes a Family* is as a kind of composite album that narrates the centrality of family issues to queer politics as the century draws to a close. These are portraits of a decade in which the fight for gay marriage made national news. These are portraits of a decade in which the children of the lesbian baby boom enrolled in elementary school, then junior high. They are also portraits of a decade in which households headed by gay

men and lesbians came to occupy a key position in discussions of how families are changing across the United States (Mason et al. 1998, Peletz 1995, Stacey 1996).

Not so long ago, the thought of any kind of family album for people who identify themselves as lesbian, gay, bisexual, or transgender ("LGBT") would have struck many people as a contradiction in terms. Gay men and lesbians, it was often assumed, had to forego parenthood. Heterosexual parents worried that a lonely, childless life awaited their queer children. Even those with children from a previous marriage had to contend with the ever-present threat of a custody suit that could challenge their fitness to parent on the grounds of sexual identity alone.

Then, in the early 1980s, the winds began to shift. A number of developments brought to public attention the fact that LGBT people can and do, indeed, create families. Anti-gay diatribes by the religious right ironically served notice that queers were out there washing the breakfast dishes, paying the bills, and arguing over the kids' education, "just like" their heterosexual neighbors. Information about donor insemination began to be widely distributed up and down the coasts. LGBT people entered into a variety of coparenting agreements, sometimes with partners, sometimes without. Gay fathers and lesbian mothers organized support groups. Family friends arranged to take the kids for a weekend to give overworked parents a break. Dinnertime conversations in LGBT households drifted toward topics such as day care, diaper services, and the advisability of giving in to youthful demands for the "action figures" promoted at local toy stores.

Meanwhile, LGBT people went to court for the opportunity to become foster parents and to adopt. LGBT advocacy groups moved family issues to the top of their lists (Achtenberg 1990). How-to books for prospective parents cropped up in the "gay studies" and "gender studies" sections of bookstores.[1] Mixed groups of heterosexual and homosexual friends gathered around bassinets, aahing and oohing over little bundles in rompers. The most unlikely people suddenly felt the need to childproof their apartments. In time, the children of LGBT parents began to organize in their own right to discuss their experiences amongst themselves (see Rafkin 1990).

The majority of LGBT people, who for reasons as varied as themselves had elected not to have children, greeted the baby boom of the 1980s with mixed reviews. Some applauded the challenge that the baby boom seemed to represent to the popular prejudice against allowing homosexuals to come into contact with kids. Some immediately set about becoming uncle or auntie to the children of friends. Some kvetched about sidewalks choked with strollers or about old buddies who now spent all their time with the little ones at home. Many LGBT people of color, who had long argued that family ties were important to racial and ethnic identity, said "good riddance" to the historically anti-familia stance of certain "community" organizations (Muñoz 1996). A few people even talked about encountering new pressures to have children from their own parents, who had brightened up at the slightest suggestion that grandchildren might be in the offing.

Of course, children are not all that makes a family, and in any event, LGBT people had been having children all along. What made the 1980s and 1990s different was the way in which so many LGBT people laid claim to family as something they had and something they wanted. Sometimes they laid that claim by availing themselves of newly institutionalized technologies (donor insemination offering just one case in point). Sometimes they laid claim to family by gracing relationships of long standing with new names. Ex-lovers, the children of partners, and the closest of friends might all, under the right circumstances, come to be considered kin. In each instance, people worked to legitimize and legalize ties that gave meaning to their lives, knowing all the while that these were ties many people in the larger society still questioned.

If there is one issue that this ongoing struggle for legitimation brought to the fore, it is the issue of what makes a family. Does a family have to have two parents of different sexes, or are families made in the making? Is love required? Is love enough? What if people from different ethnic and class backgrounds mean different things by "love"?[2] Can a family span multiple households, with different members living in different locations? Can friends "really" be family? What about ex's? Do children need adults of the "opposite" sex around? What about differently gendered adults of the "same" sex (women who are sports-minded, women who wear nail polish, women who fix engines, and women who can cook)?

As the photographs in this collection testify, lesbian and gay families have come up with some ingenious, sometimes contentious, responses to what are, after all, questions that trouble a broad spectrum of people in the

---

[1.] A genre that widened during the 1990s to include paperbacks specifically targeted at lesbians and gay men (e.g., Clunis and Dorsey 1995; Martin 1994).

[2.] See Yanagisako (1985). On the diversity of family forms and conceptions of family among lesbians and gay men in the United States, see Allen and Demo (1995), Asten (1997), Lewin (1993, 1998), Nardi (1992), Sherman (1992), and Weston (1997). For a critical account of the increasing prominence accorded to family rhetoric and family issues within LGBT "communities," see Robson (1994).

United States. Nor have gay men and lesbians set about making their families in isolation. Their sisters make up a proportion of a growing number of single mothers; their parents have introduced them to the concept of blended families with each successive remarriage; their cousins struggle with the after-effects of divorce.

Gay families simultaneously ride the wave and swell the wave of recent changes to kinship in the United States.[3] But recognition for the familial character of the ties that many LGBT people create has not always followed, whether it be recognition on the part of coworkers, television audiences, or the state. And where recognition has followed, it generally has not come without a fight (Weston 1995).

Given the lack of social and legal standing accorded to gay families, it should not be surprising that the present book—like the national debate on what makes a family—focuses on family composition rather than the processes that create kinship. This is a book of family portraits, not a collection of "action shots" that propose to capture the look on the face of a parent who has just spent the last six hours doing the laundry, or to follow the children as they race through the spray from fire hydrants with friends who might or might not be privy to the sexual identity of their playmates' parents.

A family portrait addresses the twin issues of authenticity and existence. Its first order of business is to establish who belongs with whom. Taken together, the images presented here counter stereotype by highlighting the incredible diversity of the relationships that LGBT people make for themselves. Above all, the framing of these photographs as family portraits conveys the sense that these are families, real families, not only in the camera's eye, but in the eyes of those who have brought them together. Individually and collectively, the images stress "realness," composition, and affiliation. Only in the text of the accompanying interviews does a reader begin to get a fuller sense of how the members of these families think about their affiliations, and what they think they are up against.

These are not just couples with kids in which both parents "happen" to be of the same sex. The families pictured here sometimes include an assemblage of adults, most (if not all) of whom have assumed responsibility for raising a child. There are interracial families. There are families that embrace ex-wives. There is the Borkowski/Halvorsen family, which encompasses close friends as well as the parents of an "ex," who in turn have remained grandpa and grandma to the couple's thirteen-year-old daughter. There are families that cross national borders, not to mention the borders that distinguish one household from another. There is the family in which Daddy gave birth before he transgendered his body. There is Laurie Castonguay, coparent to a family of twelve "biological" and foster children, who describes the way her family has grown with the wry comment, "Sometimes I come home to a surprise." There are even families in which the dilemmas of everyday life include not only how and when to come out to your kids, but also how to break the news to your mother that your mother-in-law is a lesbian.

Clearly we have come a long way from the two mommies/two daddies model of lesbian and gay parenthood. In terms of composition alone, many of the families photographed here are much more complicated than that. They are sheltering and educating children who have meaningful access to multiple adults, with all the additional resources (as well as occasional vexations) such arrangements entail. Here again the interviews take up where the photographs leave off, emphasizing the texture and quality of the relations among family members over any abstract calculus that could be used to determine family composition. "I grew up with a mother and a father," Shirley Riga, a lesbian mother, explains, "and

3. For an overview of recent changes in ideologies of family and the practice of kinship in the United States, see Coontz (1992, 1997), Skolnick (1991), Stacey (1991, 1996), and Weston (1997).

there was much more dysfunction in my own childhood than there is in my present blended family."

Matters of family composition are not set in stone. All sorts of events can call into the question of what makes a family, or at least what makes this family. For Ken Watson's ex-wife, Lisa Watson, the ambiguities and fluidities of family membership became especially evident once it came time to decide whether she would vacation along with Ken, his current lover, and the two children that she and Ken had had together. For Perry Voscott, family composition coalesced in places like the supermarket checkout line, where people would ask him about his son's racial identity by saying, "What does his mom look like?" For others interviewed here, the membership (and battle) lines were drawn when they were refused family discounts in stores or had to struggle to receive a family affiliation at their local temple. Even the act of gathering together before a camera can influence people's sense of who's out and who's in.

There is also a sense in which the images in this book serve as passport photos, obviously not as kin to those state-sponsored mug shots that nobody cares to display, but rather in the extended sense of a passport into recognition. These photographs not only document the historical moment that seeks to legitimate lesbian and gay families; they also participate in that bid for recognition. Look at these families, the photos seem to say. These are people who laugh, who worry, who cry. Quite unremarkable, actually, and that is the point. Undoubtedly they have their financial problems and their squabbles, their child geniuses and their ne'er-do-wells. For the most part, however, they go about the business of doing what millions of others do to survive in a consumer economy that offers minimal social services and looks to families to pick up the slack.

Thus these photographs do a particular work in the world with and through their publication. If the images and text sometimes strike a celebratory tone, that can be understood as a response to a society in which many hetero-

sexuals argue that gay people should not have children because having a gay parent is bound to be hard on a kid. (So is poverty, but in these mean-spirited times, no one seems to be in much of a rush to protect children from that particular fate.) Grade school teachers and day-care workers, fearing unemployment, remain understandably loathe to reveal anything other than a standard-issue heterosexual identity. Custody battles continue to flare, with equivocal results, and joint adoptions, which grant more than one person of the same sex legal standing as a parent, remain rare. In such a context, to make and then hold this kind of family together constitutes no small feat.

It's no wonder, then, that people try to put a good face on their family lives without prompting from an interviewer. When you live in a society that reserves the right to restrict your access to reproductive technologies and to take your children away, you tend to speak cautiously and to think before you show. For all the commonalities that LGBT parents share with their heterosexual counterparts, from helping the kids with their homework to supervising the chores, says Bonnie Zellers, "the fact that people fear us does make our lives significantly different." Not to mention the differences that LGBT parents work hard to value and to create.

Scholarly studies on lesbian and gay parenthood tend to share these parents' concerns, albeit implicitly, through the way that they frame their topics for investigation. What studies there are often center on the question of whether gay men and lesbians make good parents. The findings? Not even fair to middling, but as good or better parents than most.[4] The focus of these studies speaks not to the issues that confront LGBT parents and their children in the course of everyday life, but instead to the preconceptions, fears, and institutions of a heterosexually ordered society.

But there is another side. The interviews that accom-

[4.] See, for example, Bozett (1987), Sasse (1995), and Tasker and Golombok (1997).

pany these photographs begin to shift the focus a bit, away from the question of composition: who and what make a family? and toward the question of process: what exactly is it that families make? Mother after child after father after coparent after family friend makes it clear that families are not just about membership and affiliation, but about negotiations conducted in a daily cadence. If love makes a family, so can conflict. So, too, can grieving, uncertainty, grave-tending, desire, sacrifice, comfort, and the rituals of obligation.

"When Marquita and her girlfriend have an argument, the girlfriend comes right to me," explains Marquita's grandfather, Wallace Holman. "She'll be angry at Marquita, and I will say, 'What did Marquita do this time?' The girlfriend calls me 'Granddad,' too." This is an example of family in the making, one that cannot be grasped with a discussion (however important) of rights and recognition. What do the interviews and photographs have to say about people working their way through adversity, misunderstanding, and the less commonly understood perils of unanticipated good fortune? What can attention to process and negotiation contribute to the understanding—and the living—of family? What can it contribute to knowledge of how lesbians and gay men handle encounters with schools, government agencies, advertisements that reach right into their family rooms and continue on through the bedroom door? How does someone make a family—according to whose vision, whose standards—in a world that would rather she not?

When Dorothy Allison talks about turning down a college teaching job because of anti-gay adoption statutes in the place where the college is located, she is talking about legal rights, to be sure, but also about linkages between sexuality, class, employment, and decisions hedged in by the state. When Marcelle Cook-Daniels and Loree Cook-Daniels discuss screening sperm donors in an attempt to ensure that their child will look racially "mixed," they describe just one of many encounters with the racist assumptions embedded in

snap judgments about who belongs with whom. "We didn't want Loree to be hassled by people saying, 'Are you really that child's mom?'" When a seventh-grader discovers that not one but both of his formerly married parents are gay, he's obviously got much more to deal with than family composition.

There is a shift in emphasis here from who and what to how, as people learn to resolve (or perpetuate) conflicts and to create possibilities from constraint. It is a matter of doing connection, under difficult conditions. In this sense, the interviews offer the textual equivalent of another kind of family album. Organized with regard to process, such an album might include images of a gay man receiving a court order that terminates his visitation rights; an application from someone's lover to a consulate, stamped "Visa Denied"; a woman who has just learned that her daughter is a lesbian reaching for the telephone, or a drink; a child bringing home a report card that requests the signatures of papa, mom, and dad.

Such images go beyond even the dailiness of "Mom, is there more food?"; "But why can't I have a puppy?"; "We're proud of you, son"; and "Turn that damn music down!" With their emphasis on process, these images mark the continuous, often hidden effort required to negotiate sexual identity in the course of making kinship ties. At issue is not so much sex per se, but the multiple ways in which sexuality, once constructed as an identity that brings people into an ongoing relationship, becomes taken up into kinship. As Regina Dyton so eloquently puts it, in the pause between the cooking, the cleaning, and running to drop off the kids: "If the thing that defines us and makes us different is who we have sex with, then I can hardly find time to be a lesbian!"

In the pages that follow, interviews frame photographs and photographs frame interviews, until the framing operation itself dissolves into the dynamics of life in a gay family. Reading one against the other, you can glimpse the usual fights over bedtime and whether the kids have to finish the food on their plates. But you can also watch the reaction when a greeting card from relatives arrives, addressed inclusively for the first time to self, lover, and kids. You can almost hear the family conference called to discuss what to do after a group of kids start calling one another "faggot" on the way home from the game. As the aperture clinches, you may wonder how a second-grader who would be pitied by some for having to grow up in a queer sort of family has learned to transform stigma into specialness. (Apparently not everyone gets to have more than one mom.) You have an opportunity to join in the deliberations of the lesbian couple who has to decide whether to sell the family's transportation (but of course, a motorcycle) to fund needed home repairs. You can share the pleasure when Crystal Jang's mother agrees to give Crystal's child a Chinese name, just as she did with all the other grandchildren. You can sweat out the uneasy compromise reached when parents agree to turn their gay-themed books backwards on the shelves, at their teenagers' request, so that the children won't feel embarrassed in front of their friends. And you can revel in the unexpected, as Dorothy Allison explains how becoming a parent created a bridge between siblings divided by class mobility: "It was the first thing I ever did that they understood."

This side of family life is about paradoxes and contradictions. Imagine being Sheila Benjamin and Bonnie Zellers, lesbian parents who have both worked for the government in a society that routinely—though mistakenly—associates homosexuality with child molestation. Or picture yourself as the nurse's aide who spends her days taking care of an elderly anti-gay woman, yet fears to come out to her client. Or consider the ironies of living as a transgender parent in a family that, to all outward appearances, incarnates the cultural ideal of a happily married heterosexual couple with kids.

This side of family life is also about power, humor, ambivalence, and struggle: Children deciding when and whether to pass. Children deciding when and how to ask,

"Mom, are you gay?" A new lover getting rebuffed when she tries to discipline one of the kids. The search for other twenty-somethings with gay or lesbian parents. A debate about how to complete tax and census documents. The catch in a woman's voice as she tries to explain to a partner from a different cultural background that individual actions can reflect back upon an entire family. The exchange of glances as parents attempt to make their kids feel safe after the family car is vandalized with anti-gay slogans. The search for other butch-identified single mothers. The search for a fashion statement for the pregnant butch. Hours of agonizing over how to convince Mom, Tío, or Cousin George to treat the kids you coparent as their relatives. Hours of invention in order to come up with a narrative of family resemblance that does not rely upon a rhetoric of biology and genes. ("Let me tell you why I think you take after your other father. . . .") Last but not at all least, what to say to the nine-year-old pest who confesses to "bugging [her mother's girlfriend] because I want her to marry my mom."

Such is family life the morning before and the morning after the photo sessions that produced this fine array of family portraits. Morning finds LGBT people creating family as they make it, with or without the support of employers, friends, and relatives, and almost certainly without the support of the state. Hands collide on their way to grab a tortilla or a pancake. Dishes tower ominously in the sink. Eyes track from the milk dribbling down Junior's best shirt to the dog pawing frantically at the door. While these families may differ greatly in composition, in practice they are far from composed.

Mornings also redirect the gaze outward, this time not toward the camera, but toward the institutions that regulate family life. There are jobs to go to and jobs to seek; day care available or (more likely) not; prices of household goods falling and rising in tandem with economic trends; forms waiting to be filled out, with spaces that never seem to fit this family. Through it all, LGBT parents build relationships using cultural materials that are often as familiar to heterosexuals as themselves. (What they do with those materials is another, more complicated, story.)[5]

Like all parents shut out from certain forms of privilege, LGBT parents face the daunting task of raising a child, in Dorothy Allison's words, "to believe that he belongs on this planet." With any luck, these parents will join their fortunes to those of others who know how to brush back oppression with a look or a kiss and the reminder that no one person can always be strong.[6] Eventually they may put together family albums of their own, so that when it comes time to narrate the photographs, a child will be able to point and say, "That's the woman my grandma is married to." In the best of some possible worlds.

[5] For more discussion of the question of whether there is anything distinctive about families headed by lesbians and gay men, see Benkov (1994), Lewin (1993), Slater (1995), and Weston (1995, 1997).

[6] See Regina Dyton's comments in this volume on her relationship with Kim Grogan: "I had always seen myself as many black women do—as someone who has to be strong. Kim was the first person who ever knew I was tired, or that I needed a rest or a kiss or something sweet."

REFERENCES

Achtenberg, Roberta. 1990. *Preserving and Protecting the Families of Lesbians and Gay Men.* 2nd ed. San Francisco: National Center for Lesbian Rights.

Allen, Katherine R., and David H. Demo. 1995. "The Families of Lesbians and Gay Men: A New Frontier in Family Research." *Journal of Marriage and the Family* 57:111–127.

Asten, Maureen A. 1997. *Lesbian Family Relationships in American Society: The Making of an Ethnographic Film.* Westport, Conn.: Praeger.

Benkov, Laura. 1994. *Reinventing the Family: The Emerging Story of Lesbian and Gay Parents.* New York: Crown.

Bozett, Frederick W., ed. 1987. *Gay and Lesbian Parents.* New York: Praeger.

Clunis, D. Merilee, and G. Dorsey Green. 1995. *The Lesbian Parenting Book: A Guide to Creating Families and Raising Children.* Seattle: Seal Press.

Coontz, Stephanie. 1992. *The Way We Never Were: American Families and the Nostalgia Trap.* New York: Basic Books.

———. 1997. *The Way We Really Are: Coming to Terms with America's Changing Families.* New York: Basic Books.

Lewin, Ellen. 1993. *Lesbian Mothers: Accounts of Gender in American Culture.* Ithaca, NY: Cornell University Press.

———. 1998. *Recognizing Ourselves: Rituals of Lesbian and Gay Commitment in America.* New York: Columbia University Press.

Martin, April. 1994. *The Guide to Lesbian and Gay Parenting.* London: Pandora.

Mason, Mary Ann, Arlene Skolnick, and Stephen D. Sugarman, eds. 1998. *All Our Families: New Policies for a New Century.* New York: Oxford University Press.

Muñoz, José. 1996. Comments delivered as part of the panel, "Enriching the Landscape of the American Family: Contributions of Lesbians, Gays, and Bisexuals," John T. Patten Memorial Lecture Series, sponsored by the Ackerman Institute for the Family, New York.

Nardi, Peter. 1992. "That's What Friends Are For: Friends as Family in the Gay and Lesbian Community." In *Modern Homosexualities: Fragments of Lesbian and Gay Experience*, ed. Ken Plummer. New York: Routledge.

Peletz, Michael G. 1995. "Kinship Studies in Late Twentieth-Century Anthropology." *Annual Review of Anthropology* 24:343–372.

Rafkin, Louise, ed. 1990. *Different Mothers: Sons and Daughters of Lesbians Talk about Their Lives*. Pittsburgh: Cleis Press.

Robson, Ruthann. 1994. "Resisting the Family: Repositioning Lesbians in Legal Theory." *Signs: Journal of Women in Culture and Society* 19(4):975–996.

Sasse, Birgit. 1995. *Ganz Normale Mütter: Lesbische Frauen und Ihre Kinder*. Frankfurt am Main: Fischer Taschenbuch Verlag.

Sherman, Suzanne, ed. 1992. *Lesbian and Gay Marriage: Private Commitments, Public Ceremonies*. Philadelphia: Temple University Press.

Skolnick, Arlene. 1991. *Embattled Paradise: The American Family in an Age of Uncertainty*. New York: Basic Books.

Slater, Suzanne. 1995. *The Lesbian Family Life Cycle*. New York: Free Press.

Stacey, Judith. 1991. *Brave New Families: Stories of Domestic Upheaval in Late Twentieth Century America*. New York: Basic Books.

———. 1996. *In the Name of the Family: Rethinking Family Values in the Postmodern Age*. Boston: Beacon.

Tasker, Fiona L., and Susan Golombok. 1997. *Growing Up in a Lesbian Family: Effects on Child Development*. New York: Guilford Press.

Weston, Kath. 1995. "Forever Is a Long Time: Romancing the Real in Gay Kinship Ideologies." In *Naturalizing Power: Essays in Feminist Cultural Analysis*, ed. Sylvia Yanagisako and Carol Delaney, pp. 87–110. New York: Routledge.

———. 1997. *Families We Choose: Lesbians, Gays, Kinship*. 2nd ed. New York: Columbia University Press.

Yanagisako, Sylvia Junko. 1985. *Transforming the Past: Tradition and Kinship among Japanese Americans*. Stanford: Stanford University Press.

FAMILY PORTRAITS

Clockwise from top: *Cody, Barbara, Robin, and Hannah*

THE
ALLEN/JURS
FAMILY

BARBARA ALLEN & ROBIN JURS

HANNAH JURS-ALLEN (10)

CODY JURS-ALLEN (7)

BARBARA
(Chiropractor and Producer)

When I was in high school, I was heterosexual. My boyfriend was captain of the baseball team, and I was a prom queen my senior year! In college there were two women "who were gay," and nobody really talked to them. We heterosexuals isolated them because we weren't educated about lesbians and gays and we were afraid of them. It wasn't until the end of college that I was able to sort out who I really was. Finally, I came out.

Heterosexuals can legally get married and have weddings, and we cannot. Despite this, Robin and I had a joyful commitment ceremony with over one hundred guests, a dinner, a band, and a dance in 1985. Our cake had two women on top.

At the ceremony, we saved the front row for our families and we gave each family member a flower to wear. My parents did not come because of their religious beliefs. My oldest brother, Jim, came with his wife, but they wouldn't let their children, aged ten and twelve, come because they didn't want to expose their kids to "this lesbian thing." They did sit in the front row with other family members, but they refused to wear flowers.

My sister sang, our friends read some special poems, and Robin and I exchanged promises and rings. Then anyone who wanted to could say a few words to us. Robin's

"We have two great kids who are living their lives with the understanding that they have a perfect right to be who they are with their two moms, their two dogs, and their many friends who love and adore them. Is that enough? We think so."

— *ROBIN JURS*

mother spoke first and offered her love to both of us. When she finished, my brother stood up to speak. I instantly panicked and thought, "Oh no, trouble is coming."

Jim spoke slowly and thoughtfully as he described what had happened to him that day. He said that he had come to our ceremony because it was a family obligation, but after listening to me and Robin and our friends who spoke, he had finally gotten it. He had realized that lesbians do have long-term committed relationships, and that two women loving each other is wonderful. He wished Robin and me the same nineteen years together that he and his wife had experienced thus far, and said he regretted not wearing a flower.

From around the room, people threw flowers to him, which he and his wife proudly pinned on. It was truly a magical moment! That was my brother's coming out when he realized that love is simply love.

Since then, we have had two great kids, Hannah and Cody. Each of us gave birth to one child, and each of us has legally adopted our nonbiological child. Our children have visited with their donors, and we are all very thankful to these two great men who, as an act of love, donated their sperm to us so that we could have our two wonderful children.

It is important to understand that families come in all shapes and sizes and not to assume that everyone is heterosexual, or that everyone has a mom and a dad.

I love my family deeply, and I am committed to making the world a safer place for all of us.

ROBIN
(Teacher)

I was the fifth of six children, so family has always figured rather large in my heart, mind, and experience. When I was five I already knew that I wanted to be a mom. I would grow up, get married, and have babies. What other options were there back then?

The families portrayed on the television shows "Leave It to Beaver," "Father Knows Best," or "The Donna Reed Show" all made a strong impression on me. Imagine my surprise when it began to dawn on me that I wouldn't be June Cleaver or Donna Reed.

For years, I went through scenario after scenario of just how I could realize my dream of having a family without being in a traditional heterosexual relationship. It took me quite a while to know that I could stay true to myself, love a woman, and have the family I wanted. I was so excited that I could hardly contain myself.

When I was planning my first date with Barbara, a close friend said to me, "When you go out with Barbara, do not immediately blurt out, 'Hi, my name is Robin, and I want to have children!'" I contained myself and waited until my second date with Barbara to start planning our family. Well, maybe it was the second month, not the second date.

So, here we are thirteen years later: Barbara, Robin, Hannah, and Cody. What a

"I like my family because I think the world needs diversity. My biological mother Robin, and my non-biological mother, Barbara, love me as much as a mom and a dad would love their kid, and maybe even more."

— HANNAH JURS-ALLEN

combo! We recently moved across the country from California to New England, where we are finding new friends, new traditions, space to breathe, and dramatic weather. We spend more time together now. We are closer. We laugh and struggle in more intense ways. We know each other better, and we love the parts we know as well as the parts we continue to discover about one another.

We have two great kids who are living their lives with the understanding that they have a perfect right to be who they are with their two moms, their two dogs, and their many friends who love and adore them. Is that enough? We think so.

CODY
(Second-Grade Student)

I think it's different having two moms, and I think it would be really boring if everybody just had a mom and a dad. It's really special how I have a mom and a mama!

It's kind of weird being the only boy in the family, but everybody loves me. My favorite brothers are Austin and Bisbee, but they are our dogs!

My favorite things to do as a family are sledding, getting ice cream, and going to the lake house. My favorite things to do with my moms are being read to at bedtime and snuggling.

HANNAH
(Fifth-Grade Student)

I love having two moms, and I don't agree with people who say having two moms or two dads is wrong. Everybody is different in different ways.

I like my family because I think the world needs diversity. My biological mother Robin, and my nonbiological mother, Barbara, love me as much as a mom and a dad would love their kid, and maybe even more.

When I was three years old and my brother was very young, my parents went to court. Mama adopted my brother and Mommy adopted me, so they are both my legal parents. I love my little brother Cody, but he can be a little annoying.

When I was growing up, my parents had lots of lesbian and gay friends, so I didn't spend my first three years in a world that was very different from mine. All of the schools I've gone to so far have been very supportive of me and my family.

I wrote a poem that I read at a public hearing about the domestic partnership ordinance. My poem says, "I want you to know I think my family is great, so why don't you people just stop all this hate? I know that love comes right from the heart. My parents taught me love from the start."

"I think it's different having two moms, and I think it would be really boring if everybody just had a mom and a dad. It's really special how I have a mom and a mama!"

— *CODY JURS-ALLEN*

Dorothy

16

THE
ALLISON/LAYMAN
FAMILY

DOROTHY ALLISON & ALIX LAYMAN

WOLF MICHAEL ALLISON LAYMAN (3)

DOROTHY
(Author)

Family means two different things to me. One is the family of my birth. It's my nation. It's the people I trust and understand, even when I don't trust them for a minute. "Family" is a big word, but very painful. The word "family" hides everything—including the people that you are despised by and yet hang on to, and the people to whom you do not want to give your address. It's a big word. I hang on to my birth family pretty hard, sometimes over their protests. I've also built a completely separate family, which includes my lover, Alix, our son, Wolf, our Daddy donor, Dan, Wolf's godmother, Claudia, and GrandMary. We've constructed a family—and it's a family of people who have become related by dint of having a child together. It's also a family of friends, which is pretty much something I discovered in the lesbian and gay community.

Down south we say, "Who are your people?" By that we mean, "Who is in your family?" I remember the first time I asked someone I just met, "Who are your people?" She didn't think I meant her family of origin. She meant her people—the people she loved and trusted—and they were basically a handful of other lesbians. I thought, "My God, that's not right." It took me some time to figure it out, and then I decided that I loved the

"The nurses handed me my son and said, 'Do you want to carry him to the nursery?' I walked down the corridor carrying him. I looked down at him and he opened his eyes. I started crying. I fell in love."

— DOROTHY ALLISON

concept. So for a while, I had this concept of a family of affinity. I knew damn well that all other lesbian and gay people were my family of affinity.

I knew I was queer growing up. I just knew. One thing I knew for sure was that I was not interested in boys. The adolescent thing that happens to girls never happened to me. It never switched over. There is so much emphasis on it in southern culture that it was perfectly obvious that I was "that way."

I had a lesbian aunt, but I didn't actually find out about her until I started to hunt down some information. As a child, I had heard stories about her, but my family never made it clear that she was a lesbian. The stories were always descriptive. "She drove a truck." Or, "She was a mechanic." I didn't put it together until I went to college. Then when I tried to get information from the family, it was just impossible. Either they didn't know or they didn't want to tell me. I always wondered if they were keeping the information just from me. They might have told somebody else in the family about this aunt, but they would never have told me because they somehow knew I was queer. I've talked to other southern lesbians who have had the same experience. Oh hell, yeah. When I came out to my mother, she was like, "Honey, we knew that." Jesus God, they knew it before I knew it. They always do.

Making my son was the weirdest thing I have ever done, and, in terms of my sisters, it was the first thing I ever did that they understood. My sisters didn't graduate from high school, and the idea that I went off and then went to college and became a writer—it's just outside their realm. As far as they're concerned, lesbians, people who go to college, and writers are all creatures too strange for words. So when Alix and I got pregnant, I was finally doing something that they knew more about than I did. My sisters would call me up and lecture me. They'd say, "Dorothy, do you know about cradle cap?" Cradle cap was a biggie with them. Or, "Dorothy, that baby will get dandruff, you know." And they'd ask me questions like, "Have you thought about whether the baby is going to sleep in the same bed with you? Why, you'll roll over on that baby and smother him to death!" They kept saying to me, "Dorothy, you don't know what you're doing!" My sisters loved me and felt superior to me because they had made their babies when they were teenagers.

When Alix was pregnant, we both would say that we were pregnant. God knows, I felt like I was.

There are lots of butch moms. The big thing for them is the fashion crisis . . . C'mon, a pregnant butch woman! What clothes can they wear? Alix kept saying to me, "I ain't putting on those smocks." So I went looking, and my final solution was overalls. When I was doing my book tour for *Bastard Out of Carolina*, I met all these butch women who wanted children. They'd ask me, "What's your pregnant girlfriend wearing?" "Overalls," I'd say. You should have seen them—it was like a light went off in their heads. "Hey,

Marge," they'd say to their lover, "we can do it!" I think the revelation of overalls was the biggest thing I contributed to lesbian motherhood. As soon as Alix got that baby out, she said, "I ain't putting those overalls on again. They make me look like a dork."

Alix and I are so determinedly out. We're these big dykes. We marched into the hospital, went to Lamaze classes, and picked our doctor. First thing, Alix announced to the doctor that this baby couldn't be born if I wasn't in the delivery room. She got them all to swear that I would be allowed in there. Problem is that everything went wrong. Alix went into labor two-and-a-half months before Wolf was due, and she had to stay in bed for the rest of the pregnancy. Put Alix in a bed for two-and-a-half months, she gets right irritable! Alix had gestational diabetes and the baby was huge. The doctors misjudged, so the baby was two weeks late and no sign of Alix going into labor. They tried to induce for twenty-four hours and got nowhere. The baby went into distress; so we're going into the caesarean, and Alix is yelling, "Dorothy's coming with me!"

Then we lucked out. It turned out that the anesthesiologist was gay, and he said to me, "Come stand by me, honey." Then they just opened Alix up and pulled out this giant pink and white basketball. And this giant basketball just opened up like a flower. It was the most beautiful thing I'd ever seen. Baby Wolf was ten-and-a-half months old! He was finished past finished. He was fat—ten pounds, four ounces. The nurses handed me my son and said, "Do you want to carry him to the nursery?" I walked down the corridor carrying him. I looked down at him and he opened his eyes. I started crying. I fell in love.

Oh, God. It's unbelievable. There were days when Alix and I were so exhausted and so crazy and we were so poor, we couldn't do a thing. For entertainment, we'd just lay on the bed and smell the baby. Smells like bread, like bread baking.

Sure, we had concerns about Wolf having lesbian moms. I got offered a job in South Carolina, but their legislature had passed a law that says gay people cannot adopt children. Well, I ain't going to South Carolina with my son. I wouldn't risk my baby. I wouldn't let nobody mess with him. I got that mama thing. "You mess with my boy, you walk very carefully." It's amazing how fast it comes out! Instead, we moved to a queer-friendly community, in part because of Wolf.

All of a sudden a lot of your important life decisions get based around your child. There are things we won't do because they're not safe for Wolf. And there are things we're doing in the construction of a home life—we sold our motorcycle to pay for electrical work! How many lesbians you know would do that? But we needed the wiring in the baby's room. Priorities change.

Wolf is being raised as a southern boy with the largest extended family you ever saw. He's in day care with all these other kids, a lot of whom come from broken homes—single mothers raising kids, single fathers raising kids. Wolf says, "Well, I got Mama

"Yes, we are different. I don't want to pretend we're just like two straight parents. It doesn't mean we're better or we're worse —you simply have to judge us as people."

— ALIX LAYMAN

Dorothy, and Mama Alix, and GrandMary, and Daddy." At this point, he's real proud that he's got Mama and Mama.

Before we had Wolf, Alix and I would say, "We're not going to let him watch any television, and we ain't gonna have no weapons in the house." Now Wolf is a child who watches Disney videos, and when he didn't have no little plastic guns, he shot me with the vacuum cleaner.

Ahh, darlin', I couldn't do this without Alix. One of the problems with southern mothers is that we become like butter on a biscuit. We do not provide enough. We don't raise grown-ups. We raise boys. Alix is raising a grown-up. She gives him absolute love and confidence, and she gives him discipline. She's got a sense of boundaries. I'm over there thinking too much, "Should I say 'no,' or should I say 'yes'?" For example, early on, I'm giving Wolf a bath, and he grabs his penis and says, "What's this, Mama?" I completely froze. I screamed, "ALIX!!!! What're we calling his penis?" "We're calling it a penis, Dorothy." "It's your penis, son."

Wolf. He's big. He's blonde. He's got green eyes or hazel—they change. He's smarter than we are, and it's going to be a problem! Oh God. Got the prettiest little dimples on his knees that I ever saw. He's beautiful.

I intend to take Wolf down south, but I don't want to let him near the men in my family till he's old enough to understand them. Some of the men in my family, they got that wicked southern boy charm, you know. You think that they are the slickest, happiest, best things on the planet. But you look close, and those people are desperate, mean, and hurt. I don't want my son to be like that. Hell no, I'm raising myself a happy, middle-class child. Oh Lord, I'm raising him to believe he belongs on this planet. I always thought that I was from another planet. I want Wolf to believe that he's got a place where he's absolutely safe and at home. I want to see what happens when you raise a child who's never afraid. I want to see who he becomes.

ALIX
(Music Teacher, Trombone Player)

I was raised middle class, but I hit the streets, got in trouble, and wound up in the juvenile court. I knew I was queer from as early as I can remember. My mom sent me to a psychiatrist to try and cure me. I think she got to tolerance, but never to acceptance. I think by now she would have learned to accept me, but she died in 1984.

When I was around fourteen, this amazing girl from Oklahoma came into our school one day. She spotted me instantly. I had never talked with anyone about being gay. I was in a room with the other kids from the marching band, and she came stomping up to me and burst out, "So, are you gay?" It was inconceivable to me that anyone would say that in front of people, so I thought she had said something else. I said, "What?" And she said it again even louder. "Excuse me," I said real loud. Then she shouted it out again at the top of her lungs, "Are you gay?" I grabbed her, hustled her out of the room, and said, "Yes! But have you lost your mind? Don't ever say that in front of these people again!" This girl's mother was gay, and she had a lover who drove a motorcycle. I just idolized the lover. After her family moved away, this girl and I wrote letters for years. Later on, I went to Texas and met up with her again. She was quite a gal. I still have her letters.

Being pregnant was like massive hormone rushes. I have this theory about hormones and butch women. We have a lot of testosterone, so when you throw estrogen into it, it throws you for a loop. You don't know who you are. I was feeling so un-butch. Once I broke into tears and cried to Dorothy, "You got me fat and pregnant, and then you'll leave me." She cracked up. You become insane for nine months.

We live in a wonderful town where being gay doesn't matter. It's not a gay enclave. Everyone mixes together—it's the most integrated, relaxed-about-being-gay place I've ever been, and it's drop dead gorgeous. I'm still concerned that Wolf will get harassed in school. That's part of the reason I named him Wolf. You know the old Johnny Cash song about a boy named Sue who grew up to fight and be tough. So, I decided I was going to give our baby a real strong name because maybe it would help.

Wolf is thirty-eight inches tall. He's a blonde, hazel-eyed, cocky little guy, convinced the world is in love with him. He'll see a picture of a whale and say, "That whale loves me." He charms the hell out of everybody. Wolf is convinced the world is his potato, and I hope to make it possible for him to keep believing it. He's got good manners. He says, "Please" and "Thank-you." We're trying to raise him right.

Yes, we are different. I don't want to pretend we're just like two straight parents. It doesn't mean we're better or we're worse. You just have to judge us as people.

Allan and Dana

22

THE
ARNABOLDI
FAMILY

ALLAN ARNABOLDI

DANA ARNABOLDI (26)

ALLAN
(First-Grade Teacher)

When I was growing up, I felt very different from most of the other boys. I didn't know what that difference was about, and I felt nervous that somehow I didn't fit in. I wasn't into sports or cars or sexual conquests. I wasn't into a lot of typical male things, so kids made fun of me and called me a "sissy."

I married when I was twenty-three, and my wife and I had one daughter, Dana. We were divorced when she was seven. At that time I was trying to decide whether I was gay or straight or bisexual. When Dana was about twelve, I realized that I was gay, and I told her. Dana lived with me half of each week until she was about fifteen, and then she went to live with her mom full time because she needed to be closer to her school. It was around that time that I first became involved in a long-term relationship with a man.

I am a first-grade teacher. When I teach the family unit in my classroom, I always send a letter home telling the parents that in addition to the traditional nuclear family we will also learn about all kinds of alternative families, including families with gay and lesbian parents. Over the years, a few parents have expressed concerns because homosexuality was counter to their beliefs. I have said to them, "There are children in my class who have families with

> *"Being gay doesn't mean that you're a certain kind of person. It doesn't change the kind of person you were before you came out. All the things that had always been true about my dad were still true after he came out to me. I knew he was still this wonderful person. . . . For me, my dad is not my 'gay dad.' My dad is just my dad."*
>
> — *DANA ARNABOLDI*

23

gay or lesbian members, and they need to know that our classroom is a safe place for them to be. We are talking about families, not about sex." After this explanation, these parents were fine.

One year there were two kids in my class—a girl and a boy—who often kissed each other on the playground. One day, another student came into the classroom saying, "They're fags! They're faggots!" It was clear he didn't know what those words really meant. I called the class together and asked if anybody had a definition for the word "faggot." Nobody really knew. I said, "Does anybody know what 'gay' means?" One child answered, "It's when two men love each other." Then I asked them if anyone knew the name for two women who love each other. When they didn't know the answer, I told them that the word is "lesbian." I explained that "faggot" and "fag" are words used to make gay people feel bad. I talked about racist language and compared it to that. I taught them that the words "gay" and "lesbian" can be used in positive ways.

I talk about lesbians and gay men in the context of families in a very matter-of-fact and positive way. I deal with gender stereotypes as well. One year we were reading *The Farmer in the Dell*, and I said, "There's something I noticed about this book. It shows that the farmer is a man, and that he takes a wife. Can you only be a farmer if you are a man?" The kids weren't sure, so I asked how many of them knew women who liked to garden. Many did. "Well," I said, "a farm is like a big garden. So, do you think a woman could be a farmer?" They all said, "Yes," and I said that we could read the book again and put a woman into the story as the farmer. Then one of the kids said, "It's a woman farmer, and she can take a wife, too." Then another child piped in and said, "Oh, that's like so-and-so's two moms." To the kids, it's just so natural.

Heaven forbid that a child should do something that is not stereotypical behavior for her or his gender! Kids learn early on that it's not okay for boys to be too interested in the arts or music or anything that might be considered "feminine," or for girls to be too interested in sports or cars or anything that might be considered "masculine." Someone might call them those feared words, "lezzie," "dyke," "fag," or "queer," regardless of whether or not they are actually gay.

There is such an unjust myth about gay teachers recruiting children. Being gay is not a choice.

I think if gay people can be "out" and be positive role models, then children who grow up to identify themselves as gay or lesbian or who have gay or lesbian parents can become healthy, happy adults who are proud of themselves and of their families.

If we were more open to accepting people as who they are, this world would be a better place. We would all be respectful of each other. We would accept all the variations that we see.

"If we were more open to accepting people as who they are, this world would be a better place. We would all be respectful of each other. We would accept all the variations that we see."

— ALLAN ARNABOLDI

LOVE MAKES A FAMILY

DANA
(Graduate Student in Secondary Education)

I have two families. I have my dad, and I have my mom, stepfather, stepbrother, and stepsister.

Once when Dad had marched in the local Gay Pride march, a friend told me that her mother had seen him. I said something like, "Well, that parade is also for people who support homosexual people. It doesn't mean that you're gay if you march in it." Even though I didn't admit it, I was worried about what people would say if they found out my dad was gay.

As a teenager, I lived most of the time with my mom, so in terms of telling friends, I was let off the hook. I would have had more of a problem having to constantly explain things if I still lived with my dad. In junior and senior high, I didn't really talk about it or tell my friends. The funny thing was that my best friend's mother was a lesbian. I don't know why I didn't know that because we talked about everything else. But in the process of getting to know someone, how do you work into the conversation that, by the way, your dad is gay? Yet, with my close friend it would have been natural that I would have told her. Finally, I asked her if she knew that my dad was gay. She said, "Well, actually I did know. But did you know my mother was a lesbian?" It turned out that our parents knew each other. We thought it was pretty funny. Once I graduated from high school, it stopped being an issue. All my friends know about my dad now.

When I heard homophobic remarks as a teenager, I didn't feel traumatized. I would just think, "I'm so much more enlightened than these other kids. They are so ignorant." But I wasn't the kind of teenager who said, "No. You're wrong. Let's talk about this." I think I'm more likely to do that now.

Being gay doesn't mean that you're a certain kind of person. It doesn't change the kind of person you were before you came out. All the things that had always been true about my dad were still true after he came out to me. I knew he was still this wonderful person. Having a gay family member makes you realize that discrimination and prejudice are not acceptable in any form. For me, my dad is not my "gay dad." My dad is just my dad.

If you are worried that a gay teacher will recruit kids or influence kids to be gay, then you might as well worry if your kid's teacher is Catholic or Jewish, or any number of different things. It seems so silly! If someone is a good teacher, they don't influence students one way or the other. As a teacher myself, one of my goals is to create a classroom environment that is open and accepting of all differences.

Left to right: *Tommy, Beth, and Karen, with foster child*

THE
BELLAVANCE-GRACE
FAMILY

KAREN BELLAVANCE-GRACE & BETH BELLAVANCE-GRACE
TOMMY BELLAVANCE-GRACE (6)
FOSTER CHILD (9 MONTHS)

BETH
(Co-owner of Pride and Joy Giftshop, Photographer, Foster and Adoptive Mother)

When I was six, a group of my mom's college friends were traveling a long distance to visit at our house. At the last minute, one of them couldn't make it because her partner was very ill. I was told that her partner was a woman and that they were lesbians. I remember feeling relieved that there were other people like me.

When I was fourteen, I asked my mom if I could see a therapist so I could talk to someone outside the family. At that time, she didn't want me to see anyone. When I was sixteen, I met my first girlfriend, and luckily everything was fine for a year. Then she went off to college, and I was so distraught that my parents finally allowed me to talk to a therapist, although they didn't know exactly why I needed one. Just talking to this therapist about my life, about feeling alone, made a huge difference to me.

I remember going off to college feeling so scared, wondering whether I would find other people like me. But all it took was one preseason soccer practice to alleviate my fears. It's better for youth coming out now. At least there are people to talk to, people to look up to, and gay people on almost every television channel!

"I am not trying to say that we are 'normal,' as in, 'just like straight people.' I mean we are normal lesbian parents. We have a lot to offer our son, our foster children, their schools, and our community. When are people ever going to let go of the belief that difference is negative?"

— BETH BELLAVANCE-GRACE

27

I am a more sensitive parent now because I remember that part of my past when I had the overwhelming feeling of being alone, of thinking I was the only person like me. That kind of fear can really mess up a young person's head as well as heart, and I think my experience has a lot to do with my drive to let the children in my life know they are not alone. For that reason, Karen and I started a group called Valuable Families so our children could get to know lots of kids in families like ours.

I think the fact that I am adopted has a lot to do with why I have chosen to adopt. I help my children celebrate their differences, all the while letting them see their connections to others around them. When I was in my late twenties, I went to a meeting of adoptees. For the first time in my life, I was in a room full of people who had felt just like me.

Of course it didn't take many more meetings before it became obvious that we all had our differences, but there remained one very powerful connection: we all had felt alone and different as children. Maybe if adoption wasn't so hush-hush and taboo to talk about when I was a kid thirty-five years ago, we all could have seen how many other adoptees there were out there, thus preventing all those years of therapy as adults.

I would say the same thing about being a young dyke, a label I feel proud of using now to describe myself. If it didn't have to be such a secret back when I was growing up, all those years of torment from adolescence through early adulthood could have been avoided. It gets me pretty upset to think about it, but I am also realizing how my earlier trials in life have really helped shape me into a wonderful parent as well as person.

I want children in my life. I want to raise children and have a bigger family, but I don't feel like I need to have a biological connection with a child to feel like it's my child. Being a parent and a foster parent helps me feel whole.

I used to work at a substance abuse treatment program for homeless mothers and their children. The women would occasionally be asked to leave the program, or would take off to use drugs, and their children would be sent into foster care. I remember one of the hardest parts of the job was seeing the kids really thrive and open up within the structure, safety, and love of the program and then have to be torn away from relationships they'd formed and sent off to strangers because of a choice their mother had made.

There were two children in my town who were sent to a foster home over an hour away from their family's home, to a town where the eight-year-old was the only African American child in her school classroom. Another staff member and I went to visit these kids on their second day in foster care. I was so saddened by the whole situation. I asked why these siblings couldn't be in a foster home in the community where they had started to make connections and they could attend the same school. I was told that there were only two foster homes in our town and that they were both full. What a rude awakening. I assumed that there were lots of people out there taking care of foster children, but here in our caring, progressive community, there were only two foster homes! I talked with Karen, and we agreed we would try to find out how to become foster parents.

We finally got into foster parent training. Karen and I were both really excited, and pretty blown away when we got a call to take a child before we had even finished the ten-week training class. The evening Tommy came to our house was so incredible. I remember opening the door and there were these huge round blue eyes looking at us! Two women introduced us, handed us a bag with a dirty pair of pants and tee shirt and a pair of sneakers at least several sizes too big, and a small baby bottle. Tommy had a teddy bear they had given him at the hospital and he wore yellow Looney Tune hospital jammies. That was close to five years ago, and we've had him ever since except for one month when there was an unsuccessful effort made to reunite him with his birth family. We've had seven foster children altogether and calls for dozens more who needed placement. It's always hard to say no when you know there is a child who could blossom in your house.

For me, one of the hardest things about being a foster parent is when people, even strangers, say "How can you do that? I could never give them back after I fell in love with them!" I can't tell you how many feelings that brings up. Most of all, for all those thousands of beautiful children deserving love and care, needing safety, full of fear, the least I can do is risk that feeling of loss. There are about half a million children in foster care in the United States and not nearly enough homes for them to go into. Given what most of them have experienced in their short lives, the possibility of my falling in love with them and having to let them go seems not so terrible.

Lesbians and gay men have to go through so much planning to bring children into their lives, and I know it's not my business, but I wonder why so few of them consider foster care and public agency adoption when there are so many children ready and waiting for families. Maybe people are afraid of parenting a child who has been through trauma or isn't a tiny, "perfect" newborn. Or maybe they're afraid the child won't bond with them or vice versa. We have foster parented two infants, four toddlers, and one teenager. Our son was twenty-one months old when he came to live with us. Every one of these children is lovable and every one of them deserves loving parents and safe homes. For these reasons, adoption from a public agency was our family's first choice.

I get really infuriated when people ask ridiculous questions about whether gays and lesbians should be allowed to be foster parents or adopt children. What is it that heterosexual people think we do, anyway? Karen and I are normal, everyday people: we are parents; we run a business together; we are fortunate enough to have a mortgage to pay; we do laundry; we pay the bills; we've started a family support group in our area with a monthly newsletter that goes out to about six hundred gay, lesbian, bisexual, and trans-

"It's hard to hear some people say that having gay or lesbian parents is not in a child's 'best interests.' We know only too well that having married, heterosexual parents is no guarantee of a happy, safe childhood. The majority of kids in foster care come from heterosexual birth parents. Your sexual orientation is not a true indicator of what kind of parent you will be."

— KAREN
BELLAVANCE-GRACE

gender families and allies; we started Foster Dignity, an organization that collects suitcases, essentials, and clothing for children going into foster care; and we chaperon field trips and volunteer in our son's classroom.

I am not trying to say that we are "normal," as in, "just like straight people." I mean we are normal lesbian parents. We have a lot to offer our son, our foster children, their schools, and our community. When are people ever going to get over the belief that difference is negative?

KAREN
(Co-owner of Pride and Joy Giftshop, Foster and Adoptive Parent, Activist, Writer)

I had broken off contact with my family of origin, long before my wife, Beth, and I decided to become parents. My father died when I was a teenager and neither my mother nor my sister could understand my sexual orientation. They weren't willing to attend counseling with me or to visit PFLAG meetings or to read anything I wanted to share with them about the topic. We have not spoken in about a decade. It was sad for a while, but I think things happen for a reason. I have hope that someday we will be able to talk again; in my mind, the door is always open. For now, though, it is important that the people in my life are willing to know and love me as a whole human being.

I have found unconditional love among my family of friends and with my in-laws, who have completely accepted me as part of their family. Now that I am a parent, it is hard for me to imagine what it must be like for my mother to know that she has a daughter and a grandchild out in the world with whom she has no contact. It's hard for me to imagine the kind of fear my mother must live with which blocks her from keeping our connection intact.

My father's sister and her husband are my godparents, and they remain a part of our lives. We don't see them as often as I would like, but they were there when Beth and I had our wedding ceremony and at Tommy's adoption ceremony. Even before the adoption, they sent Tommy gifts on his birthday and at Christmas. They are strong allies, and I am so grateful for their continued love and support. It provides a link to my family and to my father that I wouldn't otherwise have.

We are really active in our son's education, and are strong supporters of the public school system. I have done some work with the PTO in our school, and I volunteer in Tommy's classroom one day each week. In every situation, from dealing with social workers, pediatricians, school personnel, karate teachers, and even in the grocery store, we are visible and verbal about who we are and who is in our family.

We are lesbian parents in a predominantly heterosexual world. We are adoptive parents by choice. We are foster parents in a world where work isn't always valued and understood. My experience has been that if we let people know about who we are in a conversational, no-big-deal way, then that is how the information is received. People are able to take it all in stride when we let them know it really isn't a big thing. It's just who we are.

At the time we decided to become foster parents, I was still pretty ambivalent about having children. We saw this as a good way to experience ourselves as parents for a time and then have our adult relationship back in between placements. Of course, it didn't turn out to be that simple.

We've had children in our home non-stop from the time we became approved as foster parents five years ago. We've had seven foster kids ranging in age from three months to seventeen years. The shortest placement was overnight. Our first foster child, Tommy, became available for adoption, and four years after he first arrived in our home, he legally became our son. He had been adopted in our hearts and by our families long before.

Foster parenting is my proudest achievement and the single most rewarding experience of my life. The children we have worked with have been extraordinary. They are lovable and loving; they are treasures, every one. It is gratifying to be able to see that you can have a positive effect on a child's life even in a short time span.

We had a two-year-old who had already been in and out of foster care six times when he arrived at our home. We were told he was aggressive, angry with good reason, and dangerous to pets. We had two cats and were warned not to leave him alone with them. We spent the next five months with him, working on giving him words for his feelings, and we got him a special toy that he could hit whenever he felt angry. By the time he left us to live with his grandfather, he could tell us when he needed to be left alone and when he needed to find his "Bang Up Bunny." It may not seem earthshaking, but I feel better knowing this child now has a tool he can take with him, no matter what the future holds for him.

Many people ask us if it's hard getting attached to children and then sending them off. It's really been a lesson in living in the present moment and enjoying the time you have with a child. These kids are going to be in foster care anyway, and they might as well be here with us where we know they will be safe and have a fair share of attention, maybe for the first time in their lives. Of course, to do the job right, you have to get attached, and really put your heart on the line. Yes, it's really sad to say good-bye. But when it gets really sad, we just remind ourselves that we have tried to do our best to break the cycle of violence somewhere. We have been able to provide a model of a loving relationship that these kids might remember someday. They might know that there is another way to be a parent when they grow up.

Beth and I really believe that we all bear responsibility for the next generation of children in our communities. Sweet Honey in the Rock sings a song which says, "Your children are not your children. They go through you, but they are not from you, and

> "Foster parenting is my proudest achievement and the single most rewarding experience of my life. The children we have worked with have been extraordinary. They are lovable and loving; they are treasures, every one. . . . We have been able to provide a model of a loving relationship that these kids might remember someday."
>
> — KAREN BELLAVANCE-GRACE

though they are with you, they belong not to you." All of these kids are our kids; how can we not invite them into our home?

It's hard to hear people say that having gay or lesbian parents is not in a child's "best interest." We know only too well that having married, heterosexual parents is no guarantee of a happy, safe childhood. The majority of kids in foster care are coming from hetero-sexual birth parents. Your sexual orientation is not a true indicator of what kind of parent you will be.

Parenting is really hard work. It's not for everyone, and it's especially difficult for people who have not been well-parented themselves. We have been foster parents to kids who are the second or third generation in foster care. Parenting kids who have been abused or neglected is definitely not easy. It takes lots of patience and you have to be able to provide strong structure in a loving way. It's not for everyone, but it is for a lot more people than pursue it now. I know so many gay and lesbian people who would make great foster families. The need is so enormous. I wish more people would consider it.

When Tommy was about four years old, I overheard him talking to the grocery bag-ger, telling him we were getting one cereal for him, and the other cereal for his mommy Beth. "I have two moms, you know," he said, without the slightest thought that someone might find that shocking or unusual. "Well, aren't you lucky?" said the bagger, without missing a beat. I'm proud that he is learning the power of honesty, and I hope he'll never feel like he has to hide parts of himself to be accepted.

Tommy has such a strong sense of himself, it amazes me. Part of it, I know, is just who he is, but part of it also comes from having two devoted parents who love him up to the moon and back. I hope that the strong foundation we are trying to give him will help him stay centered as he grows into the wider world.

TOMMY
(First-Grade Student)

It feels like it's really good to have two moms because two moms is different than other people, and I think that sometimes it's good to be different.

Adoption means you stay with the parents you're with right now and it feels like they are my birth parents even though they're not.

Family means people that really love each other and want to stay with each other forever.

Left to right: *Bonnie, Marc, Sheila, and Elan*

THE
BENJAMIN / ZELLERS
FAMILY

SHEILA BENJAMIN & BONNIE ZELLERS

ELAN BIKO BENJAMIN (15 MONTHS)

MARC BENJAMIN (18)

SHEILA
(Family Service Advocate, Child Sexual Assault Unit)

Bonnie and I were co-investigators of child abuse cases in the state of Maryland. We formed a relationship in 1990. When we got together, I knew that Bonnie was the one I wanted to be the mother of my children. I saw that she was sweet and kind and tender, and I knew that was what I wanted to bring into my family. I was so right.

My son Marc was already fourteen when I got together with Bonnie. He developed his own friendship with her. I never told him that he should start looking to her as another mother, but he made that transition on his own. He wanted us to become a family as much as Bonnie and I did.

Even before Bonnie moved in with us, she and I were both dealing with a lot of harassment and homophobia at our workplace. We decided to find a healthier place to live and work, and although our new community is not as racially diverse as I would like it to be, there is support for alternative families.

I remember having crushes both on girls and on boys all through my school years—but they didn't feel the same. In fifth grade, I remember feeling jealous when a girl I liked talked to me about a boy she had a crush on. At eighteen, I had my first real girlfriend. I felt ashamed

"We watch Sesame Street every morning. We eat pancakes together on the weekends. We go for walks in the woods, swim in the summertime, read books, and visit our friends, just like heterosexual families. However, the fact that people fear us does make our lives significantly different."

— *BONNIE ZELLERS*

Sheila, Elan, Bonnie

and guilty. We had our own little world off someplace, and then we'd go back to the regular world and pretend that everything was the way other people expected it to be. The loneliness was intense.

Finally I decided that I had to be true to myself. I called my brothers and sisters together and told them that I loved Maria. My youngest sister, who was thirteen, said, "You can do whatever you want. Just don't have a sex change operation!" In her mind, if I loved a woman, I had to be a man. That was just the beginning of their process. Now they all accept me, and they respect my relationship with Bonnie just as I respect their relationships.

I remember talking to my mom and telling her that my girlfriend and I were more than friends. She said, "I know." And I said, "We're lovers." She said, "I know." I said, "How do you feel about that?" She said, "It's your life. I trust your decisions, and if you're happy, I'm happy. You are happy, aren't you?" "Yes, ma'am," I said, and that was basically it. Dad just kind of sat there and nodded his head. Over the years, they were always very inclusive of my partners. My mom tells Bonnie, "If you need something, you call me. You're family."

Planning for the birth and having Elan has been so exciting for us. We used alternative insemination with an unknown donor because of the medical and legal protection it offers. My mother's first response to the news of our pregnancy was, "Oh, that makes thirteen grandchildren." There were no questions about biology or methods. Just as my mother had taken in Bonnie as a member of our family, she knew that our children would be her grandchildren—however they came to be. A lot of lesbian and gay parents aren't as lucky as we are.

BONNIE
(Human Services Counselor)

I grew up with my parents, a brother, and two sisters in small, all-white towns in Pennsylvania. The images I had of gay culture were those of dirty, sex-crazed, dangerous people, mostly men, who literally would hide in dark places to stalk children and each other. The love I felt for my girlfriends contrasted with these images I held of gay people, and I was confused.

I was in college when I finally felt the freedom to sort through the layers of my personal experiences, religious teachings, and fears, and arrive at a place where I could claim my lesbian identity. I can only say that once you've gone through intense self-examination, there can be an opportunity for a great personal celebration. You can develop the inner strength to stand up to the inevitable criticism you will face. Now my life is quite calm, and all of that pain seems like it took place during another lifetime.

My parents' process of coming to terms with my lesbianism may actually have been harder than my own because they are invested in a homophobic system of beliefs. My father, who is a Lutheran minister, told me in no uncertain terms that I was a sinner for whom there would be no redemption, and that he was embarrassed by me. My mother tried to figure out what had "gone so wrong" in my life that caused this "perversion," and she encouraged me to get "straightened out" in therapy. I think my parents have made progress during the last fifteen years, but they would still rather I meet the "right man" and have a "normal life."

Marc and Elan

Extended family relationships and social networks change after a lesbian or gay family has a child. Those individuals who had silently disapproved before now feel compelled to intervene "on behalf of the impressionable child." We are, in turn, compelled to speak out for ourselves in a new way, as a family rather than as individuals.

It is ironic that like many lesbian mothers, Sheila and I feel a need to protect our sons from racism and homophobia while other people feel a need to protect our sons from us just because Sheila and I love each other. We want nothing more than to help our sons love themselves and to become healthy, happy, well-adjusted adults. It hurts to know that there are so many people in the world who believe that our love for each other renders us incapable of doing that, and that they will tear away at our children's egos by telling them so.

As a general rule, lesbians don't have children by accident. Whether we conceive through alternative insemination, adopt, become involved with someone who is already a mother, or come to terms with our sexual identities after bearing children, we generally put an enormous amount of conscious effort and love into each step of becoming a family. I think our children are very lucky. Marc and Elan, like all the children in our circle of friends, are cherished.

The laws prohibiting legal marriage for gays and lesbians deny us information during medical emergencies, require that we pay much higher rates for medical insurance, and don't allow us to qualify for family discounts. We can still lose our jobs, our homes, and our professional credibility. In the event that our partner should die, we may not even be allowed time away from our jobs to grieve. Scariest of all, we have very little protection against having our children taken away from us. And then there are the little things like being kicked out of a campground or not being able to fill out the forms they give us in schools because the questions and titles don't apply to us.

We watch *Sesame Street* every morning. We eat pancakes together on the weekends. We go for walks in the woods, swim in the summertime, read books, visit our friends, just like heterosexual families. However, the fact that people fear us does make our lives significantly different.

Our children have a very serious challenge ahead of them. They are being taught to be proud, open, honest, and as free of prejudice as possible, but they still live in an unjust and conservative culture which would rather keep us invisible. I would not be at all surprised if they become the freedom fighters of their generation.

MARC
(Student)

I was fourteen when my mom and I got to know Bonnie. I saw right away how happy Mom was with her, and I hoped she would stay around. Bonnie helped me with homework, listened to my problems, gave me rides, and taught me many things. We all laughed together a lot. I learned to trust her and eventually saw her as my other mom. I always liked the idea of becoming a family, and I always wanted a brother or sister. I only wish I could have had one sooner.

I think it's cool that one of my moms is black and the other is white. There's no room for racism in our family. That's how it should be.

Growing up with lesbian moms wasn't easy. Some kids teased me and tried to beat me up. They thought that I was gay just because my parents are. That's not true. Still, sometimes,

I don't tell people about my family. It's hard to bring girlfriends home because I don't know how they will react. Despite this, I'm really proud of my family. My moms have helped me understand women, and they are good to talk to about girl problems. They have taught me that violence begets violence, and that everyone deserves respect. They have helped me to learn to respect myself. I know they will always be there for me, and I will always be there for Elan. I hope that someday gay people will have as many rights as everyone else.

Chris, Kathy, and Gretchen

THE
BORKOWSKI/HALVORSEN
FAMILY

KATHY BORKOWSKI & CHRIS HALVORSEN
GRETCHEN CHUPP (13)

KATHY
(Historian, Stilt-walker for Uppity Women)

Our family includes my partner, Chris, our daughter, Gretchen, and me—along with a few four-legged creatures. Gretchen is my biological daughter from a former marriage. Our extended family also includes our friends Bonnie and Pat and my "mother- and father-in-spirit," Barb and Rich, who are the parents of a former partner. We are very close to them, and Gretchen calls them Grandma and Grandpa.

We try to be very open and honest about our family. On my desk at work, I have a photo of the three of us, and Chris attends "spouse-included" functions with me. When everyone at work talks about what they did with their family over the weekend, I talk about Chris and Gretchen in the same way. It's no big deal.

Both my parents died when I was a teenager, but I'm out to my extended family including my two brothers and my younger sister. Dealing with family members is often a "work in progress" in any family, and mine is no exception. Because I was married to a man before I was with Chris, they had to make some dramatic shifts in their concept of who I am.

At first it was scary to come out to Gretchen's teachers and to the parents of her friends. I didn't want her to suffer the repercussions that might follow. But it is very

> *"When I was walking down the hall one day at school, this boy said to me, 'I heard this rumor that your parents are lesbians. Is it true?' I said, 'Yeah, it's true. What's your point?' His jaw just dropped down to the floor. It was so funny! He didn't know what to make of the fact that I didn't seem to care."*
>
> — GRETCHEN CHUPP

"We learned to stilt-walk a few years ago at the Michigan Womyn's Music Festival. We enjoyed it so much that when we came home, we built our own stilts, and we were off! We named ourselves, 'Uppity Women' and we began to perform at many events and parades all over Wisconsin."

— KATHY BORKOWSKI

important to be honest with children. They easily sense a lie and that sends the message that there is something wrong with their family. So being honest with Gretchen ultimately meant being honest with all the people in her life.

Chris and I always go to parent-teacher conferences together at the beginning of the school year. I put Chris's name on all the school forms that ask for the parents' names. The reactions from teachers have ranged from being very welcoming to being simply tolerant, but I've never regretted my openness with them. We are who we are.

If I had to describe our family in a single word, it would be "fun." We laugh a lot, especially at dinnertime. We do lots of things together—bike-riding, roller-blading, ice-skating, and, of course, stilt-walking.

We learned to stilt-walk a few years ago at the Michigan Womyn's Music Festival. We enjoyed it so much that when we came home, we built our own stilts, and we were off! We named ourselves "Uppity Women" and we began to perform at many events and parades all over Wisconsin. Stilt-walking is a great thing we do as a family. There aren't too many things you can still do with your parents at thirteen that are cool, but Gretchen loves it as much as Chris and I do.

CHRIS
(Data Analyst, Stilt-walker for Uppity Women)

When Kathy and I first got together, Gretchen welcomed me into her heart so easily that it almost scared me. I felt this enormous responsibility to be entrusted with a child's love to such a degree, and I was afraid of hurting her by parenting her too quickly or by letting her down in some way. I still feel that way, but now I've accepted that I'll make mistakes.

Gretchen and I do have disagreements, but that's normal. We also have a lot of fun. After all, I'm the parent who makes her laugh so hard she spits out her milk at dinner!

I've been out to my parents for fifteen years, and they are pretty accepting of me now. However, I think it's another whole step for parents to really recognize and integrate their gay child's family into their lives. In some ways my parents still treat me like I'm single, expecting me to make trips to visit them by myself and not really acknowledging my parenting role with Gretchen. Fortunately, things are improving. Last year, they sent birthday cards to Gretchen and Kathy, and this year, for the first time ever, my mom wished me a happy Mother's Day. The more we share with my parents, the more they understand us as a family.

Stilt-walking has been a completely unexpected blessing in our lives. If a fortune-teller had told me five years ago that I was going to be dressing in these incredible costumes and performing on stilts, I would have had a good laugh! I'm slightly shorter than average myself, so to be ten feet tall is a real thrill.

Stilt-walking is a fun thing we do as a family, but sometimes we have to persevere through some difficult situations together, like a very long, hot parade. We really enjoy each other, and we know we can count on each other to be there when the going gets rough.

GRETCHEN
(Eighth-Grade Student,
Stilt-walker for Uppity Women)

Most of my friends really like Chris and my mom, and they're very accepting of us as a family. They think Chris is a lot of fun, and they think Mom is too.

When I meet a new kid at school, I find out if they can be my friend by telling them that my parents are lesbians. If they get totally turned off and say, "Yuck! You're disgusting," then I know they're not going to be my friend because they can't accept my family. I think I have pretty good taste in friends because when I tell them about my family, most of them say, "Okay, that's fine."

When I was walking down the hall one day at school, this boy said to me, "I heard this rumor that your parents are lesbians. Is it true?" I said, "Yeah, it's true. What's your point?" His jaw just dropped down to the floor. It was so funny! He didn't know what to make of the fact that I didn't seem to care.

Gretchen, Chris, and Kathy

When I meet people, I introduce Mom and Chris by saying, "These are my parents." I've gotten used to thinking of them as my parents. My dad is the parent when I visit him.

I learned stilt-walking when I was nine. I absolutely loved it. I gave a report on stilt-walking in seventh grade while I was walking on stilts, and the kids in my class kept saying, "You do that?" They had all sorts of questions.

I'm really proud of my family for who we are. I'm happy that we are so open with my friends, my teachers, and the world.

Consuelo and Falcon

THE
BURNING CLOUD / SISON
FAMILY

CONSUELO BURNING CLOUD
FALCON MEGUEL FRANK SISON (14)

CONSUELO
(Intertribal Planning Agency, Social Services Project Coordinator, Domestic Violence, Sexual Assault, and Drug and Alcohol Counselor)

My friends know me as Burning Cloud or "BC." I am an enrolled tribal member of the Nisqually Tribe. I'm also Yakima and Filipino, better known in Indian Country as "Indapino."

My sister and I were assimilated into a white foster home when I was two years old and she was five. Historically, assimilation was a form of genocide by the U.S. government where they either forced Native people to relocate, put us in boarding schools, or sent us to live in non-Indian foster homes. The foster families were generally poor white people who made Indian kids clean their houses and do other domestic work as if they were slaves. Native people who took a stand or protested would mysteriously disappear or were put in prison, sometimes for life, like our political prisoner, Leonard Peltier.

My foster parents never told me that I had a biological family or that I was an Indian. I didn't know I had parents and five brothers and three other sisters until I was thirteen. My foster parents locked all of us foster kids up in the dark and beat us with belts and made us kneel in corners for hours. We couldn't sit on their furniture. We were not even allowed to look directly at them.

"Everybody on the

reservation knows

that my mom is gay.

Other kids here used

to call me names.

Sticks and stones may

break your bones, but

words do hurt!"

— *FALCON SISON*

I thought I was a "China doll" because that's what my foster parents called me. When I was growing up in the fifties, all you saw was cowboy and Indian movies. I just couldn't stand the thought of being an Indian! Once I had a fight with my foster brother and I called him a "dirty little Indian." Our foster mother came in and said, "Apologize to him right now. Give him a hug and a kiss." I said, "I ain't gonna kiss him. He's nothing but a dirty Indian." And she said, "Well, I got news for you. You are one, too!"

I didn't know the word "lesbian" when I was a young child, but I always knew I was different. I always wanted to wear pants even though girls back then had to wear dresses. I always noticed women who looked like men and I thought they were so cool. I had girlfriends from the time I was in kindergarten, and I even fell in love with the nuns at school. I had a seventh-grade girlfriend and we kissed once. That was my first kiss. At seventeen, I cut my hair short and came out as a lesbian.

In the seventies, you were either a butch or a femme, and I did the whole butch trip. I dressed in boy's clothing for about six or seven years, which was fun. All of my friends were drag queens or butches. Most of my girlfriends were prostitutes and strippers.

I am a recovering addict and alcoholic. I was on the streets for twenty-nine years, and I've been clean and sober for almost ten years now. It wasn't until I was twenty-three and in my first drug and alcohol program that I was able to admit to myself that I was a Native American. Being assimilated, being the target of racism, classism, and homophobia all contributed to my addiction. I was medicating myself with drugs and alcohol because I was a very angry person full of hatred at that time.

My son, Falcon, was born when I was still a street person. I believe that the Creator sent my son to me to straighten up my life. Falcon is my gift. I had struggled through ten different drug and alcohol programs, but it was Falcon's birth that finally changed my life.

Falcon was born addicted to drugs and alcohol. He came into the world pretty rough at only three pounds, but he's got a real strong heart and spirit. Falcon is now in eighth grade and he's a Native American Fancy Dancer. He has an orange belt in karate and he is a talented artist.

Even though he's my son, Falcon is my really good friend. We have a completely open relationship. We can talk about everything. We play and joke a lot. I don't have to fight and argue with him about things that need to get done in our house because Falcon knows that it's just him and me. We're it!

I take Falcon to as many places as I can to meet all kinds of people and to expose him to many diverse issues including racism, classism, and sexism. I want him to be well educated street-wise, as well as academically. As a young Native man, one day he's going to have to walk out there on his own.

Falcon says, "Hey! That's racist," if someone makes a bad comment. He's been brought up mainly by lesbian and straight women of all races and ethnic backgrounds. Falcon has "aunties" who are Asian, Black, Native American, Caucasian, and Jewish. He's going to know how to hold himself as a young male of color.

Many of my biological siblings live on the reservation here, too, and we all love each other. They have known forever that I am gay. Their greatest fear is that I'm going to bring a bunch of queers up here, which I do every once in a while, but my family respects my accomplishments and my goals. Like me, they were all put in white foster homes as children, and they all found their way back home to our ancestral land. We don't hang out together much, but we do have big family get-togethers during the year.

One of my sisters is a lesbian. I didn't know she was gay when I came out, but once she knew that I was a lesbian, she took me around and introduced me to people. She and her partner of over twenty years raised her two kids together, and now their children are grown and have their own kids.

After getting clean and sober, I went back to college and got my bachelor's degree in mental health and human services. Because of my personal experience with addiction, my profession of choice is drug and alcohol counseling in the Native community. I enjoy my job even though it is painful work. I am able to bring some training, support, and education to the tribes.

I was the national coordinator for the Leonard Peltier Defense Committee. I have also been very active in the American Indian movement ever since I went to the Longest Walk in Washington, D.C., when the U.S. government was trying to end our treaty rights. At the Longest Walk, I kept looking for my Two-Spirit sisters and brothers, which is our name for

Consuelo and Falcon

gay and lesbian people. I sat in the woods and cried because I felt so isolated and alone. I wondered if there were other gay Indians anywhere, and if so, where were they?

If our people would read their history, they would know that Two-Spirit people have been here since the beginning of air. Two-Spirit people had certain traditional roles and responsibilities. There were Two-Spirit women who were war chiefs and shamans. In fact, Two-Spirit people were often given the role of tribal counselors because they were able to see things from two sides. They were considered to be very natural and normal. I feel like I'm part of this path today.

In every tribe, there is documentation about Two-Spirit people. In the Lakota tribe, they were called the Winkta. For example, the Sun Dancer who chopped down the Sun Dance pole in Lakota history was always a Two-Spirit person. When the French trappers came here, they noticed that there were feminine men and male-acting women, and they called them "Berdache," a French word meaning "kept boy."

When Native people noticed that a child was more feminine or male-acting than the norm, a ceremony was performed. They would put the child on a mat with a bow and a piece of pottery, and then they would light the mat on fire. If a female child picked up the "masculine" bow or the male child picked up the "feminine" piece of pottery, they would be seen, accepted, and raised as Two-Spirit people.

I think that some of the elders still know about Two-Spirit people, and that their history needs to be talked about more. We do have a small group of Two-Spirit women who get together once a month and sweat together. Together, our group started an intertribal Two-Spirit nation about four years ago for young people who were having problems like I did as a youth. I would also like to teach a sexuality workshop for the youth and openly speak about Two-Spirit people and see what happens! It's just not talked about enough in our communities. Homophobia is alive and ill.

Once I asked one of the young women on our reservation if she would run a youth sweat at the sweat lodge behind my house. She told me, "I can't do the sweat that you asked me to do because of what you people do in that sweat lodge." I asked her, "What do you think we do in our sweat lodge?" And she said, "Our community is straight here and we don't like what you do." I told her that all we do in our sweat lodge is pray and that she should read the history of our Two-Spirit people.

I have come home. I have come full circle. I'm back here on the reservation with my son where my ancestors once lived, and I'll be damned if anyone will push me out of here. I paid my dues to get home. The folks here know that I'm in recovery and they know my work. I think that Falcon and I have their respect. Living my life clean and sober with Falcon is an example to my community.

The kids on the reservation find our home a safe home, so I imagine if their parents

"Prejudice exists because people are scared of what they don't know. People don't really sit down and talk with gay people and consider them as individuals."

—FALCON SISON

LOVE MAKES A FAMILY

didn't want them to come over here because I'm queer, they wouldn't let them come. But they sure do come over!

I don't have a partner now. I'm a Two-Spirit bachelorette!

FALCON
(Eighth-Grade Student)

When my mom told me she was gay, I didn't really mind. I thought that it was her decision, not mine. I can't change it, so I was happy for her. She was still my mother!

I started Fancy Dancing when I was seven at pow-wows and social gatherings at school. I still love to Fancy Dance but I've outgrown my regalia.

Everybody on the reservation knows that my mom is gay. Other kids here used to call me names. Sticks and stones may break your bones, but words do hurt! Luckily, nobody teases me anymore. Now I have close friends who accept my family and they stay overnight at our house just about every weekend.

Prejudice exists because people are scared of what they don't know. People don't really sit down and talk with gay people and consider them as individuals.

If somebody asked me what it's like to have a lesbian mom, I'd say, "It's fun. I get to talk to her about girls!"

Left to right: *Mary Ann, Keely, Bryna, and Melinda*

THE
COFRIN / SHAW / MERRIGAN
FAMILY

MARY ANN COFRIN

MELINDA SHAW & MEG MERRIGAN

BRYNA COFRIN-SHAW (9)

KEELY COFRIN-SHAW (6)

MARY ANN
(Social Worker, Founder of Sojourner School, Activist, Philanthropist)

I was married to a man for over a year and had lived with him for several years before our wedding. I had thought about having relationships with women, but never had the opportunity to act on those thoughts. When I was twenty-one I met Melinda, and we immediately bonded and were living together within the first few weeks of being together. We stayed together almost thirteen years. I did have relationships with men after I first met Melinda and I went through a period of non-monogamy. I felt bisexual much of that time. It is really only now that I feel a complete identity as a lesbian. I can't say I would never be involved again with a man, but I feel it is pretty unlikely.

Melinda and I both wanted children and that was always a part of our long-term plan. We decided I would be the first to get pregnant. We chose to look for a known donor as we liked the option of our children knowing their father. I met Charles at a professional social work conference. He is a gay man who lives down south with his life partner. After I came home, I wrote him asking if he'd like to be a donor and the rest is history. He very much wanted the opportunity to have a child in his life. I gave birth to Keely, and two years later, Melinda became pregnant by him as well and had Bryna, so our girls are related

> *"I think couples with children who are breaking up should always remember to put the needs of the kids first."*
>
> — *MARY ANN COFRIN*

biologically. Charles has developed a nice relationship with both of them. He sees them twice a year and writes them letters often.

Melinda and I moved to Massachusetts from Texas when Keely was one-and-a-half years old, and Bryna was born soon after. Massachusetts was allowing lesbian couples coadoption rights and so we were able to adopt each other's biological child. I think we were the second lesbian couple in the state to attain coadoption, and it was very exciting for us. We both felt strongly that while the children were "ours" in our hearts, the legal protection was good for all of us.

In 1995, I became dissatisfied with my relationship with Melinda. She moved out and we began a coparenting relationship. The children were three and six years old and understood nothing of what was happening. It was an extremely difficult period for all of us. I felt tremendous guilt and remorse about breaking up the family.

It took two years to settle our affairs and make lasting peace with our break-up. There were legal entanglements and harsh feelings to work out, but we always worked very hard to keep the kids isolated from all that.

Melinda and I both felt strongly that the girls should always stay together. While it is tempting to each take one's biological child, I felt I could not live without Bryna, and I am sure Melinda felt the same way about Keely. It certainly did not seem fair to make them lose each other.

I think couples with children who are breaking up should always remember to put the needs of the kids first. Often lesbians don't want to use the heterosexual model of divorce, but there are some real advantages to considering it. Counseling and mediation are also useful tools in working through the hard stuff. Whatever happens, I feel siblings should not be separated from each other. Brothers and sisters never should have to experience the loss of one another.

The girls adjusted to traveling from house to house after about a year. Melinda and I experimented with different schedules and finally we have created a week-on, week-off routine that is very suitable for all of us. We also finalized a parenting agreement, a formal document to fall back on in case of disagreement. We experienced some very rocky times, some ugly times, and we have had to bite our tongues and hang in there, but I feel we are through the worst of it. I think we genuinely respect one another now. We can never expect to agree all the time and we will have to continually work on how to negotiate our different parenting perspectives. We are well on our way to a system that will serve the needs of our children, and for me, that is the most important piece of the puzzle.

Melinda and her partner, Meg, have created a new family which includes my children. Sometimes that feels hard, but I respect them as a family. I don't know if the girls think of Meg as a stepparent. I imagine they do, and I do not feel it is my place to put any definitions on their relationships with one another. Melinda and Meg and I do not do a lot of things together at this point. We do not share in celebrations and holidays, or even teacher meetings at their school. Our lives are very separate. We limit our conversations to discussing the children and only share other information if it affects the children or our lives as coparents. I doubt I will ever consider Melinda and Meg my friends. I think that would make our job too difficult. We have to work together to provide a stable growing-up environment for our kids, and to do that effectively I think we have to stay out of each other's personal lives.

I currently live by myself except when I have the children. I did have a partner shortly after Melinda and I split up. Fern lived with us for over two years. During that time, I struggled with what role I wanted her to play in the lives of my children. I know now I had not taken enough time to figure out what I wanted and needed and so the ambiguity of her role was problematic. At times the kids saw her as a stepparent and at times I embraced that. Other times I felt threatened by that role and wanted to establish my own parenting role with my kids, separate from Fern. Ultimately we broke up for many reasons.

There are many people in my extended family. I still consider Fern to be family, and she and her family members continue to play important roles in the lives of my children. We also spend holidays and birthdays together, and we often travel together with my close friends Laura, Frieda, and their seventeen-year-old son, Chris. My girls think of Chris as a brother and he thinks of them as sisters. Both Laura and Frieda have a close, almost aunt-like relationship with both Keely and Bryna. Of course Charles, Keely and Bryna's father, and his partner, Jim, are a part of our family as well.

Bryna, Mary Ann, and Keely

There are also members of my family of origin who are part of our family. I have a lesbian sister who we see at least three times a year. I am also close to my other sister and two brothers, but see them less frequently. I have had a tumultuous relationship with my parents in the past, but have established a stable and caring relationship now. They see me and the girls at least once a year.

It is important for me now that I create my own family with my children, separate from any lover I may choose. Lovers come and sometimes go. I don't believe in "forever." If I find a partner who ends up being "permanent" in my life then I will be grateful, but I am not looking for that right now. I feel I am enough for my children, and I can provide a sense of family for them. I imagine any lover I have in the future will be a friend to my children for a long time before she becomes part of our family. I feel this is a healthy model for all of us.

Left to right: *Keely, Meg, Bryna, and Melinda*

I am very active in our Unitarian Universalist Society. I feel strongly about being part of a liberal religious community. I like the ethical lessons my children are exposed to in their religious education program and I like the support we get as a lesbian family there. I also like living in my community, which is very safe and supportive. I have never had to be in the closet to protect myself or my children. I sometimes choose not to be as open as I could be, but not ever because I really expect danger, although as a lesbian, one never can be totally sure.

My kids are terrific. They are funny, happy, creative, intelligent children. They keep me challenged and entertained. I am constantly amazed how my capacity for loving them continues to grow. They teach me so many things about myself, and they help me to become a better person. They love each other immensely and I appreciate what they give one another. We have an incredibly loving family and I am grateful for the richness it brings to me.

MELINDA
(Business Owner)

I came out as a lesbian to myself when I was fourteen, and the first person I told was my younger sister Rachael. One of the first things she said to me was "Then you'll never get to have children!" Then she proceeded to cry all night. From a very early age, I always wanted to have twins. However, when my sister said that to me, I had silently agreed with her, not knowing that there was a way for two women to have a family together.

When Mary Ann and I got together in 1982, it took only a short while before we were talking about having a family. We even tried, in 1983, but I miscarried. Thankfully, we did not become parents then, because by the time we made the decision in 1988 for Mary Ann to get pregnant, we felt much more ready to take on the responsibility of having a child.

We were extremely fortunate to have found a wonderful gay man who was willing to father a child. It required very little of him, as that was the way we preferred the arrangement. Over the years he has proven to be an invaluable addition to our family. A few years later, I also used him as a donor so that the girls would be related. Keely and Bryna know him as their dad. He writes to them often and sees them a couple of times a year with his partner. Although his relationship with them has never been parental, they feel a very close bond with him.

After being together for twelve years, Mary Ann and I divorced. Since we share legal custody of the girls, we remain closely connected. Our parenting styles, I believe, are still very similar, and frequent communication seems to be the key to keeping a healthy split-family situation.

My blood family has always been very supportive of my lesbianism. They have also always welcomed anyone who is important in my life into the family. They continue a connection with Mary Ann and have welcomed into their lives my new partner, Meg.

I never dreamed that I would be a part-time mom. It was very difficult at first and is still sometimes painful to have my kids only half of the time and to miss out on the other half. It's also hard because as they grow older the girls need us as parents less and less. It sure makes me appreciate the passage of time and how valuable the time with my girls is. I feel very fortunate to have a situation that allows for flexibility with Mary Ann. I'm able to stay in contact with the girls when they are with her, so I don't feel so disconnected.

As a family, Meg, Keely, Bryna, and I enjoy doing a lot of outdoor activities. The girls love to take our boat out and drive around our lake at the Cape, water-skiing and tubing

"After being together for twelve years, Mary Ann and I divorced. Since we share legal custody of the girls, we remain closely connected. Our parenting styles, I believe, are still very similar, and frequent communication seems to be the key to keeping a healthy split-family situation."

— MELINDA SHAW

for hours. We like to ride bikes, roller-blade, and play any sort of game in the water or on land. They love to laugh and I love to see them laugh, so we can get pretty silly at times. We live in a great neighborhood for kids and I hardly ever worry about their safety. It feels like when I was a kid and I could just say, "Bye Mom, I'm going out to play!"

During the school year, routine duties can sometimes get very tiring. By the time we get home in the afternoon, most of the day is gone. Bath nights can sometimes be stressful, so whenever Meg has bath duty and any extra energy, "Ms. Frostmeyer" emerges. Ms. Frostmeyer was invented by Meg, a former hairdresser, to not only make the event more fun, but to introduce the girls to the world of high fashion in the bathtub, with her wacky hairdos! The girls love her as a stepmom, although they would love her to keep up the "Ms. Frostmeyer" act all the time.

When I first started my business, Kidsports, I did not want it to be known as a "lesbian-owned" business. I was actually pretty careful for the first time in my life to not let my sexual identity become well known. Even though our community is much more liberal than most, a business which services children could have been adversely affected by that information. As the business grew and made a name for itself in the community, my reputation as a supporter of many needy causes serving all kinds of families has also grown. My worries of being judged because I'm a lesbian are not as prevalent. People see me and my family and they know that I am a lesbian because I don't hide it. People accept me. I love kids and it shows!

MEG
(Former Hairdresser, Businesswoman in Transition)

Keely and Bryna are very special to me. My role with them has evolved during the past three years into a solid stepmom position. Of course the road was, and is, sometimes a hard one, especially when they have obvious preferences for one of their moms. But when I have no competition, they take my words just as seriously as they take Melinda's.

Keely and Bryna understand that this is our house and sometimes we don't do things the same as at Mary Ann's house. As parents, Melinda and I have our own differences too. We've been through struggles, but overall, the girls are a delight!

Before I met Melinda, I wanted to be with someone who wanted kids as much as I did. Now I have that, and it is a complete joy. We are also planning to add another child or two to our family in the very near future.

KEELY
(Third-Grade Student)

In my family, there's Bryna, me, Mum, Mommy, Meg, Fern, a little bit Charles, and Jim, a little bit.

I like movie night, going boating and water-skiing, and tubing at the Cape!

It's easier with my friends at school to have two moms because another girl in my class does too, so I'm not alone.

A lesbian is a woman who loves another woman and wants to be in a relationship with her. People who don't like gays feel that way because there aren't so many gay people and they're not in a gay family so they don't know what it feels like. The other kind of family that is not lesbian or gay was started first, and people think it shouldn't change. They think people are supposed to stay the same. I want them to know that I probably have more than they do because I have two moms and a stepmom too!

It's fun going back and forth between my two moms' houses because it doesn't get boring. Sometimes I miss the other house, but not usually. I have a huggable mommy in each house.

It wouldn't be good to have a sister at one house and not the other. It would be okay to have a new brother or sister because I have Bryna who goes back and forth with me. But it wouldn't be okay if she just disappeared or something.

A family is people who live together and love each other or who don't live together and love each other.

BRYNA
(Kindergarten Student)

I like roller-blading around the kitchen, going swimming in the summer, and riding my bike back and forth down the street.

> *"A family is people who live together and love each other or who don't live together and love each other."*
>
> — *KEELY COFRIN-SHAW*

Marcelle, Kai, and Loree

THE
COOK-DANIELS
FAMILY

MARCELLE COOK-DANIELS & LOREE COOK-DANIELS

KAI COOK-DANIELS (3)

MARCELLE
(Computer Programmer/Analyst)

As a kid, I always thought I was a boy, even though I was born a female. I was a very classic, intense tomboy when I was a child, and my physical presentation has always been more male. The problem came in puberty when I started to develop female sexual characteristics. That was very stressful and I started to think about suicide.

My parents split up when I was six, and I lived with my mother. I told her about being transgender when I was sixteen. My mother didn't handle it well. She ordered me not to tell anyone because she thought it would make her look bad as a mother. I finally decided that my mother wasn't going to be happy no matter what I did, so I decided to be happy for myself.

When I first began my relationship with Loree, I was a female. I told her that I had been taking male hormones for three years, and that I had every intention of transitioning from female to male. Loree's initial reaction was to say, "I'm a lesbian, and I don't want to be with a man." I had to make a choice between the relationship and the transition, and I chose to stay with Loree.

I was the first to broach the idea of having a child, but Loree wasn't sure she wanted one. After a while, she became open to being a parent, but we couldn't figure out how to

"Some families have two mommies; some families have two daddies; some families have one mommy; some families have one daddy; our son Kai's family has a mommy and a daddy. His daddy gave birth to him."

— MARCELLE
COOK-DANIELS

59

Kai and Marcelle

do it. As an out lesbian couple, we couldn't legally adopt a child together in Maryland, and it would have been for difficult for Loree to bear children.

As a butch, it didn't occur to me at first that I could be a biological parent, but while meditating one day, I realized that I could. We began to search for a white man with some of Loree's physical characteristics to be the donor/father. We wanted to have a biracial child who looked like a mixture of me and Loree. At the time, we anticipated living as lesbian moms, and we didn't want Loree to be hassled by people saying, "Are you really that child's mom?"

Before we conceived, Loree asked me if I still was thinking about transitioning to male. I said, "I think about it every day." She told me, "I don't want to keep you from being who you are anymore." Despite Loree's change of heart, I decided to get pregnant because I was looking forward to having a child. I also thought pregnancy might help ground me in my female body; however, I was sick during my entire pregnancy. Instead of grounding me, it made me dissociate even more from my female self.

After a sonogram we were told we were having a girl. To our great surprise we had a baby boy! Even though I had always felt like I was a male, I still harbored negative attitudes about maleness. In order to be a better parent for a boy, I realized it was time for me to deal with these feelings. Soon after Kai's birth, I decided to move forward with my transition to become a male. Now I'm glad I waited all those years because it gave me a chance to mature and to bring Kai into the world.

When Kai came along, he was my mother's only grandchild, and she loved him. Since his birth, my mother has been trying to accept me, too. She actually sent me a card on my last birthday that was addressed, "To my son." I never expected her to acknowledge me in this way.

What may make Loree and me different from some "traditional families" is that we planned and worked a long time to have Kai. He is very much wanted and loved and appreciated. What makes us the same as some "traditional families" is that we have fights over how much candy Kai can eat, about his bedtime, about when to comb his hair, and

LOVE MAKES A FAMILY

about all sorts of mundane things. We go to the Farmers' Market every Saturday and to the library to pick out books for him. We watch a lot of trains because Kai loves trains. We think about Kai's future and how to do everything we can to help him be happy and healthy. This is what parents do.

We're proud about who we are and what we've done. We've had to come a long way to get here and there's no reason to hide that. Some families have two mommies; some families have two daddies; some families have one mommy; some families have one daddy; our son Kai's family has a mommy and a daddy. His daddy gave birth to him.

LOREE COOK-DANIELS
(Free-lance Writer)

I was a very strong lesbian feminist for twenty years, and now I live in a household of men. Ironically, I've wound up becoming, in many people's eyes, a suburban wife and mother! Marcelle and I have been radicals all of our lives, but now we appear to be a traditional family. I'm still trying to figure out what it all means. It's interesting to see the differences in the ways people reacted to us as a lesbian couple in the past and as a seemingly hetero-sexual couple now.

In terms of our relationship, there hasn't been a lot of change since Marcelle transi-tioned from female to male. I was fearful that Marcelle would become macho after the transition, but he didn't.

Marcelle transitioned while I was a writer for a gay newspaper in Washington, D.C., so I had to come out. It was a very public transition. Everyone knew our whole history. When we moved to the San Francisco area, nobody knew our history and people assumed I had given birth to Kai.

When people ask me if I'm still a lesbian, I tell them that I'm a Rorschach test and I ask them what label they think I fit into. Some people feel that they have the right to define what the word "lesbian" means, so if I were to call myself a lesbian, they would say that I'm not entitled to that label anymore because now I have heterosexual privilege.

We've been here in the Bay area for a year, and I've just begun to come out about our family at work, but the neighborhood doesn't know about us yet. Last week I came out to two women at work and both of them knew other transsexuals or lesbians. It just wasn't a big deal.

I do say, "I'm queer." One of the lovely things in this day and age is that a younger generation has reclaimed that name for us so we have a nice umbrella term. I also call myself a "bridge builder" because I've been in so many minority communities. I'm part of an interracial couple, I'm a lesbian, and now I'm part of the transgender community. My work is to help point out similarities and differences and translate from one side to another.

When Kai was born, my parents were forced to be very out since I wasn't "really" married and I wasn't pregnant. They had to explain to their friends that I was in a lesbian relationship and that my partner was having the child. When we came to them a few months after the birth and said that Marcelle was going to transition, I was afraid they would be upset. I was shocked because they took it extremely well. My father was much more interested in interacting with Marcelle after the transition. I think it's because there had been something "not right" about Marcelle, and then it was fixed.

We're very open about our family, and Kai will know our history as he grows up. I think every family is different, and perhaps Marcelle and I understand that more than most people because we've been so different in so many different ways. We are going to continue to take the risk of being open as it's important for Kai to know that being transgender is not something to keep secret.

When we show Kai pictures of Marcelle before his transition, Kai just says, "That's Daddy." To him, it's just Daddy without a beard.

Left to right: *Rob holding Christopher, Daniel, and Jon holding Jessica*

THE
COOPER
FAMILY

JONATHAN COOPER & ROBERT COOPER

DANIEL COOPER (9)

JESSICA COOPER (5)

CHRISTOPHER COOPER (7 MONTHS)

JONATHAN
(President of Manufacturing Firm)

Rob and I have been together for fourteen years. After the first three years, we decided we really wanted kids. It was the only thing missing in our relationship. We thought it was the only truly negative thing about being gay. But then a gay friend of ours told us about international adoption.

We adopted Daniel first. He was followed four years later by Jessica and then by our latest addition, Christopher. We would like to adopt at least one more girl so Jessie can have a sister. We have already picked out the name Jennifer for our next daughter.

I am the coach of Daniel's soccer team. Once I was driving four or five kids home from a game and they were making fun of some kid they were mad at. One of them said, "Oh, that kid is so gay." I asked them, "Do you know what that means?" And they said, "No, not really." And I said, "Well, I'm gay and Rob's gay." They knew that Daniel had two dads and that Rob and I lived together, but they hadn't connected us with the word "gay." Obviously, they had picked up that being called gay was an insult, but they hadn't connected it to a real life situation.

Jessica is into anything Daniel's interested in, and she wants to play soccer too, but

> *"It's very important for people to understand that love makes a family. Without love, there's no family. Gay families do the same thing straight families do—which is to love each other. Gay parents have the same power of love as anyone else."*
>
> — ROB COOPER

her main interest now is ballet. She loves putting on makeup and getting dressed up. Daniel is much more the rough-and-tumble type. He's a very bright kid and loves the computer. He also loves playing tennis with my father.

We've been meaning to attend get-togethers with some local gay parenting groups, but we're always so busy. For example, this weekend we had two soccer games, two birthday parties, and homework. We even forgot to go to the annual Gay Pride march on Long Island this year because we were out shopping for furniture for the kids. We do go to the Gay and Lesbian Parents' Coalition International Conference once a year, and the kids really enjoy that. During the first gay parents' conference we attended, Daniel asked us, "Are all these parents gay?" "Yes," I answered. "Does that mean I'm gay?" "No," I said and I explained what being gay actually means.

We live in a progressive and open-minded community, and I don't think the kids have felt any prejudice yet because of our being gay. In fact, when they found out that the next gay parents' conference will be in California, Daniel turned to me and said, "Boy, I'm so glad that you and Papa are gay." I asked him why, and he said, "Because we get to go to so many great places and do so many fun things."

I felt a lot of prejudice about gays before I came out. I went through a lot of turmoil initially because my image of gay men was of people who were effeminate and I wasn't like that, so I thought I couldn't really be gay.

Some people worry that gay parents will have gay kids. Recently, there was a case that received a great deal of media attention in which Sharon Bottoms, a lesbian single mom, lost custody of her young son to her own mother. The boy's grandmother feared that growing up in a lesbian household would influence him to become gay. It's ironic because the grandmother is straight and she had already raised a lesbian daughter herself. Obviously, any parents can have gay children. My parents are straight, as are Rob's.

Sometimes strangers approach us and ask where the mommy is. At those moments, the easiest thing to do would probably be to smile and say nothing, but Rob and I make a point of explaining that we are two daddies, and that there is no mother in our family. We want to do every little bit we can to raise the consciousness level of people who may have misconceptions or stereotypes of gay people. If we do this with one person at a time, maybe that person will go home and say, "Hey, I met this nice gay couple," and then they'll tell someone else who will tell somebody else. Without exception, the reaction of people has been totally friendly and supportive.

There are forces out there that are opposed to gay rights and to the very concept of gays adopting. The battle lines are drawn, and I see ourselves as soldiers fighting that battle. I'm sure if the American people were educated by looking at all the facts, they could put aside the stereotypes and see what gay families are really like.

ROB
(Househusband)

What is going on inside of a gay home? In a gay family? When people walk into our home, it's the love that they can feel.

I quit work to stay home with the kids. It's a long day, but it's a lot of fun and very rewarding. When Jon comes home, you can see our kids' faces light up. "Daddy, Daddy," they yell as they run up to him.

I changed my last name to Jon's last name so all of us could have the same last name. I feel good carrying Jon's last name, especially because I am so close to his family. I am carrying his name with pride.

I understand that some people believe that kids should have parents of both genders, but what really does a girl have to learn specifically from a mother or a boy from a father? Some people think there has to be a mother for the daughter to become a woman. But Jessie is doing just fine.

I have so many friends who are mothers from the neighborhood. They often call and ask me for help. Kids come to play at our house and sleep over here often. Sometimes I have to say, "No, not this weekend. We need to get some sleep."

At a get-together with a lot of moms, everyone was talking about their birth experiences and I obviously could not give my personal experience. But when it comes to raising babies, I can give them lessons. They don't exclude me at all. I feel like there is no difference. We're all just parents.

Once when Daniel was little, he walked a bit ahead of me. I was watching him, but a lady went up to him and said, "Where is your mommy?" She must have expected to see his mother nearby. Daniel said, "I'm adopted. I have a papa and a daddy." And then I said to her, "I'm his father. I'm watching him. Thank you very much for your concern." It was nice to see that Daniel understood our family.

It's very important for people to understand that love makes a family. Without love, there's no family. Gay families do the same thing straight families do—which is to love each other. Gay parents have the same power of love as anyone else. All they do is love their children and try to do their best to raise a family.

DANIEL
(Fifth-Grade Student)

My two dads come on school field trips with me. When I was in kindergarten, Daddy came to my class and brought dinosaur bones that he got from my grandpa and he gave them out to my friends. Papa comes to my birthday celebrations at school and takes me to visit my friends. Daddy also coaches my soccer team. We're undefeated this season!

When I was seven, I wanted pygmy goats and Daddy said if I still wanted them when I was eight I could have them. And I did. Now we have four goats, plus a dog and a cat.

JESSICA
(Kindergarten Student)

Papa makes my bed and cleans up my stuff. We play Aladdin. It's a game. We also play with my Barbie dolls. My family goes to Disney World all together every year. We went to the animal ride and we saw fake animals.

Daniel and I wrestle, then we play, then we wrestle. Then, we say, "Stop it. Stop it. Stop it." We wrestle, and we fight, and we race. I love my baby brother, Christopher. He's a lot of fun.

Left to right: *Marquita, Laquita, Wallace, and Rafael*

THE
DRAYTON
FAMILY

MARQUITA DRAYTON

WALLACE HOLMAN

LAQUITA COWART (5)

RAFAEL HOLDER JR. (4)

MARQUITA
(Private Duty Nurse's Aide, Co-facilitator of a Gay, Lesbian, and Bisexual Youth Group)

I don't think I could ask for a better family. There's my daughter, my son, my grandfather, and my mother. My mom is pretty supportive of me. She's a churchwoman, and the church puts anti-gay stuff in her head, but she still knows I'm her daughter. I lived with my mom after her divorce, but I moved out when I was sixteen. I've been on my own since then but I see her almost every day. I also have nine brothers and sisters from my mother and five from my dad. One of my sisters is incredibly supportive, and she goes to the lesbian clubs with me.

I was in a relationship with Laquita's father during my high school years. I had a miscarriage before Laquita was born, which was very painful emotionally, and I couldn't get pregnant again for a while. Then all of a sudden it happened. Laquita was due the day before my graduation. Everyone said, "Don't go into labor on stage during the ceremony."

I knew I was a lesbian before I got into heterosexual relationships. During fourth, fifth, sixth, seventh, and eighth grades, I was attracted to girls. In junior high I started dating boys, but I still felt an attraction to girls. My mother made a comment one day, and she made it sound like it was a bad thing, so by eighth grade I pushed it behind and only dated guys. Laquita's father and I stayed together for a few years. I thought I wasn't going to date anyone after breaking up with him, but I met a very nice guy. He took me out to eat, we went on walks, and he got along with my grandfather. I got pregnant and gave birth to our son, Rafael. I really did love this guy. He was good to me, but things were just not right. I tried so hard to do everything that pleased him, but I wasn't pleasing myself. Once we parted, I felt it was time for me to be me. I decided to come out.

My sister found a support group for gay youth, and I joined it. It was great to hear other people's stories and realize that other teenagers had the same feelings I did. It wasn't just me. I am the leader of this group now.

I met my girlfriend two years ago, and my kids really took to her. It's family night whenever she comes down here.

I don't think my daughter, Laquita, knows the word "lesbian" yet, but she knows that my partner and I have a special relationship. Laquita calls her "Mommy's girlfriend," and she knows that we love each other. I never tell Laquita that she can only love boys or only love girls when she grows up. Both of my kids are being taught that you can love everybody. What she does is going to be up to her. She's her own person.

After the march on Washington for gay rights, I told my mom that I'm a lesbian. I had no intention of telling her, but during the march a friend of my mother's came up to me. I knew that if I didn't tell my mother, this friend would, and the last thing I needed was for my mother to hear something from the street. I came out to my mother! All she said was that if I could handle society, that it was on me. My mom doesn't talk about it, but she loves my partner.

When I first came out, I had a hard time dealing with it. I kept saying to myself, "God, why me? Not to be conceited, God, but I'm beautiful, so why are you going to put me through this?" But now I'm happy. It just took time and hooking up with the right people to give me support, to be there for me.

I'm part of a gay speakers' bureau and I speak at high schools. At one school where there was a lot of gay bashing, I said, "I didn't come here to argue with you. I just came here to tell you the facts." I told the students my coming-out story and that I'm a mom, which shocks everybody. There are always a lot of questions.

The high-school students often ask me and the other speakers if we are born gay. I tell them that usually people live their lives being conditioned by what they see growing up. If you grow up in a house with a mom and a dad and that is what you are taught is right, you kind of go by that model. I've met so many men in their fifties who are just coming out because they went by what they were conditioned to be. But then you have people who come out early because they're ready to deal with the world.

A lot of high-school students know that they're gay but they don't come out until

"You haven't got the church in your heart if you can't accept things. This is where churches fail their mission. It just has to be in your heart. If you can't accept anything in your heart, then you're not a truly religious person."

— WALLACE HOLMAN

LOVE MAKES A FAMILY

later on in life because school is not a safe environment. Who wants to live a life being screamed at and being called names every day?

People always say that they don't know anybody gay, but the individual working next to them or sitting next to them at school who they think is so nice can be that gay person.

I'm a nurse's aide. I do private duty, and I take care of a lady who is eighty-something years old. The other day we were watching *Love Boat* together and they had all these ladies in bikinis on the show. I'm sitting there massaging her feet with lotion and I go, "Umm, I'll take her home." She says, "What did you say? What are you? Gay or something?" I said, "No." And she said, "Oh, good, because I could not handle that." I work with this lady for an hour seven days a week. She can't live without me. She depends on me more than anyone else. I do things I don't have to do for her. Now I know I'll never come out to her because she'd be crushed. My girlfriend takes care of her yard, so if this woman finds out she has lesbians taking care of her, she won't know what to do.

I'm fine with the word "lesbian," but if you call me anything else, I'm ready to fight. I'm not a "dyke." I'm a lesbian. My gay friends use the word "dyke" very freely, and that's cool, but I can't handle it if heterosexuals use it. They mean it differently. They don't mean it in a good way. It's very much an insult. It's no more right to call someone who is gay a name like "dyke" or "fag" than it is for someone on the street to call me the "N" word. That's the only way I can really sum it up.

WALLACE
(Grandfather)

I've got thirty-three grands and thirteen great-grands. Rafael and Laquita are great-grands.

My daughter is Marquita's mom. She called me right after Marquita came out to her. I said, "Well, if Marquita's happy then God bless her." My wife really couldn't accept or understand it. She just went to pieces. I said, "Marion, you can't go around choosing people's lives. You haven't got the church in your heart if you can't accept things. This is where churches fail their mission. It just has to be in your heart. If you can't accept anything in your heart, then you're not a truly religious person."

When Marquita and her girlfriend have an argument, the girlfriend comes right to me. She'll be angry at Marquita, and I will ask her, "What did Marquita do this time?" The girlfriend calls me "Granddad" too. She keeps in touch with me. Sometimes she comes over and calms herself down. She's a great girl. I like her. We talk to each other and I try to help her iron out the problems. Marquita's very strong-headed. She was a track star. She was a champion.

I grew up in Durham, North Carolina, for the first sixteen years of my life. The people across the street had a daughter who was a lesbian. Her family had one of the biggest meat markets in Durham during the Second World War. They would supply the whole neighborhood. This girl was one of the best butchers I've ever seen in my life. One day I asked her about her partner and she said, "She's just my friend." I just let it go.

Eventually someone's going to come up to Rafael and Laquita as they grow up and throw it in their faces that their mother is a lesbian, but I think they'll be strong enough to handle it. Marquita will have taught them to handle a situation like that. She'll get them squared away. They'll be ready.

Left to right: *Regina, Kim, Rayna, and Edward*

THE
DYTON / GROGAN
FAMILY

REGINA DYTON & KIM GROGAN

RAYNA WHITE (16)

EDWARD WHITE (12)

REGINA
(Human Services Consultant at a Teen Prevention Program)

Ours is an interesting family, to put it mildly. My first husband, the father of my kids, is gay, and I'm a lesbian. He and I were together for fourteen years before we divorced. Kim is my partner now, and we are planning to get married.

I remember being very clear about having romantic feelings toward other girls at the age of twelve. I was real close to my girlfriends in high school, closer than people usually are. I remember checking myself and trying to censor my thoughts by saying to myself, "Oh, that's wrong." Also, I was a victim of incest, so I thought that making a sexual advance was a mean thing to do. Straight people often think that incest or sexual abuse makes you become a lesbian. For me, being a victim of incest stood in the way of my realizing I was a lesbian earlier in my life because I had labeled sex as "bad."

Rayna was the first child born from my marriage. I had many dreams during my pregnancy. I saw her come in on a ray of yellow light.

"Our family is very structured, and I get mad when people assume that it isn't, simply because we're a lesbian household. People think lesbians spend all day having sex. If the thing that defines us and makes us different is who we have sex with, then I can hardly find time to be a lesbian! Cooking, doing laundry, taking the kids back and forth, fussing at somebody who didn't do their homework, going to a teacher's meeting, taking the animals to the vet. That's our day."

— REGINA DYTON

That's why her name is Rayna. Three days after I birthed Edward, I was driving on the highway with him in a car seat in the back. He was screaming and crying and would not stop for anything. I did all the things I could do to comfort him while I was driving; but finally I got off at an exit, picked him up, and got him out of the car. Three seconds later, the car blew up. There was a fire under the hood. Edward saved my life!

Recently, Kim and I went to a beautiful heterosexual wedding. The bride was a short, blonde, petite American beauty. In contrast, I had an image of myself as the "AIDS Ministry Lady"—just work, work, work. I saw myself as being big and brown, and I didn't expect anybody to ever see me as sweet or romantically attractive. At some point in my life between being abused by my father and going to school with people who didn't think anything about me was beautiful, I had decided that only petite black or white girls with little high voices had something that would make people adore them.

I was forty before anybody gave me a ring—and that was Kim. I cried all the way back from the jewelers. I started to get to know and not be afraid of the really sweet part of myself. I felt sweet and pretty when I was around her. I had always seen myself as many black women do, as someone who has to be strong. Kim was the first person who could see when I was tired and needed a rest or a kiss. While we were watching that wedding, I thought that I was as sweet and lovely as that bride, and I wanted to be Kim's bride. I asked Kim to marry me. I told her that she loved me with a love that I thought was reserved for small, hazel-eyed, high-voiced, light-skinned girls.

My kids didn't accept Kim at first. I think they thought I belonged absolutely, totally to them because I had raised them alone for such a long time. The big breakthrough came when I was away, and Kim stayed with them for a week. She made bacon cheeseburgers! I consider myself quite a cook, but it seems that Kim's bacon cheeseburgers broke the ice.

Both of my kids do well in school. For example, Edward wrote a book that won an award from the State Department of Health when he was only eight years old. It's called *You Don't Have to Be Afraid of AIDS*. He's always been real deep, real good. When straight people know the kids before they know me and Kim, they make a lot of assumptions about what wonderful parents the kids must have. And it's true. But when they find out, they either try to ignore that I'm a lesbian, or they start looking for big psychological defects in the kids.

Our family is very structured, and I get mad when people assume that it isn't, simply because we're a lesbian household. People think lesbians spend all day having sex. If the thing that defines us and makes us different is who we have sex with, then I can hardly find time to be a lesbian! Cooking, doing laundry, taking the kids back and forth, fussing at somebody who didn't do their homework, going to a teacher's meeting, taking the animals to the vet. That's our day.

KIM
(Recovering Drug Addict, Public Speaker)

I met Regina because she asked if I'd be on a panel as a former intravenous drug user who is HIV positive. I speak to a lot of different groups because when a label has a face that you know, it's a lot harder to just hate. When I tell people that I'm part of a family, and that I have feelings as well as people who love me, it brings us all a little closer.

I'm proud to be part of this family. The kids are great. They are real, true, and honorable. They are clear about what they think is right and they stick up for it. I've heard Rayna argue with people about their homophobia. I always tell Regina that I'd like them whether they were her kids or not. I feel loved by them, too.

My parents accept Regina, Rayna, and Edward as my family. They buy Christmas presents for the kids and my mother has a picture of me and Regina in her wallet.

RAYNA
(Eleventh-Grade Student)

My grandpa majored in biology in college, but he wasn't allowed to teach at a high school because he was black. Not long ago, I spoke on a panel at a high school with my mom. This guy in the audience told my mom that he wouldn't want her to teach his kids because she is a lesbian. It reminded me so much of what happened to my grandpa. I think homophobia is like any other "ism." It's the racism of today. Like racism, you learn it from the people you grow up with, from your parents, from television, and from society.

When I was twelve years old, I told my mom that she was a lesbian. My mother was becoming friendly with a woman who lived down the street, and then they started hanging around each other a lot. She was here all the time! She wouldn't go home. Once I wore her socks by mistake. It was just ridiculous. So I asked my mom, "What is your relationship with her?" And she said, "Oh, we're just good friends." I said, "I think you are a lesbian." She said, "Well, I haven't done anything yet, but I'll let you know." And I said, "Watch, in about three weeks you're going to come back and tell me." And she did.

My mom had told me about my father being gay a long time ago, but I had blocked it out of my head until then. So I thought, "Both my parents are gay." I was upset because when you're twelve years old, your own sexuality starts to become more enhanced. I began to wonder what kind of role models I had. And there was the whole idea of popularity, of trying to fit in. Basically I knew that homosexuality was not accepted in our society, so it was hard for my twelve-year-old mind to accept the situation.

I didn't tell anybody about my parents because I knew I'd be treated badly. I did have

"My grandpa majored in biology in college, but he wasn't allowed to teach at a high school because he was black. Not long ago, I spoke on a panel at a high school with my mom. This guy in the audience told my mom that he wouldn't want her to teach his kids because she is a lesbian. It reminded me so much of what happened to my grandpa. I think homophobia is like any other "ism." It's the racism of today."

— RAYNA WHITE

a few friends whose parents were gay who knew, but none of them went to my school. Middle school is really mixed up. No one ever says anything like, "Did you hear that Josh likes Mike?" It is always, "Joanne likes Michael." I just knew I would get teased if people found out. I don't think the kids at school would have tried to understand. They would probably have said, "Oh, Rayna was raised in that kind of home."

My brother and I have always been very protective of our mother, but she's fairly out. She doesn't walk around with a T-shirt that says, "We're queer. We're here. Deal with it." But if you just hang around long enough, you can pretty much figure it out.

My high school is as conservative as my middle school. I have a couple of friends who know. My boyfriend knows. When someone starts to figure it out in their own mind and stops calling me, I say, "I think you know anyway, so I'm telling you, and if you have a problem with it, that's fine. You don't have to hang around me anymore. I'm a part of my family, and my family is a part of me. If being gay is something you can't accept, it's just too bad." If you're being discriminated against as an adult, you can move on, or you can file complaints, or you can sue your firm for discrimination. I can't do that in high school.

In my human rights class at school, we are studying gays, lesbians, and bisexuals and I'm learning how incredibly homophobic our society is. If you have any kind of moral issue about it, you can be excused from taking this class. Even as we're shifting into a more diverse culture—or, in theory we are—a lot of people still have a lot of hang-ups about sexuality. I recently learned about the laws against sodomy. That just cracked me up. I didn't know that there were states where you can get arrested if they catch you doing something. Even heterosexuals. It just seems to me you have to be bored to think up stuff like that.

Our household reminds me of a normal one—that is, what society calls "normal"—except that we tend to have more liberal ideas, and we're a lot more accepting. I still get in trouble with my mom if I come in late. I still have a job. You don't see whips and chains all over the place.

Growing up in this family, I've learned how to stand up for myself and to express my opinions. I think I'm more open-minded than many of my friends, and I have the power to change people's thinking. If my friends realize that gay families get up in the morning, get dressed, go to work, do chores, and have bills and responsibilities like everyone else, then I've changed some people's minds.

EDWARD
(Seventh-Grade Student)

I was twelve when I found out my dad is gay. I already knew about my mom being a lesbian. I was kind of mad and confused. I thought, "How can I have two gay parents?"

When I first found out that my dad was gay, I didn't feel like he was a man anymore. I don't know why, but he just seemed different to me. I still loved him the same, though. I loved my mom all the time I knew she was a lesbian, so I couldn't say to my dad, "I don't love you now," because that wouldn't be right. I love him now. We see him four times a year and in the summer a lot. I think he understands me. My dad and I can relate and talk about anything with each other. But I can talk to my other friends' fathers about girls better than I'm able to talk with my dad. I think this is because he's my father, not because he's gay.

Sometimes I am afraid to bring friends home. One of my friends asked me if my mom was gay and I said, "Yeah." I thought he wouldn't want to be here anymore, but it didn't matter. I was happy. I knew I was still going to have a friend, and it was easier having him over without having to worry about him finding it out.

I hear a lot of anti-gay stuff at school. People stereotype other people by how they act. In my school right now in sixth grade, a lot of kids call this boy "gay" because he acts like a girl. But I never would have guessed that one of my mom's friends is gay. Being gay doesn't show in the way he looks or dresses or acts.

Left to right: *Michael, Justin, Doug, and Zachary*

THE
ELSASSER / ROBINSON
FAMILY

MICHAEL ELSASSER & DOUG ROBINSON

JUSTIN ROBINSON (12)

ZACHARY ROBINSON (9)

MICHAEL
(Textile Designer)

Doug and I met over sixteen years ago on a stalled subway train underneath the East River in Manhattan. We became good friends and eventually we became partners. Doug had already adopted his son, Justin, and I became Justin's godfather. When I moved in with Doug about ten years ago, there was a transition time when I went from being Justin's godfather to becoming his "Poppy." He was two then, and the adjustment took about a year. There was also an adjustment time for me and Doug in terms of defining ourselves as a family. We really didn't have any guidelines for how to raise kids in a family with gay parents, and we didn't know whether to come out to people.

Doug and I heard about a group of gay and lesbian families, and we decided to go to one of their events. From the first day we met them, it became very easy to define ourselves as a family. Meeting other families like ours and sharing stories was a very freeing experience! We soon became the "answer people" for a lot of folks who'd call us up and ask us how we had talked to Justin's teacher or his doctor about our family.

Two years later, Doug and I got a phone call from a child welfare agency. They said they thought they had the perfect child for us. They did, and his name was Zach.

"I always draw parallels between my experience growing up in the fifties and sixties as an African American, and being gay in America in the nineties. . . . The most important thing is for every gay person in this country to come out. Straight people would be really shocked to see how many of us there are, and where we are. We are their neighbors."

— *DOUG ROBINSON*

If you want a child, you have to accept the fact that you're going to be out. You owe that to your child, and besides, children bring you out. They tell their friends, classmates, teachers, doctors, and the cashier at the supermarket. They tell everyone, "I have two daddies." You don't want to tell your children that they have to hide or be silent, because you don't want your children to be ashamed of their family.

In first grade, Zach had a homework assignment to make a family tree. The teacher had sent home a traditional family tree—with a mother, a father, and four grandparents. So I had to redo it. The teacher called me the next day and apologized for having been so thoughtless. She said, "I shouldn't assume that every child in my classroom has this specific type of family structure." When we feel that we are not included in school, we point it out. There's no need to make a big issue about it. People are just not aware and need some help in adjusting. They're not used to families like ours.

Doug adopted both boys. I would like to adopt them too, mostly because in case I die, they would receive my Social Security benefits. Emotionally it would be good for all of us. I haven't adopted them yet only because it has been such an expensive process. Fortunately the cost is coming down, so I'm hoping to do it soon.

Since kindergarten, I had known I was gay, although I didn't know how to name it. I entered the seminary when I was fourteen, and was with the Carmelite Order for thirteen years. My being gay was acceptable to my parents because I was confined by church structure and the religious life. But when I left the seminary to live an openly gay life, they couldn't deal with it. They stopped talking to me. I told them about the kids and Doug, and they met Justin once when he was two years old, but issues of race, sexuality, and their insecurities were too much for them. There were just too many issues for them to deal with.

My father recently died and unfortunately nothing had changed before his death. Though it was difficult, all of us attended the funeral. It was important to me that my children as well as my family see that we belong, that we are compassionate and stronger than the fear and prejudice that held my parents captive.

Doug and I feel we need to pay back the greater community, so we do volunteer work. Grief is a part of life, but the loss of a pregnancy or an infant can be quite painful. So for more than ten years I've co-run a bereavement group with a nurse in Brooklyn for couples who have had a still birth or an early infant death. Predominantly straight couples come to the group, though I've worked with a few lesbian moms, too.

When people see Doug and me, some of them say, "Oh look, there's a gay couple, and I have problems with gay couples." Others say, "Oh, there's an interracial couple, and I have problems with interracial relationships." We strike up a lot of interest as a family because we tap into other people's fears and prejudices just by our existence. In terms of who we are and how we see ourselves, this is just our family.

Zach and Justin are being brought up in a unique time. Life is challenging and we grow from meeting those challenges. Any child who has parents who have struggled to make their dreams a reality is bound to benefit in many ways.

Where does the fear, hatred, and anger toward gays come from? It runs very deep in people, and they can't name where it originates. That's why it causes so many problems. Even in the lesbian and gay community, we don't often name our own fears and self-hatred. This questioning is a process people need to go through, and those who risk asking themselves these kinds of questions open themselves up to a blessing in life.

DOUG
(Computer Programmer, Gay Activist)

Family is very important to me. It wasn't important for me to have biological kids, just to have kids. I also had grown up in a family where giving back to the community was very important, so I decided to adopt children from the foster care system. Where we live, and throughout the country, the majority of children in the foster care system are African American or Latino. I guess the rest is history. We have two beautiful boys. In our home, they flourish and bloom.

Michael and I could not imagine living without children. It's a wonderful experience to see new life and to watch the boys develop and mature. Watching Justin begin to walk was amazing because he walked at such an early age. He was an incredible walker when he was only ten months old! And Zachary at two years old was standing on his head! We loved being there on the day each of them learned to ride his bicycle.

Our family life is a very traditional American one—early morning getting up, eating breakfast, getting dressed, making sure everyone has matching socks, getting the boys off to school, and then going to work. At night, it's homework and getting ready for bed. Weekends, I coach Justin's soccer team. We've been class parents in Zach's and Justin's classes every single year. We feel we want to be there for our children all the time to advocate for them.

I came out when I was a sophomore in college. Nobody believes this, but I think I was between three and five years old when I knew I was different, although I had no idea what that difference was. I had no label for it. By eleven or twelve, I knew I was gay and that being gay was something that everyone thought was immoral.

My mother's major fear when I came out to her was that I was going to become a hairdresser. That's the image that she and so many other people in this country have of gay men—that they are hairdressers. There's nothing wrong with that profession, but gay men have many different types of lives and careers. My parents became comfortable with me being gay when they realized that it wasn't my intention to become a hairdresser. When Justin and Zachary came into our lives, my parents were elated.

"If you want a child, you have to accept the fact that you're going to be out. You owe that to your child, and besides, children bring you out. They tell their friends, classmates, teachers, doctors, and the cashier at the supermarket. They tell everyone, 'I have two daddies.' You don't want to tell your children that they have to hide or be silent, because you don't want your children to be ashamed of their family."

— MICHAEL ELSASSER

Michael's parents have never accepted the fact that we are a family. They met Justin just once, but they had never met Zach. Recently Michael's father died and we all attended his funeral. There were relatives at the funeral who didn't even know who we were. They asked us, "Who are you to the family?" Others walked past us purposely and wouldn't speak to us, and there were some relatives who were very nice. It went from one extreme to the other.

At the funeral, Michael's two oldest siblings did the eulogy, and it was very moving for them and for everyone in attendance. On the other hand, I kept feeling angry because they talked about how their father was such a wonderful grandfather and how he had taught their children to fish and spent so much time with them. He had never done that with our kids. Exactly at that point in the service, Zach started to cry. Later on, he told me he was sad that he had never gotten a chance to talk to his grandfather.

The religious right say gay people shouldn't have families because it will affect and hurt our children in bad ways. But we aren't the perpetrators of hatred. We are the ones who are living our lives trying to pass on the same good values that our families passed on to us. These folks who are against us are the ones who are hurting our children, not us. We have to overcompensate and help our children understand that these people are wrong and that we have to live our lives with pride. If anything, these negative attitudes about our family bring us closer together, but it takes a lot of work to fight this stuff.

Justin is just approaching adolescence now and he wants to be accepted by everyone, so he doesn't like to talk about any issue that makes him different from other kids. He was teased about having gay dads early on in his life, but the few times it happened, we jumped on it immediately. We talked to the parents of the kids who teased him and to the school officials. Those experiences always turned out positive. It's the experiences that he and Zach don't talk to us about which worry me. I want them to share such things so we can help rectify them.

Gay parents have to overcompensate and be "in your face" all the time to make sure that we protect our children. It's not much different for African Americans. My parents did the same thing for me when I was raised in the fifties when racism was so incredibly overt. They had to be "in your face" protecting me and my siblings and teaching us skills so we could handle prejudice when they weren't there. Over the years, we've taught Justin and Zach ways to handle difficult and uncomfortable situations and we've even practiced acting them out, but in real life, when something actually happens to them, it's a whole different experience.

I'm one of five openly gay school board members who were elected in New York City. I was the first African American gay official elected in New York. Some people see me as the gay person who fights for gay issues. Some see me as fighting for African American causes. Some see me as a person who fights for the people in my district on the Upper East Side of Manhattan. But what I try to fight for is the quality of education and the protection of kids who might be otherwise forgotten—children of gays and lesbians, gay and lesbian kids, kids of color, and poor kids of any color who might not have advocates. So I wear a lot of hats.

People are afraid of gays and lesbians because they fear the unknown. They don't know us. I always draw parallels between my experience growing up in the fifties and sixties as an African American, and being gay in America in the nineties. Our family was the first one to integrate the town I grew up in. My brothers were the first black kids to join the YMCA. People thought that everything was going to go haywire, and that all the work the white people had done to make our town a community would all go downhill when the blacks integrated it. But after meeting us and figuring out who we were, it wasn't the big deal that some people made it out to be. I think it's the same thing with gay people—it's not a big deal. We're just like everybody else.

Left to right: *Michael, Justin, Doug, and Zachary*

The African American community does have a lot of homophobia, but homophobia is prevalent throughout our entire society. It does seem especially hard for African Americans to look at gay rights as a civil rights issue and to see homophobia as parallel to their experience of oppression. Oppression is oppression no matter what form it takes, regardless of whether folks discriminate because of color, gender, or sexual orientation. I think it is partly because people of color are very identified with Christianity, and the church, in general, hasn't been great with gay issues. It's so important to realize that you shouldn't scapegoat another group if, in fact, you are a group that has been scapegoated. Some African Americans feel that homosexuality is different from race because it's a choice. As we all know, being gay is not a choice. I didn't choose to be gay. It was just clear that was who I was.

The sexuality piece is such a small piece of who you are as a person. But most heterosexuals don't seem to get it. They don't get that they were immediately attracted to someone of the opposite sex and that their attraction to people is just a small part of who they are in the bigger picture of how they live their lives. The bigger things are, of course, our moral values, our civic values, how we perceive ourselves, and how we contribute to our community, our country, and our society. Those things make us who we are regardless of our gender, our cultural background, and our sexual orientation.

What expands and enriches Zach's and Justin's lives is not only that we are a multiracial family with two dads, but also that Michael and I bring so many different perspectives into their lives. As in a mosaic, what makes our family beautiful and unique is the many different patterns and shapes which together create a whole picture.

The most important thing is for every gay person in this country to come out. Straight people would be really shocked to see how many of us there are, and where we are. We are their neighbors.

JUSTIN
(Sixth-Grade Student)

My name is Justin Tyler Robinson, and I'm in the sixth grade. I like going out for lunch and gym the best. I play all sports except for hockey, including soccer, baseball, and basketball. I play handball every day. My dad Doug coaches some of my teams.

I used to say I wanted to be a soccer player when I grew up. I'm really good and I'm also a good runner. I just finished my track season. I've also wanted to be in the Olympics as a runner. I do well in school, but I'm not sure now what I want to be.

In our family we like to go to the movies together. I haven't seen the film *Godzilla* yet, and I want to see it really bad. I keep missing it. I was camping, then I had a report to do, and I was invited a third time but my grandfather died so I couldn't go.

I like living in New York City. There's more to do here than living in the country. There are a lot of tourist attractions to see. I like having so many people around me. I don't really like when it's quiet, and I like having all this noise around me.

A family is people who love each other.

ZACHARY
(Fourth-Grade Student)

My name is Zachary Maurice Robinson, and I'm in fourth grade. I always make the beds. I clean up our bedroom; Justin cleans up the playroom.

I like to go to the movies with my two dads. My pop, Michael, usually brings me to karate and basketball. We all go to the Ninth Avenue street fair every year. We like to go to amusement parks and do lots of things together.

I like basketball and track the best of all the sports I do. I also like learning karate. My dad Doug used to be a coach on my soccer team and on my baseball team. My pop Michael watches all of my games.

I like Christmas best of all holidays as a family because you get all these presents and you get to open them and you don't know what's in them because my dads have spent the whole night stuffing these boxes full of good things. Last Christmas, our whole family got my pop Michael a breadmaker. And this year I knocked a shelf over and crushed my dad Doug's favorite lamp, so we all bought him a new lampshade for Christmas.

A family is my dads and the big guy—my brother, Justin—and our dog Yondo.

Left to right: *Jay, Al, Kerry, and Mark*

THE FERREIRA/CROWELL/DONOVAN FAMILY

AL FERREIRA & JAY CROWELL

KERRY DONOVAN

MARK O'SULLIVAN (26)

AL

(Director, Project 10 East, Cambridge Public Schools; High-School Photography Teacher; Former Education Co-chair, Governor's Commission on Gay and Lesbian Youth)

I met Kerry when I was a college freshman, and she was pregnant with her son Mark. When Mark was two, Kerry's marriage broke up, and Kerry and Mark moved into an apartment in my building. Our doors were always open to each other, and we were constantly going back and forth.

Kerry wanted Mark to grow up with positive role models, both heterosexual and homosexual. She encouraged me to be openly affectionate with the men I was dating so Mark would see that two men could have a loving relationship, just as a man and a woman could.

Before Mark came into my life, I had been reluctant to be around children at all because of my own homophobia. Some heterosexual people don't like to have gay men around their children, so I felt uncomfortable touching children and being affectionate to them. Many people hold stereotypes of gay men as child molesters, in spite of the fact that most child abuse is perpetrated by heterosexual

"I grew up, as did most gay, lesbian, and bisexual people, in a straight household where I was bombarded with heterosexual images. My family, my church, my school, and my culture told me that I must be heterosexual because I was male. I was highly motivated to be heterosexual because it would have made my life a lot easier. In spite of all of that, I have been gay all my life. Early in elementary school, I was aware that I was gay. Being gay is part of who I am."

— AL FERREIRA

males. I had internalized these stereotypes, but Kerry helped me exorcise them. She taught me that I could provide parental nurturing, and I became a parent to Mark.

I was there throughout Mark's childhood traumas. The worst experience I had as a parent occurred when Mark was eighteen. At 2 A.M. one night, I got a call from the police when Kerry was away on a business trip. Mark had been in a car accident. I raced off and arrived at the scene where I saw a tow truck hauling away his crumpled car. Even though the police officer had told me that Mark was okay, I didn't believe him. I felt absolute terror, as if my own life was ending. When I saw that Mark was alive, I was incredibly grateful.

Mark lived with my partner Jay and me during part of his high-school years. When Mark stayed out late, it was a game for him to try to sneak into the house without my hearing him. This was impossible because I couldn't relax and go to sleep until Mark was home safely. We share a spiritual connection that is very important to me. It's a lifetime commitment, a blind, unconditional love.

I grew up, as did most gay, lesbian, and bisexual people, in a straight household where I was bombarded with heterosexual images. My family, my church, my school, and my culture told me that I must be heterosexual because I was male. I was highly motivated to be heterosexual because it would have made my life a lot easier. In spite of all of that, I have been gay all my life. Early in elementary school, I was aware that I was gay. Being gay is part of who I am.

Recently, my father told me that when I was in elementary school, he and my mother talked about the possibility that I might be gay. I said, "Gee, I wish you could have had that conversation with me. I would have felt so much better if I had known that you weren't flipping out about the possibility that I might be gay." But people didn't discuss such things then.

I was "outed" in my freshman year of high school, and was the target of physical and verbal abuse, not just from students but also from teachers. A gym teacher who identified me as a "sissy boy," rapped me on the back of the head with his college ring because I wasn't acting masculine enough. He left a big goose egg. I learned how to act masculine, and I also learned to be afraid of my feminine characteristics.

As a teenager, this internal conflict caused me to go into a self-destructive mode. I was heavy into drugs, alcohol, and promiscuity. It was a horrible time for me. My adult connections were hookers in the "Combat Zone" in Boston. Interestingly, they were the only adults in my life who were constantly urging me to go back to school. Fortunately, a teacher came into my life who believed in me more than I did in myself. With his encouragement, I went to an arts college, met all kinds of people, and realized that being different wasn't so horrible, especially in an art school.

Eventually I became a teacher myself. I probably would have stayed in the closet at the school where I teach, but then I heard that a former student of mine—a wonderful young man—had committed suicide. His girlfriend confided in me that he'd been struggling with the knowledge that he was gay. I was devastated. I realized that I was part of his isolation because I was afraid to be honest about who I was as a person. I went to the principal and said, "Look. I'm either going to quit teaching or I'm coming out as a gay man. I can't be a part of another kid's isolation."

I came out in front of three hundred teachers at a workshop on homophobia. I told them that I had been hurt by their insensitive comments, and that I wanted them to change their way of speaking. I said that I didn't want to be hurt anymore, and I didn't want them being callous and insensitive in front of students.

I have worked to promote the idea that people are not really homophobic, but rather homo-ignorant. They simply do not have knowledge about homosexuality. I believe knowledge can change attitudes. For example, one of the incoming eighth-graders in my school made a "fag" comment. An older student said, "You're going to have to change your attitude because we don't tolerate that in our school." The fact that an eighth-grader heard that statement from a high-school senior is powerful evidence that education allows people to make informed decisions.

In order to provide a forum for students, I founded Project 10 East at the high school where I teach. Our group is modeled after Project 10, an organization that was created by educator Virginia Uribe at a California high school. Members of our group include students who want to support each other as caring human beings regardless of their sexual orientation. Some parents feel that I'm undermining traditional "family values" at our school. But I stand for family values, which, to me, means keeping families together.

My son, Mark, could never do anything that would push me away from him, and I think that is a real family value. I don't understand how anybody can call themselves a loving parent and then throw their children out of their home because of their sexual orientation.

JAY
(Secretary)

Al and I have been partners for sixteen years. Al, Kerry, and Mark's relationship had always been very loving, and it was easy for me to become part of it. Mark and I have always gotten along. During high school, Mark and Kerry lived with us for about eight months. After Mark went away to college, I would send him "care packages" of food. Now that Mark is back living in the area, we generally see him on Sundays for dinner.

Al and I share loving relationships with our extended families. Al's father sends me birthday cards and signs them, "Love, Dad." That is touching and means a lot to me. My family thinks Al is wonderful too. My mother is very vocal when people start saying "queer" or "fag." She says, "They are people just like you and me."

KERRY
(Co-owner, Publishing Company)

Al was always there when I needed him as a friend and as a father for Mark. We did everything together. Mark's biological father wasn't around for all the milestones that occur in a child's life, but Al was. We laughed together at the funny things Mark said as a young child, and we worried together about his childhood crises. When I recall those times, I realize how fortunate we were to have had each other.

When he was in fourth grade, Mark asked me if Al was gay. I said, "Yes." Then Mark asked me, "Well, what exactly does that mean?" I explained the definition of the word "gay." Then Mark said, "What if people don't like that?" I told him, "If people don't like Al, they're not our friends. If they're not our friends, then it doesn't matter to us what they think." As Mark grew older, I always knew that Mark had someone besides me who loved and cared about him. Al's partner, Jay, came into our lives when Mark was eleven. We have all evolved together, and we depend on one another. That's why we are a family.

MARK
(Customer Service Representative)

Many of my friends had never met anybody who was openly gay. By being close to me, they got to know Al and Jay. This helped my friends understand that gay people aren't deviant or strange. People usually didn't hassle me, but if they did, they wouldn't be my friends. When I brought a girlfriend home, I'd explain the situation beforehand because Al and Jay were often at our house playing cards or eating dinner. Some girls were standoffish at first, but most were very casual. Actually, many of them were pretty curious, which I think is good.

Left to right: *Carolyn, Leslie, Katherine, Peter holding Sophie, and Bill*

THE
GABEL / BRETT

FAMILY

CAROLYN GABEL & LESLIE BRETT

KATHERINE ALLEN (25)

PETER GABEL-ALLEN (28)

SOPHIE GABEL SCHULTZE-ALLEN (1)

BILL ALLEN-ROSS (30)

CAROLYN
(Co-manager of Feminist Bookstore)

I am a lesbian mother and grandmother. I was married for ten years and had three children: Bill, Peter, and Katherine. Seven years after my divorce, I came out as a lesbian. When Leslie joined our family, the children were only nine, thirteen, and fifteen. Leslie and I have been together for fifteen years! We've been a family for a long, long time.

My oldest son, Bill, is gay and he's married to David. My younger son, Peter, is straight and is married to Dortlis, a German woman. They have a baby daughter Sophie, and they live in Germany. Dortlis is pregnant with our second grandchild. My daughter Katherine is single and straight.

As a lesbian mother, I felt very strongly that it was important to be out within our entire extended family. Some mothers I know stay in the closet because they are afraid of losing their children. Sometimes they don't even tell their own children that they are gay. I feel that the children do know on some level, and they are denied a safe place to talk about their feelings and to be united as a family around the struggles that they may face.

"Growing up in a loving and attentive lesbian family like ours can add an extra dose of permission to explore and be different from stereotypes. Our kids repeatedly got the message that 'It's okay to be who you are. We love ourselves, and we'll always love you, too.' Our family structure is different from a lot of other families. Differences are something worth celebrating."

— *LESLIE BRETT*

LESLIE
(Executive Director, Connecticut Permanent Commission on the Status of Women)

A family consists of the people you make your life with and the people with whom you share the best and the worst. No matter what the mainstream media tells us, it's just never been true that there is a "regular" or "standard" kind of family. Never.

I am a stepmother to Bill, Peter, and Katherine, and now I am a grandmother to Sophie. We have all made connections that I think are special, important, and different, as we came into each other's lives at different points in time.

Growing up in a loving and attentive lesbian family like ours can add an extra dose of permission to explore and be different from stereotypes. Our kids repeatedly got the message that "It's okay to be who you are. We love ourselves, and we'll always love you, too." Our family structure is different from a lot of other families. Differences are something worth celebrating.

PETER
(Teacher, Gardener)

At first, my mom's relationship with Leslie was a little difficult for me. I didn't quite understand it. But after a while, it didn't bother me. As a man, seeing two women together is not such a big deal. But the first time I was driving somewhere, and my brother Bill and his boyfriend were in the back seat kissing, I felt uncomfortable and worried that someone in the car next to ours might see them. I got used to that, too.

I had a high-school friend who was gay. Knowing a family like ours may have helped him in his coming-out process. We never really talked about it, but I assumed that he figured out that my mom is a lesbian.

My wife, Dortlis, is active in the feminist movement in Germany, so she knows many lesbians. I think she thought it was cool that my mom was a lesbian. When our baby Sophie was playing with a neighbor's little boy, Dortlis and I kidded with the other parents and said, "Maybe they'll get married someday." When we met another friend who had a little daughter, we said, "Hey, maybe they'll get married someday."

BILL
(Student in Wetlands Management)

My dad has known for six years that I am gay, and it has always made him uncomfortable. And yet, he and my stepmother, Irene, have always welcomed me and my boyfriends into their home. Even my grandparents, who describe themselves as very Victorian, send Christmas cards to my partner.

After my mother came out as a lesbian, all three of us kids were nervous that the children in our school would find out. They didn't find out at first, and then later on when they knew, they didn't tease me. Ultimately, I learned that it was okay to tell people. I didn't have anything to fear.

We refer to Leslie as "Leslie," and we consider her a second mother. The fifteen years that Leslie has been in our family feel more like a lifetime. I can't imagine a time when she wasn't a part of our lives. We also considered another very close female friend of our family to be a mother. She has passed away. I feel that we grew up in a family with several mothers—women who were very important in helping to create an extended family.

I didn't start dating anybody until I was eighteen, and I never felt any pressure from my mother and father to conform and go out with women. Some kids who know they are gay feel compelled to date women in order to fit social norms. In my family, it was okay if we didn't want to date anybody at all. My parents didn't push me to define myself, to fit a box. They allowed me and my siblings to be who we were.

I did date some girls, but they were pals. When I met my first boyfriend at the age of eighteen, it was like lightning struck. It was like night and day. With my boyfriend, our hearts were beating fast, and it was love. It was very clear, and I knew—I'm gay and I'm happy about it. I've been with my partner David for four years. We were married at a ceremony during the Gay Pride march in Washington D.C., in 1993. Leslie and Mom were there too.

I realized I was gay when I was a teenager, but I didn't feel the necessity to come out. When I was in high school, none of the gay kids were out. As I've grown older, I've been impressed by the bravery of young men and women in high school who have been able to come out. It's really extraordinary.

KATHERINE
(Store Manager)

I never told anybody about Mom and Leslie until I was a freshman in college. When I was growing up, my story to my friends was that Leslie was a student living here in our basement. I was scared of being labeled the "dyke's daughter," or of being ostracized. You just don't want to do anything that would make you different or make you an outcast. I never wanted to call any attention to myself about anything, including my family. I never had friends over to my house, and I kept my family life very separate from my social life. I always loved Leslie very much, but if she came to an event at school, I was embarrassed.

I only had one friend who confronted me in high school by asking if my mom was a lesbian. I lied and said she wasn't. Years later I told that friend the truth. Last fall, I went back to my old high school with a lesbian and a gay man, and we spoke to the students. There's this group now at my old high school called SAFE, which stands for "Sexual Awareness for Everybody." They talk about homosexuality and all sorts of things that nobody ever talked about when I was in high school. Now I finally tell the students at my old high school that my mother is a lesbian and my brother is gay.

When I went to college, I attended an open circle for people interested in talking about lesbian issues. At this meeting, everybody there introduced themselves as a lesbian except for me. I said, "My mom is a lesbian," and everybody thought it was the coolest thing. All of a sudden everything had changed. I think this had to do with the progress that lesbians and gays have made by being so visible.

Now I work for a company in India, which is a very conservative culture. Consequently, I feel less secure when I'm there. I'm still in the closet about my family with my Indian friends.

Left to right: *Jon holding Madison (foster child), Michael holding Adam, and Rosa (Madison's sister)*

THE
GALLUCCIO
FAMILY

JON GALLUCCIO & MICHAEL GALLUCCIO

ADAM GALLUCCIO (2)

MADISON GALLUCCIO (1)

ROSA (15)

JON
(Actor, Stay-at-Home Dad, Educator, Civil Rights Activist)

I pretty much felt that I was different from other boys from the time I was five or six years old, but it took until I was a young teenager to know why. At the age of thirteen I had my first relationship with another person and it was a guy. I had girlfriends up through college, but I was secretly seeing other guys. There were no out gay role models and I felt very lost and confused. I suffered from depression in high school and I assumed all along that it had something to do with me being a homosexual, but I wouldn't admit that to anyone. All the older gay men I knew were married to women and having secretive relationships with men. I accepted that as my future and it certainly didn't look pretty.

At college, I decided to pledge a fraternity for one reason—Michael. I was so attracted to him that I just wanted to be near him even though I had always been very vocal about how stupid and useless fraternities were. Michael changed my whole world. I was in love. Although I had been with other guys by then, I had never before experienced love. It rocked my world and his, too. We had to break up with our girlfriends because they got in the way of us being together. After that,

"We filed a class action lawsuit against the state of New Jersey and a separate petition to jointly adopt Adam without the state's consent. Michael and I won the legal battles in 1998, and we were able to legally adopt our son as a couple. Our landmark victory was heard around the world!"

— JON GALLUCCIO

I told my my mother and I urged Michael to tell his. I couldn't bear it alone and I don't think my mother wanted to be the only parent to deal with it. My mom was pretty good, although she did send me to see some shrink who told me he was going to change me. She claims she didn't know. Anyway, I told him that I didn't want to change and that was that.

Michael and I returned to college the next fall where we were roommates in the fraternity house. We immediately went back into the closet. It was horrible and during that semester I dropped out and went home to deal with another bout of depression. Eventually, I returned to college, but soon after, Michael and I quit school, packed up, and went to California. I worked as an actor in Los Angeles and had a wonderful time. To make some extra money, I got a temporary job with a cellular phone company. That quickly turned into a career and when we moved back east, I became a marketing manager for a similar company in New York City. I left that company because a homophobic vice-president was discriminating against me. I received a big settlement check, all very secret, and I was able to pursue acting again.

My parents always thought I would be a great father, so when Michael and I decided to have children they didn't think that being gay made any difference in my ability to parent. My mom cried because she assumed I would never have children. Now she would be a grandmother by me, and she was thrilled. Most of my family was on board right away; it was Michael's family that presented a few challenges, but even they came around eventually.

We had decided that we would adopt in New Jersey, so we headed to my home town of Maywood one Saturday, looked at all the houses for sale, picked one, and went to contract on Sunday. We picked Maywood for two reasons. First, it was close to both of our families. Secondly, the town had an openly gay councilman with two kids who had already dealt with the school system. Our thought at the time was that we didn't want to pave any unnecessary roads. Who knew?

When we first moved to our new house, we went to all our neighbors and introduced ourselves. I would say, "Hi, my name is Jon and this is my husband, Michael. We just moved into the white house down the street, and we are going to have a baby." After they shook the shocked looks off their faces, they would say "Wow, that's great. Is there anything we can do to help?" The responses from our new neighbors were almost all like that. We knew immediately that we were on the right path.

Michael and I went to the Division of Youth and Family Services (DYFS) and specifically asked if we could jointly adopt. The Supreme Court of New Jersey had recently recognized same-sex parents in a lesbian case regarding second parent adoption of a partner's biological child, so we thought it would be possible. We were told yes. We went through the required training and were approved, jointly. We found out about the foster-adopt program during this training process, whereby you become foster parents first and as soon as the child is legally free, you can proceed with the adoption. We were told it was the best and quickest chance of getting an infant; however, we were informed that most infants in this program were ill. We decided to take that route and were approved as a foster family. Placement of Adam came quickly.

Adam was born premature and very ill. He was HIV positive then, and he was three months old before we could bring him home. He had medications to take every few hours for the first couple of months along with nebulizer treatments for his lungs. He had doctor appointments and tests like you couldn't imagine. It was exhausting.

When Adam was eleven months old, Michael and I filed to adopt him and found out that the DYFS would only let one of us adopt. They said they had thought they could let both of us adopt Adam, but that they had made a mistake. Since I didn't have an income, they would only allow Michael to be the adoptive parent. The fact that I didn't have an income because I was Adam's full-time caregiver didn't matter to them. They said we couldn't adopt jointly and we said we could. Adam had two parents, so we said no to DYFS!

We retained the American Civil Liberties Union and began putting real legal pressure on DYFS. They still would not budge so we filed a class action lawsuit against the state of New Jersey and a separate petition to jointly adopt Adam without the state's consent. Michael and I won the legal battles in 1998, and we were able to legally adopt our son as a couple. Our landmark victory was heard around the world! New Jersey became the first state in the nation to have an official policy that puts gay and lesbian couples on an equal footing with married heterosexual couples with regard to adoption.

The Episcopal Church has also welcomed us with open arms. We were both recovering Roman Catholics with a lot of "church baggage." They've helped us heal those wounds. They have baptized our children; they have blessed our relationship; they have blessed and celebrated the adoption of our son. They held a prayer chain while we were in court; they

Jon and Madison (foster child)

> *"Families always have, and always will, come in many shapes and sizes. Our family is based on love and commitment, just like any other healthy family. Just because ours is not the most recognized type of family does not mean it is not a good type of family. If I had to put a label on our family, I'd call it All-American."*
>
> *— JON GALLUCCIO*

attended press conferences, and held us as we cried. They never abandoned us. On this coming Father's Day, we will enter in a Holy Union with the blessing of our bishop and with four priests celebrating. We could never have asked for all that we've received so freely.

We had no idea at the time of planning our Holy Union that it would become such a "public event," with many members of the media attending. We are quite spiritual and just a tad religious. In order to meet those needs first, we have decided to have a very private service on the Saturday evening and then a public service during church on Sunday. Why have both? It's because so many people have reached out to us and made us part of their families that we want them to be able to share in our public celebration.

Many people in our country do not have the ability to do the things we have done and are doing. We need these people to know that there is hope. Just look at how startlingly high the suicide statistics are for teens struggling with gay and lesbian issues. We recently received a letter from a sixteen-year-old boy from Texas. He told us that when he meets the man he will love and marry—if marriage between gay couples is legalized—he hopes that they will be able to proudly raise a family as we have done. He said that seeing our situation only brightened his horizons and pushed him to fight for his rights. This is why we are glad we have been so public about our family situation.

Although our Holy Union is a religious ceremony, it does spotlight the inequality of the civil rights of the gay and lesbian population. If we had access to the same civil rights as heterosexuals, this would be a legal wedding and not a Holy Union. As a result of these inequalities, our willingness to commit and profess our love to one another at a Holy Union in an Episcopal church is interpreted as a political statement. Much like two men or two women holding hands in a public place is seen as a political statement in certain parts of the country. We feel strongly that these reasons alone justify us inviting and welcoming the media to this event.

Michael gets up at 4:00 A.M. weekdays so that he can be at his desk by 6:00 A.M. and leave by 5:00 P.M. The kids wake me up when they are ready, usually Madison first at around 6:30 A.M. After I change her and get her started on some juice, I get Adam up and start his routine. We do breakfasts and diapers, run errands, read books, and play games. Twice a week Adam goes to nursery school. We have lunch, play some more, and then it's nap time, theirs not mine! I get dinner ready, straighten and clean the house. The kids get up, Father comes home, and we all have dinner. After dinner Father and Daddy take the kids for a walk or play in the yard. We then get them ready for bed; they usually drop like flies. Then Michael goes to the gym and I collapse for a few minutes before I tackle cleaning up after dinner. Michael comes home and we have some time to talk, write, read, watch TV, and then totally crash.

Our family consists, first of all, of Michael and me. We are two loving, caring, silly men who are both independent free spirits who usually travel in the same direction. We have worked hard at our relationship, at building a foundation strong enough to support each other and our children. We complement each other from our coloring to our souls. God has blessed us with each other.

Speaking of blessings, there are the children. Adam is a miracle. He is no longer HIV positive! I don't like to put pressure on him with that kind of labeling, but he is definitely a miracle. In my heart I will always believe that Adam survived all that he did for a reason. It might have been the whole New Jersey adoption victory, who knows, but God chose him to survive and thrive for a reason. He has blonde hair and brown eyes and an engaging smile that invites you to love him. It is not hard. He loves people and trusts everyone. He is also very busy, always exploring, touching, smelling. Adam already thrives on experiencing the world. He is a joy.

Madison, the latest addition to our family, is another of God's beautiful creations. On the same day we surrendered another foster son, Andrew, back to his grandparents, we retained the ACLU to fight for Adam's adoption, and we received a phone call telling us about Madison. She came home to our house in much better shape than Adam had been when he arrived, but she was tiny. Born HIV indeterminate and drug addicted, Madison required routine testing and heavy-duty nurturing. She is now a beautiful, thriving toddler. She is definitely a "Daddy's girl," and I am Daddy, so I just love that. She is very bright and advanced at eighteen months. She is quite the talker! She already shows a flair for the dramatic, and with one look, Madison can captivate you for hours. She enjoys copying everything her brother does, so I often call her "Monkey Do." She is still our foster daughter. We hope she will soon be our adoptive daughter.

Our extended family includes Michael's parents, grandparents, and siblings, my parents, my birth parents and birth siblings, some very close friends, and our next-door neighbors. From baby-sitting to helping with the house or running errands, they all have been and continue to be there for us. We have cried on all of their shoulders at one point or another through our legal struggles with Adam's adoption.

I was adopted by my parents when I was only thirteen days old. My adoptive parents never received any genetic information or medical history regarding the circumstances of my adoption. The only thing my parents were told was that I was 100 percent Irish. Thirty-three years later I found out that this information was totally wrong. Without any information for all those years, I always felt uncomfortable deep inside. I knew, however, that I, too, would adopt someday. I'm not sure why, but I think it was a sense that if I did it too, it would mean I was okay myself. I do know that Adam's adoption process put me over the edge in the curiosity department regarding my own adoption. It was during our fight with the state of New Jersey that I began the search for my biological parents. Much to my surprise the search only took three weeks. I met my birth mother over a year ago, and her other son a few months later. We are all extremely close now.

The path we had been on before our court case was that of a private little family life in suburbia, but that was not the plan God had in mind for us. In the name of our children and children all over, we continue to stand up to discrimination. We have been urged to produce both the literary and film versions of our life and struggle to adopt. Hopefully I'll act in the movie not as myself but maybe in some smaller role. We have begun traveling around the country lecturing at colleges and organizations about what family is really about, about how hate, no matter how it is packaged, still is hate, and that, above all, the only truth is that love makes a family.

Families always have, and always will, come in many shapes and sizes. Our family is based on love and commitment, just like any other healthy family. Just because ours is not the most recognized type of family does not mean it is not a good type of family. If I had to put a label on our family, I'd call it All-American.

MICHAEL
(Businessman, Educator, Civil Rights Activist)

Jon and I met in college in 1981 when he attended a party at my college fraternity. We spoke briefly, didn't really get along, and went our separate ways. At the time, I had a girlfriend, and she and I were considered the "campus love affair." She was the varsity cheerleader captain and I was on the executive board of the "big fraternity." I assumed that she and I would get married after we graduated.

Early the next semester Jon turned up again, this time as a pledge at my fraternity. I spent the next several weeks being as mean to him as possible. Typical fraternity stuff. Soon, we became friends . . . sort of. Our girlfriends were in the same sorority and we did things all together. Before long . . . somehow . . . I ended up falling in love with Jon. In April of 1982, it became apparent that Jon and I were a couple and we broke up with our girlfriends in order for us to be together. We kept our relationship a secret. We were very young and very scared.

Unfortunately, I never had the courage to tell my girlfriend why we were breaking up. I made up some lie and wasn't very nice about it. It took a while before she found out the truth from someone else, and I never discussed it with her. Funny though, when Jon and I hit the national media during our legal battles to jointly adopt Adam, she was one of the first people to contact us with her support. She told the press, "I loved Michael because I knew he would be a great father. I still think he must be." We stay in pretty close touch now and we've gotten together with her and her husband and had a wonderful time. At our first

"All in all, we are a regular family with a huge support network. Our lives are rich and full. There is never a dull moment."

— MICHAEL GALLUCCIO

meeting, I apologized for my horrible actions back in college, and she was amazingly forgiving. She admitted that she had hated me for some time, but eventually she had realized how scared I was way back then.

Jon and I had been together for a few months when he told his family about us. I was terrified to tell my parents. I knew it would be "the end" of my family, and I was afraid of what might happen. Jon and I spoke many times about it, but I still wasn't convinced it was the right thing to do. One day during an argument with my mother, she asked me if I was gay. I started to cry and so did she. She said she needed to call my father. When she left the room, I ran out of the house and went to Jon's. I was twenty years old.

When I realized I was gay and was going to stay that way, I gave up my religious life. In my mind, the only God I knew hated me and had turned away from me. I was spiritually alone with no hope of salvation. Unfortunately, I didn't realize then that this was just the Roman Catholic version of God and that not all religions have the same version of God. So I left God behind, with much sadness, for thirteen years. My family felt the same way about me as the church did. I was an abomination to God and would be damned forever. They prayed for me. They cried for me. In their minds, they had lost me not only in this world but for eternity.

Adam and Michael

Once Jon and I matured, we both began to look for religion again. We thought that there must be someplace we could go. We found the Episcopal Church. They preached of a God who loved all people, not just a select few. This is a God who created and loves all of us. The church supports us as a loving parent would support its children who are being harmed. We took time to reeducate ourselves in religion; then we took the time to do the same with our families. Jon and I now have a strong spiritual life. Our families also seem to have drifted away from their rigid Roman Catholic doctrine. They question their old belief in a vengeful, restrictive God and are leaning more toward believing in a loving God. Our

"If a stranger comes up to us and asks where the mommy is in our family, it is our duty to correct them and tell them openly that there is no mommy in our family. Our kids are watching, no matter how young they are. If they see we are ashamed of ourselves, how are they supposed to feel about their family? To date, this method has worked very well. No one has reacted negatively to a family with 'just two dads.'"

— MICHAEL GALLUCCIO

relationships with our families have become very strong with religion acting as a binding factor instead of a separation between us.

After Jon and I had been together for over twelve years, we were sitting in our Manhattan apartment following a full day of fun in the city. We started into a typical "thirty-something," life-evaluating conversation. We asked each other, "Where are we in our lives, and are we happy with where we are?" At the time, we were living the exemplary "gay lifestyle." We knew the right people, hung out in the right places, and had the right address. We were both successful in our work. During this conversation, we both decided that we were very happy where we were and we had no regrets. It was after a short silence that I turned to Jon and said, "You know what? I do have a big regret. I really regret that I will never have children." Jon looked me in the face with utter shock and said something like, "You would want to have children? I would love to be a father. It's probably my only regret, too."

The can of worms had been opened and we were on our way. Before long we were grappling with all our internal homophobia, which was telling us that it wasn't right for gay men to raise children. It took some real soul-searching before we could get rid of our inner beliefs that we were less than everyone else in some way. Everyone else straight, that is. Once we shed the shame we had been living with, it was just a matter of deciding how and when to become parents.

It was decided that Jon would be a stay-at-home dad because he was working as an actor at the time and had more time to dedicate to parenting, while my job seemed more likely to be able to financially support a family. He began the research . . . the rest is history. We've been together sixteen years now, and we have a beautiful son, Adam, whom we adopted jointly in December 1997. We also have a foster daughter, Madison, who, with the grace of God, will join the family permanently very soon. Her biological sister, Rosa, visits with us on weekends and may come to live with us someday, too. In retrospect, Jon is better qualified to be the stay-at-home dad anyway. He is far more patient than I am. His ability to nurture and care for our children could not be surpassed in any way by me. Our kids are lucky to have Jon as the main influence in their lives.

I had a job which involved quite a bit of traveling and I was gone many nights. I was away on business when my son, Adam, had his first birthday. My whole family was at my house singing "Happy Birthday" in New Jersey, and I was in a hotel room in Texas singing the same song and crying. I swore that day that I wouldn't be that kind of father. Two weeks later I quit that job for one that didn't involve traveling.

When Jon and I decided to have kids we also decided that we would be the type of parents who would not change our lives because of children. Our kids would go to all the events we went to. Right! It's funny how your life adapts to your children's needs so quickly. Well, we still do a lot of things most people normally don't do with young children like go to art galleries and travel. We still spend time in the city and visit our friends. But the kids come first. Most of our time is spent running around with them, reading to them, acting silly with them, and singing the alphabet song.

We have a ritual in our family that every night after dinner we all play. Whether inside the house or outside, we run around and make noise. We laugh and carry on like . . . kids! Then we sit and read a book or two. The kids choose the books. Since the kids are only one and two years old, the same books usually get read over and over. We all look forward to that time of day.

One of the main philosophies in our family is to be proud of who we are. There was a long period in my life where I was very ashamed of myself for being a gay man. I know the pain of shame and the loneliness, and it would be a terrible thing to push that onto a young child. Jon and I decided very early in our journey of family-building that we would need to come to terms with the feelings of shame we harbored within ourselves. We strongly believed that our biggest mistake would be to raise our children in an atmosphere of self-loathing in which many gay people exist without even recognizing it. We decided to be out at all costs.

If a stranger comes up to us and asks where the mommy is in our family, it is our duty to correct them and tell them openly that there is no mommy in our family. Our kids are watching, no matter how young they are. If they see we are ashamed of ourselves, how are they supposed to feel about their family? To date, this method has worked very well. No one has reacted negatively to a family with "just two dads."

I never even thought about changing history when we began the process of fighting a legal battle to adopt Adam. We just wanted to move to the suburbs, get this adoption done, and get on with our lives. I was completely against the idea of talking to the media back then, and I yelled at the ACLU that I didn't trust them. I didn't want them dragging my family into the spotlight. But I soon realized that talking to the media was the only way we were going to get done what we needed to get done. It started as a necessity, and I went into it grudgingly. Then as we got more and more well known, I got scared. We had an alarm put on the house and I notified the police that we were going to be the focus of a lot of public attention. Then it became really cool because most everyone we heard from was in support of us.

From the time our lawsuit hit the news, my parents have asked me why my family has to be in the media spotlight. Why us? At first, I didn't have any answer other than it was the best way to assure we would be able to adopt Adam. Recently, Jon and I were talking with my parents about our upcoming Holy Union. They asked me again, "Why can't you just go and live your life? Why do you have to deal with the media now that you've already won the lawsuit." I was finally able to explain it to them. I said, "Mom, can you imagine what it would be like if your family were illegal? Just imagine what it would feel like if you and Dad went away and it was against the law for both of you to stay in the same room. Imagine that there are people who believe you shouldn't be allowed to raise your four kids. How would you feel about that?" I also said to her, "Do you know what it's like to be sixteen and hate yourself because all you've ever been told is that everyone, including God, thinks you're disgusting? Imagine how it feels for teenagers to realize that they are gay in that kind of atmosphere. It's my responsibility to do this media stuff because people are listening to me and Jon. You would do the same thing for your kids. It's my responsibility to Adam and Madison. What if someday my kids find out that they are gay, wouldn't it be much better that I did this now so it wouldn't be as hard for them? Do you know how many kids kill themselves because they are gay? I don't want my kids to be one of those kids. I don't want my kids to have to go through what Jon and I went through."

My mom just sat there listening. She's usually the big supporter and Dad is usually very quiet. This conversation changed everything. It was clear that something went off and clicked for him. By the time I was done speaking, he was the one who said he completely understood and that we were doing the right thing. He said to me, "I hate it when you make so much sense." Then he offered Jon and me their house for the party after our Holy Union even if it meant the media would be there, which is so totally against what my family was into before we had that conversation. The local paper is doing a big article on my father and me for Father's Day with my dad's permission. I was one step from dead in my family's eyes and now my parents really respect me and my family.

Jon and I gave a talk at Princeton University and there were over a hundred kids in the room. We just told the story of our lives, and it's kind of a soap opera story with real highs and real lows. At the end, a college student stood up crying and said, "You won't believe how you have changed my life. You're doing what I want for my life. Thank you so much." Jon was also crying hard at this point. Those are the kinds of things that just floor me.

When we were on the Larry King show with Jerry Falwell, even he couldn't say anything bad about us. He did say he believed firmly that homosexuals shouldn't have families and that gay families should not even exist, but he couldn't attack us personally. There's nothing to attack. Well, I do have a cousin who is publicly speaking out against us. Someone sent me a tape of a television show he did in Colorado in which he declared that he was a homophobic, right-wing radical. He talked about his cousin Michael adopting this baby and what a travesty it was. In response to a question, he said he thought gay-bashing was cool. I think he wanted to get in on something that was popular and would bring him some attention.

The most important thing to me is that I'm a parent and the main responsibility of parents is to make the world a better place for their kids, whether it's buying them an extra toy, making sure they have food, or making a major social change. At this point in our lives, Jon and I feel we can make a significant change in the world.

We have a huge number of friends and acquaintances. We are very close with our families, even our third cousins. We are active in our church, where we are lay readers. We are close with many of our neighbors, and I have many close friends at my job. We have even kept in touch with some of our friends from high school and college including my ex-girlfriend. All in all, we are a regular family with a huge support network. Our lives are rich and full. There is never a dull moment.

Vivian, Lillian, and Armando

THE GONZÁLEZ/CARLO

FAMILY

LILLIAN GONZÁLEZ & VIVIAN DALILA CARLO

ARMANDO CARLO-GONZÁLEZ (2)

CELÍN ALEJANDRA CARLO-GONZÁLEZ (IN UTERO)

VIVIAN
(Professor of Multicultural Education)

My parents are both from Puerto Rico. They met in New York and started their family in the early 1930s. I was the youngest of four children, born fourteen years after my oldest sibling. Our entire extended family lived in New York. Everybody was struggling. My father got a job offer in a quilting factory in Chicago, so my mother and my two sisters, my brother, and I moved to Chicago when I was four.

My mother and father had an intensely passionate relationship. They adored each other. They were married in their late teens and renewed their vows on their twenty-fifth anniversary and again on their fiftieth. They kept marrying each other. My father was incredibly romantic around my mother. My mother was very, very affectionate, touching him all the time and talking about the wonderful way he smelled. I had this image that this was the way I wanted to be in love when I grew up. I just accepted that I was heterosexual like my mother, and that I was going to find some wonderful man, get married, and have kids. When I did marry, it was really my husband who pointed out to me that I was much more complicated than that. He was a very nice guy who helped me find myself. His support helped me realize that I'm a lesbian.

"We actually formed our family close to sixteen years ago, although I don't think society necessarily viewed it as a family because there was no formal ceremony or public acknowledgment. But within our hearts, we knew we were forming a family, and we've gone through a lot of changes, challenges, and wonderful times together in these sixteen years."

— *LILLIAN GONZÁLEZ*

In the mid-seventies, I played in a woman's percussion band in Boston, and Lilly was very good friends with the leader of the group. One night we went out, and there was a disk jockey at the bar who had developed a little repertoire of records by Latin artists. We started dancing, and we danced great together. She was twenty-three, and I was thirty-four. We connected. We became one while dancing.

Lilly and I have been together almost sixteen years. She always wanted to have children, but I wasn't so sure. Lilly didn't push me to decide. Rather, she gave me a lot of room to consider what this might mean to me in my life. That freed me up tremendously, and I was able to say to her, "Let's do it." When Lilly was pregnant with Armando, I used to go to sleep at night with my hand on her tummy. Before I fell asleep, I would send wonderful thoughts into him. I would think, "intelligent, bright, creative, funny, active, humorous, loyal." I had nine months of adjectives. They just got better and better all the time.

I had never spoken the word "lesbian" to my mother, but I hadn't hidden my life from her either. She knew I'd been living with Lilly forever, but when Armando was born, my mother sent a card to Lilly. She wrote, "Lilly, congratulations on Armando's birth. It is so wonderful that this has happened to you." On the same card she wrote, "Vivy, it's so wonderful that Armando has come to live with you." That felt like I had a roommate, so I thought, "No, no, no! This cannot happen. This is not how my life is going to be now. This has to change."

I sat down and wrote my mother a ten-page letter. In it I said, "Mom, I've always protected you because I was afraid to use the words with you. But I realize I can't protect you anymore because I want you to be as happy about the birth of my child as you are about the birth of any of your grandchildren. I need you to know that Armando is your grandchild." I told my mother how much I loved her, and how much I loved Lilly.

My mother, being the wonderful person she is, didn't call me to talk about my letter. She talked to my sisters about her feelings first. She said to them, "The problem is not that Vivy's with a woman, it's that she wants me to regard Armando as my grandchild." My sisters, being who they are, said to her, "Ma, if she adopted a child, would that child be your grandchild?" When my mother heard that question, she said, "Seguro!" Of course!

A few weeks later Lilly and I went to see my family in Chicago for Thanksgiving. My mother and I still hadn't spoken about my letter. When we arrived we stayed with one of my sisters. My mother came over and handed me a bag. In it were three small boxes. I opened the boxes and there were three Christmas tree ornaments. One was for Lilly, one was for me, and one was for Armando. Every year she gives her grandchildren ornaments. She had written on his, "For my Grandson Armando, Love Grandma."

Culturally, Lilly and I come from a tradition of understanding family in a very deep, meaningful, poignant way. We both knew that once we moved away from our own extended Puerto Rican families, it would be important for us to replicate the values of the family that we grew up with. We have tried to create a sense of family with our friends who are lesbians and with our friends who are heterosexual as well.

I don't think attitudes toward gays and lesbians are the same in Puerto Rico as in other Caribbean countries. Although homosexuality was not considered the norm, I never felt a very strong taboo against it when I was growing up. For example, my older sister married a man who had a gay brother. This was back in 1954, and I can remember going to dinner at his house when I was around seven years old. The brother cooked and his lover showed us toys we could play with. I was getting a message from my parents that I could break bread with gay people.

I believe my father knew I was a lesbian before my mother did. Even though he died before I talked with him about it, I believe he accepted that about me. When he met Lilly, he took her off to the side of the room to check her out—to see what her job was and to see if she would be supportive of me.

Vivian and Lillian

We have the same anonymous donor for both Armando and our soon-to-be-born daughter, Celín. We tell Armando that even though we don't know who his birth father is, we do know that he's a really generous person because he knew that there were two women who wanted to have children, and he was willing to help.

I think Celín is going to have a very different personality than Armando, and, like Armando, she's going to enrich our lives. We're going to have the best of both worlds, having a boy and a girl. We'll love her as much as we love Armando. Sometimes, I want to have a third child.

I've learned over the years to use words that Lilly can understand when I'm feeling emotional, and Lilly has learned to accept my emotions and express more of her own. We have been a positive influence on each other. I've gotten my doctorate with Lilly's help, and Lilly was able to get a master's degree in taxation with my help.

Lilly has a terrible sense of direction. She never knows where she's going when she gets into the car, and I have a great sense of direction. But Lilly is so ambitious; whatever she wants to do she does. I always tell her, "Lilly, if I stick with you, we'll go places. But if you stick with me, at least we'll know how to get there."

LILLIAN
(Certified Public Accountant)

We actually formed our family close to sixteen years ago, although I don't think society necessarily viewed it as a family because there was no formal ceremony or public acknowledgment. But within our hearts, we knew we were forming a family, and we've gone through a lot of changes, challenges, and wonderful times together in these sixteen years. I think the addition of a child makes people realize, "Oh yeah, this is a family because there's a child." But I feel it's important to acknowledge the fact that we were a family before we had a child. And after the kids grow up and leave the house, we'll still be a family.

There's an African saying, "It takes a village to raise a child." I think this attitude has been instilled in our Puerto Rican culture as well. If you need something, you can rely on aunts, uncles, and cousins to help. Even your second and third cousins are always involved with everybody, and everybody keeps tabs on each other. People deal with each other as one big family. In a Puerto Rican extended family, children are always around, and we all deal with them. It's not an "I have to," but it's something that you do because you want to. I find in the white American culture that taking care of the kids is often seen as a sacrifice. If someone called me to ask if I could watch their kid for two hours, even if I already had plans, I'd say, "Sure, she can come along with me." In white culture, people might say, "No, I have an appointment and I can't cancel it." We Puerto Ricans integrate children into our lives.

One of my favorite expressions about having kids is, "It's the toughest job that I've ever loved." Vivian and I have both learned so much. As much as we're trying to teach Armando good values, he teaches us every day how to be better parents, how to be better people. He's very self-assured; you can see that in his demeanor.

Armando knows he's loved. When I ask him, "Do you know how much I love you?" He opens his arms wide and says, "Like this!!!" It fills my heart with joy.

Left to right: *Hera, Kirstin, Carl, Bill, and Scot*

THE
GOODRICH/CORNWALL/
OPPERMAN
FAMILY

HERA GOODRICH

SCOT CORNWALL & BILL OPPERMAN

KIRSTIN GOODRICH (13)

CARL GOODRICH (7)

HERA
(Orientation and Mobility Specialist, Teacher of Visually Impaired Children)

Fourteen years ago, my partner, Pamela, and I wanted very much to have a family. At that time, we didn't know of any other lesbians planning to have children.

I had dated Scot in high school and college, and we had remained very close throughout the years. He was gay and involved in a long-term relationship with Bill. Scot had once said that his only regret about being gay was that he couldn't have any children. Pamela and I wanted to know our future child's father, and we agreed that Scot was the obvious choice. Without telling him why, I asked Scot to go out to lunch with me. I was very nervous. We talked about other things until it was time for him to go back to work. Then I blurted out, "Pamela and I really want to have a baby. Will you be the father?" He said, "I have to talk to Bill about it." A couple of days later,

"Before we made the decision to have our first child, a psychiatrist told us, 'Hey, there will be twice as many parents. It will be twice as good for the children and half as hard for you.' He was right. It's really good when we go places—three adults on two kids is a pretty good ratio as far as keeping an eye on them. One parent gets to breathe."

— *BILL OPPERMAN*

we received a phone call I'll never forget. "In a word, yes," Scot said. Then Pamela and I looked at each other and said, "Oh, my God. What have we done now?"

Although Pamela and I split up when Kirstin was two, Pamela has remained very close to Kirstin over the years. Several years later, when I decided that I wanted Kirstin to have a sibling, I spoke again with Scot. This time Scot and I decided that Bill would be the biological dad.

Our next door neighbor was an old, rigid Yankee-farmer type person, with conservative politics. Periodically, he and Pamela used to talk garden talk. After Pamela left, he asked me, "Where's your buddy? I haven't seen her around." Although I'd never spoken a word about our relationship to him, I said, "Well, I'll tell you, it's the saddest thing that has ever happened in my life. Pamela is the person that I loved and still do love, and she's left." Then my neighbor talked to me about his relationship to his wife. Perhaps this was his way of saying that he understood my feelings for Pamela. It shows that if somebody knows you as a person, and then they find out other things about you that they might not approve of, it doesn't always matter.

Scot, Bill, Pamela, and I agree on most parenting issues. If they have any qualms about an issue, they are very good about letting me make the final decision since I live with the kids most of the time. There really haven't been any major issues—only minor ones—and we talk about them. We are four very peaceful people.

SCOT
(Librarian)

We had trouble with the nurse when Bill and I both wanted to visit our son Carl in the newborn nursery. Bristling, she said, "You're going to have to decide who the father is." I said, "Go ahead, Bill."

My very conservative aunt called me before a family reunion and said she wanted to do an update on our family genealogy. She intended to include everybody who was going to be at the reunion, but she was a little concerned about including Bill, Hera, Kirstin, and Carl. After I discussed this with her, she titled the genealogy, "The Cornwalls and Allied Families," and she felt comfortable with that.

A couple of years ago, Bill and I came to one of Kirstin's school plays. We were slightly early, and a whole bunch of her classmates surrounded us, saying, "Which one is Daddy and which one is Papa?"

BILL
(Computer Technician)

Carl had a fantasy that Scot and I would move next door to them, and then they could come to our house to watch television. Hera doesn't have one, and we have thousands of videos they like to watch.

Before we made the decision to have our first child, a psychiatrist told us, "Hey, there will be twice as many parents. It will be twice as good for the children and half as hard for you." He was right. It's really good when we go places—three adults on two kids is a pretty good ratio as far as keeping an eye on them. One parent gets to breathe.

KIRSTIN
(Seventh-Grade Student)

A friend of mine asked me, "How is your family different from having just one mother and one father?" Basically, it's hard for kids to really understand how there could be a family with two mothers and two fathers. I tried to explain it to her, but I said I couldn't compare my family to any other family because I had never lived in another family. Sometimes I wish I could know other families just like ours.

It's fun to have a bunch of parents because they take me and Carl on different sorts of trips and we do different stuff with each parent. We go camping a lot in the summer with Mama. We go to museums a lot with Daddy and Papa. It's like there's more variety in our family.

Once some kids at school were talking about how many grandparents they had. One girl said her parents were divorced and that her father is remarried, so she had six grandparents. But I have eight grandparents!

Sometimes I wish that my fathers lived a bit closer to us because two hours is a long drive. Maybe one hour away would be okay.

CARL
(Second-Grade Student)

Every summer Mama, Kirstin, and I go to the Thousand Islands. We have a motor boat. During the school year, I see Daddy and Papa every other weekend and during school vacations. If I could change anything in my family, I would have all my parents live closer together.

Linda, Anna, and Molly

THE
HELLER
FAMILY

LINDA HELLER

ANNA HELLER (27)

MOLLY HELLER (25)

LINDA
(Social Worker, Therapist, Feminist/Lesbian Activist)

Coming out is not an event. It is a long process. When a parent comes out, the whole family is affected. Our homophobic society has done tremendous damage to so many human beings. What we need is people to understand what a family really is.

I've often wondered why there's so much fear and hatred of lesbians and gays. I think it's because people have fears about their own sexuality. I believe that everyone is on a continuum of sexuality. Some people are at the extremes and others fall more in the middle. I remember having a crush on a female teacher in first grade and being attracted to other women as I grew up. But being a lesbian wasn't an option. It never really occurred to me. I was heterosexual when I married. During my sixteen-year marriage, I began to realize that I was possibly bisexual. Then, when I fell in love with a woman, it was clear to me that I was a lesbian. I felt like I was coming home.

All families have challenges. Our children have the challenge of dealing with rampant homophobia. For the last eight years, my daughters, Molly and Anna, have been actively working to help other children of gays and lesbians become comfortable and proud without having to keep any secrets. I think that the work Molly and Anna do is part of healing our

"I don't have a problem with religious people, but when people tell me that my family is bad and is going to hell because there's the wrong kind of love in it, it makes no sense to me. All I can ask them is, 'Why don't you meet us first, and then make a decision?'"

— ANNA HELLER

planet. My children have educated people and opened people's hearts. They are activists because they have lived with prejudice. They have heard it; they have seen it; they know it.

Molly and Anna understand that families are about love, commitment, and the willingness to face challenges together. I believe that all children know this unless adults teach them to hate. We are all activists in our family because the most important thing we can do is to promote change and healing for all people.

MOLLY
(Graduate Student, Gay-Rights Activist)

When I was eleven, my mom brought a woman home and introduced her to me as a new friend. At eleven o'clock that night, I heard them talking in my mom's room. Being a nosy kid, I snuck out of my room because I had to know everything that was going on. I thought, "Uh oh. This woman's not leaving. She's staying overnight. Oh my God, my mom's a lesbian!"

I couldn't tell my sister, Anna, because she had gone out for the night and Mom's girlfriend had snuck out early before I woke up. When Anna came home, I told her but she didn't believe me. We went back and forth. "Mom's gay." "No, she's not." "Yes, she is." "No, she's not." "Well, let's find out the second she comes home." When Mom walked in from work, she didn't even have a chance to put down her bags. We were waiting for her at the top of the stairs. Simultaneously, Anna and I both asked, "Mom, are you gay?" She said, "Girls, we need to talk."

Anna and I met Mom's girlfriend a few days later, and we drove with them to meet her girlfriend's family. Anna and I were in the back seat of the car, and Mom and her girlfriend were holding hands. Anna and I stuck our fingers down our throats and pretended we were throwing up because we thought it was so weird and gross. How could they do that? In spite of this, we had a great time. It took us no time to warm up to this woman. She was just the neatest person.

I didn't tell anyone for seven years that my mom was a lesbian. I used to ask her not to wear Birkenstock sandals because I thought that they were "lesbian shoes," and that everyone would know my secret. I even had a boyfriend for four years in high school whom I didn't tell, and we were very close. He kept asking me, "Where does your mom's friend live? Where does she sleep?" I would just make up a new lie every time. "Oh, she lives in the basement," or "Oh, she's just a good friend."

I was afraid that my classmates wouldn't like me, or that they'd think I was gay if they knew that my mom was a lesbian. I was worried about being rejected and not fitting in. I was also afraid that my friends wouldn't like my family. I knew that people wouldn't understand that we had a wonderful family.

It wasn't until I was eighteen that Anna called me up and said, "There's this great conference we can go to for free if we take care of the little kids." That was our first Gay and Lesbian Parents Coalition International Conference. It was the first time we met other kids who had gay parents. We realized that there was a lot that we weren't dealing with. We cried for three days. There were eight kids in the room, and every kid was crying. We just passed around the tissues. We spoke about the secret. It's awful to keep that secret. We realized we were not alone.

After the conference, I started a support group for teenagers with gay or lesbian parents. Anna, another woman, and I currently co-lead a group for younger kids of gays and lesbians.

When people ask me about my sexual identity, I always say, "I'm straight now, but who knows? I could come out someday." If I were to come out someday, I would be the luckiest gay person on the face of this earth because I know I would be accepted totally by my family.

ANNA
(Gay-Rights Activist)

When I was in fifth grade, I remember saying to my mom, "Oh, that's so gay." Mom told me, "That's not nice. You're talking about people, and it's not nice to make fun of other people." I asked her, "Are you gay?" She said, "No, I'm not, but I have a lot of friends who are." I believed my mom, and it made sense to me not to make fun of people, so I dismissed that idea forever. When Molly told me that Mom was a lesbian, I remember thinking, "But Mom told me that she wasn't, so she can't be."

When we confronted Mom about being a lesbian, Molly and I were hysterical. We were crying. All of us were crying. And we were pissed. We said, "Why can't you two just be friends?" Then Mom, Molly, and I went out for dinner because that's what we did whenever we were in crisis in our family. That's what we still do.

Although we didn't like the fact that Mom and her girlfriend were lesbians, for the first time in our family there was a lot of love and laughter and talking and listening. Our father was a very loving parent, but we didn't see much happiness in our parents' marriage. Even though Molly and I ended up keeping Mom's lesbianism a secret outside of our home, we wanted her lover to live with us. And, in time, she did.

Mom and her lover worked different hours, and when we came home from school, we knew that 90 percent of the time there was going to be a love note on the kitchen table. So, every time we came home with a friend, we were very anxious. How were we going to get into the house, get to the kitchen table, and remove the note without looking completely ridiculous?

I didn't tell anyone about Mom until I was out of high school. I found out later that

"Our homophobic society has done tremendous damage to so many human beings. What we need is people to understand what a family really is."

— *LINDA HELLER*

everybody knew! All of my friends knew! But I spent my high-school years terrified that people would find out and not like me anymore because they would think that homosexuality wasn't okay.

A girlfriend in high school once said to me, "Anna, I would love you even if you were gay." She said it in front of all my friends, and I remember thinking that it was really a weird thing for her to say to me. Years later, she and I decided to live together as roommates. At that time, it was important to me that I didn't have to live with a secret anymore. I told her about my mom, and she looked at me and said, "Anna, I knew about your mom when I was sixteen." I said, "Why didn't you tell me that you knew?" She said, "Because I wanted you to tell me yourself. I didn't think it was my place to ask. And it never mattered. I always loved your mother."

The gay jokes at my school were constant. As I got older, I would stand up to the jokes and just start screaming at my friends. If someone told a racial joke, or said something that was offensive to any people in any way, then we knew we could never tell them about our mom. We had feelers out for people who were open and accepting, so that when we told somebody, it wasn't as much of a risk for us. Children of lesbian and gay parents go through a similar process to what gay and lesbian people go through when they are coming out and testing the waters.

If all young children were taught about different types of families, children of gay parents wouldn't have to live in fear that they would lose their friends just because their families weren't the "norm." High school is too late to begin learning about different kinds of families. This education needs to start young. The younger the better.

There are people who believe the Bible literally and say that they have this love for God and that they love everyone, and yet they have so much hatred for people they don't know anything about. I don't have a problem with religious people, but when people tell me that my family is bad and is going to hell because there's the wrong kind of love in it, it makes no sense to me. All I can ask them is, "Why don't you meet us first, and then make a decision?"

Left to right: *Marcelo,
Wendy, Kristin, Lily,
and Judith*

THE
HICKMAN / STEVENSON
FAMILY

LILY GEE HICKMAN & JUDITH STEVENSON

WENDY BOWERS

MARCELO ERNESTO LEON

KRISTIN GEE HICKMAN (11)

LILY
(Elementary School Teacher)

I divorced my husband when our daughter, Kristin, was very young. She was four years old when I met Judith, my partner, and we've been together for eight years. Judith has four daughters from her previous marriages, including Wendy. Marcelo is Wendy's husband.

Judith and I formed our relationship very slowly and intentionally because we both knew that solid relationships had to be developed with each one of our daughters. It couldn't be forced.

My parents are exceptional people, and even more so because they emigrated from China to America. I marvel at their ability to overcome and modify their Chinese up-bringing and the Chinese culture's sense of right and wrong. They have Chinese friends who disowned their children when they married white people, but despite their anguish and heartbreak, my parents did not disown my sister when she married a white Jewish man. By the time I married a white person it wasn't a big deal as three of my older sisters and one of my older brothers had already done so.

When I came out as a lesbian, I knew that I couldn't expect my parents to accept it. I thought it was too much to ask of them, as they would have had to rethink and modify

> *"I think kids who are raised in a lesbian family may have a harder time, but in the long run I believe they have more compassion than kids raised in a 'traditional' family. From my perspective, my daughter is living in the ideal world of the future. Only she's living in it today."*
>
> — *LILY GEE HICKMAN*

their Chinese sensibilities even more fully. At first, my mom cried a lot, but my parents didn't disown me. My mother told me that gay people in China did their familial duty by getting married and having children. She said I should honor our family by either staying married to my husband or by marrying another man.

My mom has very gradually come to accept my relationship with Judith because she and I have been together for so long. My brother, Young, is also gay and he has been with his partner, filmmaker Arthur Dong, for almost twenty years. Our parents didn't disown him either when he came out. But even after my brother had been with Arthur for ten years, my mom would still tell Arthur, "You need to find Young a nice Chinese girl to marry." My parents don't talk to their friends or relatives about the fact that I'm a lesbian or that Young is gay. They would lose face.

Judith comes from a white European background, and I come from a fairly traditional Chinese background. The first time we had a culture clash was not pleasant, and it made us realize how different we are. Now, things are better and we share our traditions. For example, in every house in China there is a built-in altar. My parents have an altar in their house in America, and Judith and I have built an altar where we place photos of our ancestors in our house, too. We celebrate Chinese New Year together by following the Chinese customs of burning money and making wishes.

I teach at an elementary school, and most of the staff know that I'm a lesbian. A few years ago some kids came back from a field trip and told me that they'd seen a photograph of me on the front page of the *San Francisco Chronicle*. Judith and I had been photographed kissing on Valentine's Day while registering as domestic partners. The kids at my school thought it was cool, and their teachers did a marvelous job of explaining the photo to them.

A lesbian mom is like any kid's mom. I make Kristin clean her room. I make her brush her teeth. I make her do her homework. I make her do her chores. I make her go to bed at a reasonable hour. I think kids who are raised in a lesbian family may have a harder time, but in the long run I believe they have more compassion than kids raised in a "traditional" family. From my perspective, my daughter is living in the ideal world of the future. Only she's living in it today.

JUDITH
(Director of Operations, Residential Treatment Services)

I came out in 1977. Twelve years later, I met Lily at a Metropolitan Community Church forum on parenting. I had already raised four daughters and was looking forward to the time when I could be an independent woman in the world. For that reason, I had reservations about dating a woman who had a young daughter. However, over the course of three or four years, Kristin and I walked kind of slowly into a family relationship.

During our years together Lily has given me a lot more support involving my issues with my four daughters and grandchildren than I have needed to give her and her issues around Kristin. Kristin has two strong parents—her father is very involved in her life—and she has a huge family of grandparents, aunts, uncles, and cousins.

After I came out to my daughters, my second daughter, Karen, decided to live with her father and essentially disowned the rest of the family during her high-school years. I went to court and fought a "lesbian mother battle," but I lost, and she stayed with her dad. I didn't know whether we would ever see Karen again, and I gave her up for lost. Happily, she came back into our lives after she turned eighteen, and we have a very healthy, mutually affirming relationship.

My youngest daughter was lost to me for a period of years as well. She would often tell me, "You just don't know how hard it is to have a lesbian mom." But this same daughter is in college now, arguing with her law enforcement professors when they say that the "homosexual lifestyle" isn't natural. She takes them on and has called me up in tears saying, "I can't live in a town like this."

There was a period of time when each of my four daughters was just rageful and wanted me to be married to a man and not be a lesbian. I don't think I ever lost my belief that they would come through it.

We live in a kind of family that isn't shown very often on television or spoken about in Sunday schools. Our children grow up knowing that it's okay to be different, and I can't help but believe that this knowledge makes them better people.

Every time there are newspaper articles like the ones about Melissa Etheridge becoming a lesbian mom, I send copies to my older daughters. I write, "Show this article to your children. It's very important that they have these role models when you talk with them about me."

One of my granddaughters visited here for a month. When she went back home, she showed her friends some photographs of our family. They asked her who Lily was, and she told them, "That's the woman my Grandma Judith is married to."

KRISTIN
(Sixth-Grade Student)

Lily is my biological mom. Sometimes I tell my friends at school that Judith is my mom's roommate. But with my friends who know about our family, I call Judith my stepmom. I didn't tell my best friend that my mom is a lesbian, but she kind of figured it out. Then I talked with her a little bit about it, and now she accepts it.

Some friends say homophobic things, so I don't really talk about our family that

"Some friends say homophobic things, so I don't really talk about our family that much. Sometimes I ask my friends, 'What's so wrong about being gay?' I would like to tell them that my mom is a lesbian and that gay people are just like regular, everyday normal people. There's nothing wrong with them."

— KRISTIN
GEE HICKMAN

much. Sometimes I ask my friends, "What's so wrong about being gay?" I would like to tell them that my mom is a lesbian and that gay people are just like regular, everyday normal people. There's nothing wrong with them.

At school during sex education class, we were learning a bit about gay and lesbian people. When the teacher said, "You know, you can never tell when a gay person is out in public," one girl said, "You can always tell when gay men are out in public—they always dress so wild." I whispered to her, "Have you ever seen any gay or lesbian people out in public?" And she said, "Yeah, and they always dress so weird." I said, "Well, if they dressed regular, how would you know if they were gay or lesbian?" She just kind of shut up. Kids stereotype gays because they pick it up from their parents or from their religion or from television. They don't really know anybody gay.

I like having Judith in the family because when my mom gets mad and narrow-minded about some things, Judith helps calm her down. She also helps me with a lot of things. Without Judith, I'd have nobody to do my makeup and my hair when I go to ice-skating competitions.

WENDY
(Human Resources Professional)

I didn't come out about my family to any of my friends in high school, and I always introduced my mother's partner as our roommate. Some years later, I realized that my friends knew my mother was a lesbian, but at the time I was much too uncomfortable to talk about it. Even though I wasn't consciously trying to hide a "horrible secret," I instinctively knew that I didn't want to tell my friends. When I went to college, I immediately told all my friends and it wasn't a problem.

I lived for many years with my dad. It was very sad not living with my mother on a day-to-day basis, but I loved visiting her. My mother's household was always filled with music, singing, and lots of women. Meeting her strong feminist women friends was extremely important in my development.

I think my mother is exceptional, and not just because she's a lesbian. I just think she's a wonderful person. Being a lesbian has probably shaped who she is, in part, and made her more open and accepting of differences. My mother has profoundly shaped who I am, the values I hold and those I don't hold.

I think it's nice to see your parent in love with somebody. It's not about who she loves; it's just about being happy that she loves somebody and that somebody loves her back. This example is very good for Kristin.

MARCELO
(Student and Teacher)

I met Wendy in Chile, which is my home. She told me that her mother was a lesbian, and in my country, this is taboo. It is not acceptable to be gay or to live with a gay family. If there are gay families in Chile, they are very hidden.

Wendy and I lived with Judith and Lily when we first came here. I couldn't speak any English then. Zero English. Judith and Lily were very supportive of me, and we became very close. When I had problems, they were very patient, especially Lily, who helped me a lot because she is a teacher. Judith is amazing, too. I like being a part of this family.

I haven't told my mother that my mother-in-law is a lesbian because my mother is a very old-fashioned, conservative woman. To live in a gay family is new and different for me. But the great thing for me is that I have two new friends. I have two wonderful mothers-in-law!

Abbie, Abbie Marie, and Karen

THE
HILL / HOFFMAN
FAMILY

ABBIE J. HILL & KAREN M. HOFFMAN

ABBIE MARIE HILL (7)

"I like our family because it's a nice family and it's a good family. I like having two moms because it's different, and I like my family being different."

—ABBIE MARIE HILL

KAREN
(Firefighter)

In 1987, Abbie and I got together, and we hit it off right away. A year later we had a commitment ceremony. I originally wanted three kids, but we ended up with one. We used donor insemination at home, so you could say that Abbie Marie was homemade. The donor is anonymous to Abbie Marie, so she's grown up knowing that she has two moms and no dad.

The kids at school sometimes try to put me in the father role because I'm 6'2" tall and masculine looking. Lots of times kids will ask me, "Are you a man or a girl?" I answer, "Neither. I'm a woman." Their eyes get really big. Given my career choice, I must seem much more masculine than some of their fathers. I like being a firefighter. I especially like helping kids.

I haven't come out to my parents or to my two younger sisters. I'm sure they suspect I am a lesbian but we haven't ever talked about it. I guess I don't have the guts to come out to my family members, although I've told strangers and people at work. I work with nine men at the fire station who all ask me how my daughter is doing. It's no big deal.

I'm angry because my family is so weird about everything, not just about gays and lesbians. I come from a family where my father told me if I showed up with a black boy at the front door, he'd shut the door in his face. So, I just didn't bring any boys home!

It's like *Sesame Street* where we live. Almost every family in our neighborhood is different in some way, and all of the straight people are very accepting of us. It's almost like they want us to be in their circle so they can expose their children to lesbian families! They feel like we're good people and good role models, and they feel safe when their kids are playing at our house.

Even the eighty-year-old Irish Roman Catholic couple who live next door to us like us. They once asked us who was the boss in our family, but that was their only question. They love us because we keep our property up, and we don't play loud music, and when they fall down we help them and drive them to the hospital.

The school that Abbie Marie goes to is very good, and several teachers there are gay or lesbian. We're completely out at her school, and the staff and teachers treat me like I'm Abbie Marie's mom, which is how I view myself.

ABBIE J. HILL
(Entertainer, Tourism Worker)

Before I had Abbie Marie, I volunteered in my community to be a "Big Sister," but I was turned down. You couldn't work with kids in those days if you were gay. I felt that I had something I really wanted to give to a young person, and I was afraid I might get too old to become a mother. I felt very sad about that possibility.

When I met Karen, she told me, "You can have everything you want." I told her that I wanted to be a parent. I knew from my experience as the oldest of four siblings that raising a child is a hard job, and that I couldn't do it alone. I needed to share this responsibility with someone who was very committed.

In many ways Karen and I are like a heterosexual family. We got married before having a baby, and we have a very deep commitment to each other. Karen loved the fact that I was pregnant. She fed me venison during my pregnancy so the baby would be strong and healthy.

We had a difficult time picking out a name for our daughter. I would like a name but Karen wouldn't. Finally Karen said, "Well, your name is a nice name." I agreed, and we named our baby after my grandmother. My family came over on the Mayflower, so it meant a lot to carry on a traditional family name.

My mother was very hurt when I first came out to her when Karen and I got married in 1988. She said, "I feel betrayed." To this day, I'm not sure whether she was upset because I had taken so long to tell her or simply because I'm a lesbian.

There's been some progress. My mother recently visited us for a week. We told her about friends of ours who were thinking about having children, and we used the words "artificial insemination." We even told some lesbian jokes in front of her. At one point, my mother grabbed little Abbie Marie and said, "Oh why don't you just let Grammy take you away out of this crazy household?" It was good because she didn't say it in a serious way. She was just teasing.

In the past my mother has said to me, "If you die, don't ever think that I would let Karen raise your child without a fight." I have always replied, "Karen is Abbie Marie's mother! How can you even think that way?" I think it really helped my mother to actually visit us in our home and see our relationship firsthand.

I still sense a reserve and a distance from my family that may never be fixed. I miss them and wish they felt more comfortable around me. I don't know what else to do except just keep plugging away. They haven't shut us out of their minds and lives, so I have a feeling of hope that these barriers might be broken someday.

Once I took Abbie Marie to a film about gay families. Standing in front of the movie theater were people holding signs saying "Homosexuality Is Wrong" and "God Made a Man and a Woman, and You People Shouldn't Have Children." Luckily, Abbie Marie was young enough so I don't think any of it sunk in.

Before I had Abbie Marie, one of my fears was that she would invite her school friends for sleep-overs and they wouldn't be allowed to come over because she has lesbian mothers. Obviously that's not the case because kids love coming over here and the house is always full.

ABBIE MARIE
(First-Grade Student)

I call one mom "Momma," and the other mom is "Bubba."

Kids at school ask which mom I came out of and how I was born and stuff. I give them a little bit of the answer. I say a lot of different things.

I think it's wrong that our country doesn't want two people of the same sex to get married.

I like our family because it's a nice family and it's a good family. I like having two moms because it's different, and I like my family being different.

"It's like Sesame Street *where we live. Almost every family in our neighborhood is different in some way, and all of the straight people are very accepting of us. It's almost like they want us to be in their circle so they can expose their children to lesbian families! They feel like we're good people and good role models, and they feel safe when their kids are playing at our house."*

— KAREN M. HOFFMAN

Crystal, Cameron, and Nancy

THE
JANG / OTTO
FAMILY

CRYSTAL JANG & NANCY OTTO
CAMERON JANG (19 MONTHS)

CRYSTAL
(Middle-School Coordinator of Support Services for Sexual Minorities in San Francisco, Teacher, Counselor, Mother)

I am fifty years old now and I'm a new mother. I went to Asia ten months ago to adopt Cameron when she was eight months old. Nancy and I started seeing each other shortly before Cameron arrived.

I'm a fifth-generation San Franciscan. My mother had four kids, and I was the firstborn. I was raised by my grandmother because my mother was just starting her optometry practice. When I was growing up, I didn't know one other Asian lesbian, and I didn't know how to find any. It was a very isolating experience. In fact, I was always told that there weren't any Asian gays and lesbians.

I came out over twenty years ago at a time when Asians didn't have any gay role models. I began speaking out in public so that other gay and lesbian Asians would know that we existed. As an Asian lesbian, it is very important to be out there. Our young people need to know that they aren't alone.

When I started to speak in Chinatown, I knew that my parents would hear about it so I had to come out to them, too. It had become hard for me to sit at the dinner table with my

> "I came out over twenty years ago at a time when Asians didn't have any gay role models. I began speaking out in public so that other gay and lesbian Asians would know that we existed. As an Asian lesbian, it is very important to be out there. Our young people need to know that they aren't alone."
>
> — CRYSTAL JANG

Cameron and Crystal

family and not be able to talk truthfully about my life, so there were personal reasons for coming out to my parents as well. My mother was very stoic; she didn't say anything at all. She's still like that. It is an unspoken issue in my family.

In Asian culture, what you do is a reflection of your family. This is a tradition. Although many Asian gay and lesbian people are out to friends and to colleagues at work, they are most often not out to their families because they're really afraid of shaming them. Once I was pictured in an Asian newspaper as part of a gay and lesbian group. When my aunt saw the picture, she cut it out and sent it to my mother. However, she would never say anything to my parents like, "We saw Crystal in the newspaper. How do you feel about her being a lesbian?"

Coming out to my parents freed me to be very visible in the Asian community. I've been fortunate to receive honors for my work in the gay community, and I've been able to share this with my parents. My parents have come to a number of gay events, and I'm really proud of them for doing that.

I wanted to be a mother since I was in my early twenties, but in those days being a lesbian and being a parent was not really an option. And it was certainly not an option in my Chinese American family to be an unwed mother, whether gay or straight.

Many years ago, a male friend and I decided to coparent a child. When I brought this idea up to my parents, they said, "Absolutely not!" I set aside my desire to be a mother until I had the powerful experience of being a godmother to a friend's child, which brought me back in touch with my feelings of wanting a child of my own. As I was approaching fifty, I realized that if I didn't do it then, I'd never do it.

My mother had a difficult time when I first told her I wanted to adopt a baby. She wasn't sure I was serious about it, given my age. She's not a warm, loving grandparent, but she treats Cameron the same as she treats all her other grandchildren. My mother gave Cameron a traditional Chinese name as she did for her other grandchildren.

When the baby came, it brought about a tremendous change in my relationship with Nancy. My whole life suddenly revolved around Cameron, and Nancy and I had to renegotiate everything. She's just now beginning to take more of an active parenting role.

Having a child is much harder than I ever thought it would be, but it's also much more rewarding. Fortunately, I have a really strong support system and a lot of help from Nancy and my other friends. I worry because I'm so much older than most other parents. Nancy is only thirty-two, but by the time Cameron reaches middle school, I'm going to be nearly sixty! The age thing is more of an issue for me than the lesbian issue.

My job in the San Francisco school system is to ensure that gay and lesbian families feel safe and welcome in the schools. Over the last two years a number of Asian students have come out as either bisexual or lesbian or gay at their schools, and I go and talk with them because they feel so isolated in their families.

We've had a number of Asian students who were institutionalized by their families after they came out. I don't know if this happens because being gay is seen by Asians as a sickness. When Asian youth are deciding whether or not to come out, they're often caught between wanting to be true to themselves and protecting their families. These kids tend to be so afraid of shaming their families.

Gay and lesbian parents are just like everybody else. Because we are a family of color, we embrace diversity and we accept and respect people who are different from us.

NANCY
(Project Director, ACLU of Northern California)

My mom came to the United States from Japan when she was thirty-five. My father is from St. Louis, and he's white. When I first told my mom I was a lesbian, she became suicidal. One of her best friends, who is also Japanese, was very tolerant and understanding of gay people, and she was able to help my mom along. I think she really saved my mom's life and helped her feel less isolated with this issue. My mother even joined PFLAG, which was a remarkable step for her.

My parents are divorced, and my father has been very supportive of me. I'm even out to my family in Japan, although they don't really understand my being a lesbian. These relatives think it's a phase, and they still ask my mom when I'm going to get married.

Crystal and I got together less than a month before Cameron arrived, and neither one of us really knew where our relationship was headed. We recently decided to make a go of this as a family, which means that I have to get out of the back-seat role and become much more assertive about coparenting. Crystal has slowly introduced me to her family as someone significant in her life. We've gone to family functions, and I'm sure her mom knows what our relationship is. But it may never be spoken out loud.

I do love Cameron. She's wonderful to be with, and being part of this family is very much a gift to me. I'm evolving toward becoming Cameron's second mom, and although Crystal and I have never really talked about it, I've begun to think about second-parent adoption.

I'm still discovering the role of motherhood. It's a whole new learning thing for me, trying to figure out how I can give Cameron the best experience. It's a mystery.

Left to right: *Masha, Colleen, Leigh, and Lacey*

THE
JOHNSTON / FINNEGAN
FAMILY

S. LACEY JOHNSTON & COLLEEN FINNEGAN

MASHA FINNEGAN JOHNSTON (5)

LEIGH FINNEGAN JOHNSTON (2)

LACEY
(Computer/Technology Administrator)

Colleen and I have been together for over ten years. Before I became involved with her I had considered having children, but never in any serious way. For me, the decision-making process was a gradual one over the years. Ultimately I felt I had a lot to give to a child, and that I wanted to share my life and love with a child of my own.

We both tried unsuccessfully to have biological children through artificial insemination. Although we had always wanted to adopt a child at some point in our lives, we decided to pursue this method sooner rather than later.

Masha came home to us from Moscow when she was fifteen months old. Our first photo of her shows a fierce-looking one-year-old scowling over her crib bars at the photographer. She has lived up to this first image of her. Masha is a wild, wonderful child, full of life and adventure. We wanted Masha to have a sibling so we adopted Leigh, who was born in Wuhan, China.

The adoption agency knew I was a lesbian, but as far as the Chinese authorities were concerned, I was just a single woman. While Colleen and Masha waited eagerly at home, I went to China with six other prospective parents and learned quite a lot

"Because of our friend-ships with other families, both traditional and non-traditional, I've become aware of just how similar we all are. We have the same concerns for our children, the same day-to-day joys, drudgery, and patterns, and the same sense of family bonds."

— S. LACEY JOHNSTON

about the Chinese people and their love of children. Colleen told me that she'd never seen Masha so excited as she was the night Leigh and I were to arrive home. Leigh is a beautiful, charming, quick, and delightful child.

The two sisters have become incredibly close. Masha is the ever-protective older sister, and Leigh misses her terribly when she's at school or at a friend's house. I couldn't have wished for a closer bonding between the two girls. They have learned so much from each other. Masha has become much more affectionate, and Leigh has become quite the trooper while trying to keep up with her big sister.

Massachusetts is one of the few states that has legalized second-parent adoption by unmarried and same-sex parents. We coadopted each of the children this past year and this past summer we had a big Adoption Day party. The legalization of our coadoptions made us feel substantiated as parents, as a lesbian couple, and as a family.

It was overwhelming how much love and support we were shown at our Adoption Day party by our families and friends. Both Colleen's family and my family were present. They expressed how proud they were of us and of the wonderful job we have done with our daughters. It was a day of good wishes, appreciation, and heartfelt love.

My parents and younger brother and his family live close enough that we can visit them on weekends. My family has been extremely supportive of my relationship with Colleen, and they were delighted when I adopted Masha. She was their first granddaughter! My younger brother, sister-in-law, and nephews have also formed wonderfully close relationships with both Masha and Leigh.

Colleen's family has been supportive of our family too. Masha was their first grandchild as well, and she has had lavish attention paid to her, especially by Colleen's mother. Colleen's entire family loves having both girls visit. This past holiday season they were extremely disappointed that we wouldn't be coming down to visit. They wanted to see the girls open their presents on Christmas morning so much that they made a special trip to our house.

Colleen would like to take in foster children with the secret hope that it will lead to another adoption or two. We're starting by having a "Fresh Air" child from New York City this summer.

For Colleen and me, having children has been an on-going coming out process. Whether it be with people in the supermarket, teachers, the pediatrician, relatives, or co-workers, you are always having to explain that the girls have a mama and a mommy. We are both "out" in all aspects of our life, but every new person we encounter gives us yet another opportunity to explore our own internalized homophobia.

The fact that we are a family with two moms hasn't been an issue yet for either of the girls. Neither one of them realizes yet that it is anything out of the ordinary. We have lesbian friends who have both biological and adopted children, and we have nurtured these

"Our kids don't see any particular differences between us and the other families they know. I see many more similarities than differences between us and our heterosexual counterparts."

— COLLEEN FINNEGAN

friendships both for ourselves and for our children. It is very important for our girls to know children from families similar to ours so they won't feel isolated.

Because of our friendships with other families, both traditional and nontraditional, I've become aware of just how similar we all are. We have the same concerns for our children, the same day-to-day joys, drudgery, and patterns, and the same sense of family bonds.

COLLEEN
(Physician)

I had always wanted to have many kids. One of my favorite movies was *Yours, Mine and Ours*, in which Lucille Ball plays the mother of eighteen children. The reality of parenting in combination with my not-always-patient, more-comfortable-with-order personality has given me cause to reevaluate. In fact, I felt relieved when I returned to my medical residency training program eight weeks after adopting Masha. I said to a coworker with four sons, "Parenting is really hard!" He agreed and said, "I forgot to tell you how difficult it is!"

I now have a deeper appreciation for parents and a better understanding of people who choose not to parent. I must say, however, that I love Lacey and our two daughters more deeply than I ever imagined possible.

I grew up in Hawaii and miss the strong presence of numerous cultures and the intertwining of daily life with the beauty of the natural environment. Lacey and I are both passionate about sailing and would practically sell our souls to live on the ocean. However, we've chosen to live in Northampton, Massachusetts, an inland community where the support for gay and lesbian families and the sheer numbers of families like ours seem unmatched anywhere else.

We've found wonderful schools, child care, community events, and a church and religious education that reflect our values of inherent respect for individuals and diversity. We also have found support from others when we've had to confront bias and discrimination in our community. We could not give up this opportunity to raise our children in such a nurturing environment.

Besides our chosen community, our families of origin have also been remarkable. Both sets of grandparents have made astonishing strides in accepting our family. My mom is challenged by her ingrained Catholic opposition to homosexuality, and Lacey's parents are challenged by their traditional southern upbringing. I haven't noticed any difference though between the way our parents treat our family and the way they treat the more traditional families of our brothers.

We enjoy a special family closeness while sailing, dancing to the radio in the kitchen, performing acrobatics in the living room, and visiting with grandparents, cousins, neighbors,

"I like swimming with my moms. I love birthdays and playing with my animals. I like to go sailing with my cousins Cody and Rossi. My family is Mommy, Mama, baby sister, Leigh, and our kitty, Alexandra."

— *MASHA FINNEGAN JOHNSTON*

and friends. Our kids don't see any particular differences between us and the other families they know. I see many more similarities than differences between us and our heterosexual counterparts. We have the same struggles as heterosexual families, such as getting the kids ready for school on time, balancing our work with parenting, and keeping up with the laundry.

MASHA
(Kindergarten Student)

I like swimming with my moms. I love birthdays and playing with my animals. I like to go sailing with my cousins Cody and Rossi.

My family is Mommy, Mama, baby sister, Leigh, and our kitty, Alexandra.

Left to right: *Joann, Sol, Sunshine*

THE KELLEY / JONES

FAMILY

SUNSHINE JONES & JOANN KELLEY

JOHN QUINLAN

SOL KELLEY-JONES (11)

SUNSHINE JONES
(Community Activist, Family Life Educator)

Joann and I met and fell in love when we were both working at a battered women's shelter in Michigan almost twenty years ago. We've been in a lesbian marriage relationship based on love, fidelity, commitment, and shared spiritual faith for nineteen years.

After eight years together, we conceived our child through alternative fertilization. We delighted in every aspect of my pregnancy! Our daughter, Sol, was dreamed of, planned for, and celebrated in the context of our loving partnership.

Sol has been our greatest blessing in life. We will never forget the beautiful summer day of Sol's "Baby Blessing" when we celebrated her birth and renewed our marriage vows before family and friends. I remember my mother laying her hands on Sol's head and offering a prayer of blessing. The other people there were our extended family of love. From this experience, we recognized the power of creating a family life with rituals that reflected our values and affirmed our family identity in a culture that marginalizes us by rendering us invisible.

My mother has been a blessing in our lives. She has been there for us in love and support every step of the way. It's been a longer journey for the rest of our biological family. There has been a lot of pain and challenge, and yet there's been movement toward under-

"From studying history, I've learned that our Constitution does not say, 'All people are created equal except for gay and lesbian people and their children.' It says, 'All people are created equal.' I'm going to keep working until we live up to the founding principles of this country. I hope you will, too."

— *SOL KELLEY-JONES*

151

standing. No matter what came at us, however, we always tried to send back love in a way that honored the integrity of our family.

We remember our joy when Joann's parents, who had struggled with our relationship for years, were able to rejoice with us at the news of our pregnancy and send us hand-crocheted baby clothes when Sol was born. Joann and I try to celebrate every step, every card we receive, every small movement toward being embraced.

We recognized the need for support from other gay and lesbian families in handling the pervasive stress of heterosexism. Ever since Sol was a baby, we have gathered with a circle of gay and lesbian families for equinox and solstice celebrations and family rituals. We host an annual Halloween talent show. This year some of the kids had us rolling on the floor with their skit about a Rainbow Party politician named Gayla Pride.

I have been active in social justice work for my entire life. I knew that bringing a child into a lesbian family in this culture meant becoming an advocate for her in the institutions she would encounter. It also meant creating new support systems for gay and lesbian families. In 1989, I cofounded the Lesbian Parents Network, which provides education, advocacy, and support for over 150 families in Wisconsin. Later, I was also a founding member of Gays, Lesbians, and Allies for Diversity in Education, which advocates for our families in the schools.

We knew from our earliest experiences in parenting Sol that we needed to live visible, open lives. To deny our relationship would be to deny Sol the truth of her family. We also knew that we had a responsibility to give our daughter the protection skills that she would need to cope with prejudice, just as other families from groups facing discrimination must do.

To give Sol the foundation she needed meant conscious parenting in all aspects of her life including choosing to live in multicultural neighborhoods, reading her books with multicultural and gender-inclusive themes, writing stories together about gay and lesbian families, finding a spiritual community that was affirming of our family, and creating an extended family of love.

Sol has grown up celebrating the promise of her family's difference. Two of the strengths that Sol has received from living in our open lesbian family have been a regard for the rich diversity of life and the willingness to live life honestly. She has felt pride in her family when we have done trainings throughout the community and have appeared in newspaper stories and television reports seeking to give a human face to the debate around civil rights for gay and lesbian families. Sol has also learned that injustice is not something inherent, but stems from prejudice and fear.

I wonder if the time will ever come when I don't have to open my daily newspaper and read that being gay is "wrong," or "sinful," or "immoral." Words like these perpetuate violence against gay and lesbian people and hurt real families and real children. What some people call sin, I call a grace-filled relationship. I believe that God's heart is big enough to hold all families.

If people really knew anything about me, my marriage, our compassionate and beautiful

"To be homophobic is to have prejudice against human beings who are God's children. . . . We are real people, not a 'lifestyle,' a behavior, or a way of being."

— SUNSHINE JONES

daughter, our family service in our community, our commitment to our extended families of grandparents and siblings, and our years of responsible work, no one could include us in the same sentence with liars, adulterers, child abusers, and murderers, which we so often see in the media.

I recently told a minister from the religious right that to be homophobic is to be prejudiced against human beings who are God's children, just as he is a child of God. We are real people, not a "lifestyle," a behavior, or a way of being.

JOANN KELLEY
(Community Services Director at a Utility Company)

When I was a young girl, I knew that I was different from other girls because I liked different activities. As I grew up, I was always good with children but I never dreamt that I could be a parent. Fortunately, I met Sunshine and she shared her dream of having children with me. Now I can't imagine my life without Sol. I wouldn't trade my life as a parent in this family for anything. I've never known this kind of love before.

What makes me a mother is baking muffins at 11:00 P.M. for Sol's school party, comforting her when she's crying, creating a "math dog" to make math fun, and saying "no," even when it's disappointing to Sol.

Living in a family that is not legally recognized has emotional and financial costs. We do everything we can to take care of ourselves, but we are denied the benefits and legal protections that are so basic for most families.

I am the primary financial provider for our family, but I cannot provide for Sunshine and Sol in the same way that my heterosexual counterparts provide for their family members. For example, I cannot provide health insurance benefits for both Sol and Sunshine. The lack of fringe benefits cost our family $9,000 in gross pay in 1997. This is money that could have been set aside for Sol's education, or for our retirement, or simply to protect us during times of financial hardship.

As substantial as these hardships are, the kinds of things that keep me awake at night as a parent are the consequences for Sol if something catastrophic were to happen. Because Sunshine and I are denied marital status, Sol would be denied all the normal benefits she'd

Joann, Sol, and Sunshine

be entitled to upon the death of a parent if I were to die. Sol's parental relationship with me is also not protected if something were to happen to Sunshine. She could lose Sunshine in death, and then lose me in the courtroom.

This year, Sol spoke before a legislative committee about the same-sex marriage issue. She also spoke on a panel with Martina Navratilova about what it's like for her at school as the child of lesbian moms. For Sol, it has been an incredible blessing to be a child who is seen and heard.

SOL
(Fifth-Grade Student)

"I wouldn't trade my life as a parent in this family for anything. I've never known this kind of love before."

— *JOANN KELLEY*

Some people don't understand everything about my family. They ask me, "Who is your real mom?" I say, "They are both my real moms." I have a great family full of lots of love. That is why it is hard for me to understand why some people are so afraid of us.

I am a really lucky kid because I have two parents who love each other and love me very much. My parents are always helping me and they help lots of other people, too. My friends tell me how lucky I am because I've always had a mom home with me after school who fixes great snacks. Not everyone is lucky enough to have two great parents so I know I have a lot to be thankful for.

Once, when I was nine, I saw people carrying signs outside our church that said, "God hates gays and lesbians." It was very scary for me. I woke up crying that night because I dreamt that these same people bombed our church when our family was there. I don't want to be afraid of these people and I don't want them to be afraid of me and my family. I think we can all get along. We don't all have to be exactly the same.

Too many people remain silent about homophobia. We need to break the silence. People need to know that homophobia is hurting real people—real children and real families. I know firsthand what this is like. I have two moms, but one of my moms, Joann, is denied all legal rights of parenthood simply because she is gay. She cannot marry my other mom, Sunshine. She cannot legally adopt me in Wisconsin. Gay and lesbian families deserve the same rights as straight families.

I did a survey about attitudes toward gays and lesbians in the fourth and fifth grade classrooms at my elementary school, and I learned that there is a lot of homophobia. There are some supportive teachers at our school and some who are afraid to deal with gay and lesbian families. I feel sorry for the kids in those classes.

When I saw the results of my survey, I was surprised that 40 percent of the kids said they wouldn't be friends with anyone who had gay or lesbian parents. It helped me understand why a lot of kids in families like mine have a hard time feeling accepted in school. There is less prejudice when kids are educated about gay and lesbian families, so I bring in articles about gay and lesbian civil rights to my class and show the kids that our families are good.

From first through fourth grade, there was never one story or one image presented by the teachers that included gay or lesbian families unless I brought it in. That felt awful. Homophobic name-calling goes on all the time at school and seems to be completely acceptable on the playground. When I was little, I especially hated those times on the playground.

When anti-gay legislation passes even though we tried to stop it, or when homophobic things happen at school, my moms remind me of the power of truth and love. They say that each time we stand up for love and justice we succeed no matter what happens.

On the night before my eleventh birthday, I received the "Young Civil Libertarian of the Year" award from the ACLU. It felt really good because I have great respect for the ACLU. They not only believe in a rainbow of diversity, they also live out their beliefs by making sure that civil rights are applied equally to everyone. I want to live my life with that kind of courage even when it's scary.

In the past year, I've heard many gay and lesbian kids and families speak out with unbelievable courage, some risking their jobs and physical safety. I've also heard our straight allies speak out. I've learned so much from listening. I've learned how important it is to trust what your heart has to say. I've learned that all people from the youngest to the oldest can make a difference. We each have a part of the truth to speak and we need to find a way to bring that into the world.

John and Sol

When my moms and I traveled to New York to speak at a Gay, Lesbian, and Straight Educators conference about homophobia in schools, we took a boat ride out to Ellis Island. We leaned against the boat rail while gazing at the Statue of Liberty. Holding a golden torch of fire, she stood tall and courageous. I was glad she was green so she wasn't any particular race. I kept thinking about what liberty and justice for all meant and why I was in New York. Liberty's reflection created a long path in the water, and I knew there was a long path to go for justice for our families in America.

From studying history, I've learned that our Constitution does not say, "All people are created equal except for gay and lesbian people and their children." It says, "All people are created equal." I'm going to keep working until we live up to the founding principles of this country. I hope you will, too.

JOHN QUINLAN
(Journalist and Nonprofit Consultant)

I became Sunshine and Joann's housemate four months before Sol was born. As a gay man, I had assumed that children would never be a part of my life.

I never would have imagined it, but I found myself changing Sol's diapers, and taking her on outings to her favorite parks and the zoo. As the months went by, I was honored to become much more than a housemate. I became Sol's "Uncle John" and I will always be a part of her extended family of love. We lived together for the first six years of Sol's life, and I continue to be very close to Sunshine, Joann, and Sol.

People often assume that I have a biological link to Sol, but I don't. A lot of us who are part of the extended families of love for gay and lesbian families with kids are creating new family roles based on love, not on biology. Sol is fortunate to have many people in her extended family related both by blood and by love.

People attack gays and lesbians for threatening traditional family values. I find this ironic. In a transient society, many kids in heterosexual families live far away from their grandparents, cousins, and aunts and uncles. In contrast, the children of gay and lesbian parents are often surrounded by a circle of close friends who become "family" and care about them throughout their lives. Gay and lesbian families are actually recreating the old traditions!

It is clear that Sol's desire to make a difference comes from deep down inside her. She continues to teach the adults in her life new lessons each day. Since Sol's babyhood, I've seen Sunshine and Joann provide her with a firm foundation of love and integrity. Her moms have set the stage for Sol to shine.

Kitt and Samantha

THE
KLING
FAMILY

KITT ALEXANDER KLING

SAMANTHA LYNNE KLING (16)

KITT
(Consultant, Activist)

I was a twenty-eight-year old woman when I decided to have my first child. I got pregnant and had Samantha. She was eighteen months old when her dad and I split up. Our household then consisted of my maternal grandmother, Samantha, and me. I worked as a bookkeeper for a local factory until Samantha started school. At that point, I used my GI Bill, went back to college, and got a degree in sociology.

My grandmother passed away while I was still at college, and my mother took on the baby-sitting duties for Samantha whenever I was at school or work. Both of my parents were very helpful. They provided lots of love and support and are still very much a part of Samantha's life.

While I was at college, I became involved with the Gay and Lesbian Student Union. Although I was living in an openly lesbian relationship at the time, I always identified myself as bisexual and kept trying to explain to people that I really felt male. No one seemed to understand.

I tried to be as masculine as I could, forging new paths in the world around me. I was the first girl in my high school to take auto mechanics and the first to be suspended for

> *"When I first heard that my mother wanted to become a man, it honestly wasn't a big deal to me. . . . I do remember being frustrated that everyone else was making such a big deal, fussing over something that didn't need to be fussed over."*
>
> — SAMANTHA KLING

disobeying the dress code by wearing slacks. I did these things under the guise of "women's liberation," as I had no other outlet for expressing my masculinity. After high school, I joined the army. I thought, What better way to prove my machismo? This was a disappointment, as I did not prove my strength and ability, but faced whispers of "dyke." It's funny how the very qualities that are applauded in men are often despised and belittled in women. The only time I ever felt in touch with my "womanhood" was when I was pregnant with Sam and when I was nursing her.

All my life I felt like a stranger. I was never comfortable within myself. I was well liked and had a circle of friends, but there was always a deep well of emptiness inside of me. Waking up each morning and having to look in a mirror at a reflection that didn't feel like mine led me to the edge of insanity. A whole host of self-destructive behaviors marked my life when I was young.

A therapist once said to me, "It's okay to be a lesbian!" I already understood that, but it wasn't the point. I didn't really feel like a woman myself. I'd read about men who became women, like Christine Jorgenson and Renee Richards, but there were no accounts I could find of female-to-male transfolks. I assumed that sex changes were only for the rich and famous so I continued to live as a bisexual woman. At last I met a woman who opened my eyes to the reality that ordinary people can and do change their gender identity. I discovered that the "maleness" I felt had a name: transsexual or transgender. What a revelation! I had spent the better part of my life searching for who I was. It had been a long and rocky path, but I was finally comforted by knowing that I wasn't walking this path alone.

After gathering information, I began to transition from female to male. After the transition, I felt I was myself for the first time in my life. I'd wake up in the morning, look into the mirror and smile at the guy who looked back at me. I sang along with the radio as a tenor and not an alto. I joyously worked out so that my body would continue to metamorphose into the man who had always been there, waiting.

I keep smiling, mentally recording the "firsts" in my new life. The first time I was called "sir" by a store clerk. The first time someone didn't recognize my voice on the phone. But with the good comes the ugly. A few friends no longer call, and though my family has made a half-hearted attempt to try to understand me, they seem to be working hard to ruin everything I have accomplished. But I won't be intimidated. My newfound sense of strength and inner peace will not be dimmed or extinguished. I will stand tall, square my shoulders, and say, "This is the person you have raised me to be." If my parents cannot accept me as their son, at least I will know that I am resolved to be myself.

Despite all the trials and tribulations, Samantha and I have maintained our version of family. We are not typical, perhaps, but we've lived in the same house for fourteen years with neighbors who observed my transition and gave us total support. We've built our own

"I think many people are afraid of gay people and transfolk because people tend to be afraid of what is different. It's a very simple reason. It's a shame that there isn't a simple solution to the problem of fear."

— SAMANTHA KLING

extended family. My ex-girlfriend lives a few blocks away and stops in frequently. My current girlfriend of five years, her mom, and her brother have all accepted Samantha and me into their family. And I hope my parents are slowly realizing that I'm not some off-the-wall fool. Maybe they will begin to accept me as their child even if I'm not what they expected.

Samantha is truly my pride and joy. My heart swells with love when I think about her. She is a fantastic kid. I am so proud of her accomplishments, her empathy, her strength. It's so sad that she has seen the mean side of so many people. Yet she has touched many lives and shown others what love and family really mean.

SAMANTHA

(High-School Junior, Co-originator and President, Lesbian, Transgender, Straight, Gay and Bisexual High-School Support Group)

I know my family is considered an "alternative family," but I really don't think about it all that often. I was brought up with the idea that being gay wasn't wrong, just different, and that has carried over into other areas, including transgender folks. So I really don't see our family as an "alternative." In fact it's sort of a blessing in disguise. It's definitely harder to deal with, but who wants life to be easy if it means it will be boring? I feel like being in my family qualifies me to educate people about what it's like to be different and how to deal with bigotry.

I remember back to the day when my kindergarten teacher was asking for the work phone numbers of our mommies and daddies, and I gave my mom's number and my mom's girlfriend's number. It's always been like that. I always knew that my family was different, but it was never something to be hidden or ashamed of or anything stupid like that. As a result, I've never seen it as a bad thing, or as a skeleton in the closet.

When I first heard that my mother wanted to become a man, it honestly wasn't a big deal to me. I don't really remember having a big reaction. I do remember being frustrated that everyone else was making such a big deal, fussing over something that didn't need to

Samantha, JenE, and Kitt

be fussed over. As I said before, I was brought up to be very open-minded.

The people I consider my family include my biological family and certain others who are not related to me by blood. One example of my extended family is a transwoman I've known for many years who has taught me a lot about Native Americans. Her teachings have helped me form a great deal of my own moral beliefs. I also know a transgender girl who has taught me about individualism and introduced me to activism. My girlfriend, JenE, has also supported me and put up with the "craziness" that is my family despite her very conservative religious upbringing. The greatest thing about extended family is that no matter what your faults and foibles, they choose you. Your bio-family is stuck with you, but your extended family chooses you. I think that says a lot.

Any time anyone makes a derogatory comment about queer people, I speak up. When I defend gay people, I often get asked the "famous" question, "Do you know some of them freaks?" To which I give my "famous" answer, "My family is full of them freaks." That usually leads to all kinds of discussions. The first person I told about my family was a friend I'd known almost my whole life. One day she asked me who this guy hanging around me was. I couldn't say he was a relative, because my friend knew my family so well. I couldn't say he was my mom's boyfriend, because she knew my mom was a lesbian. So I finally told her that my mom was becoming a man. At first, she asked questions, but things between us went back to normal very quickly. She was the first person I told that I was a lesbian and she reacted wonderfully to that news, too.

I have definitely experienced homophobia and transphobia. There have been occasions when I've been out with my girlfriend, and people have made rude comments. There have been times when mothers with the classic, closed-minded glare of death have pulled their children away if they walked too close to me or transfolks around me. It is something I've gotten used to.

At times I feel like yelling at people who perpetrate these phobias. I want to tell them how hurtful their attitudes are, not just to gays and transfolk, but possibly to their own children. What if one of their children someday discovers she is gay or transgender, but then remembers that moment and lives in fear of coming out to her parents? Sometimes I like to return the glare of death and say, "How dare you condemn me!" Sometimes I simply look at them and smile as sweetly as possible, because that bothers the hate-mongers the most. They don't want to look at us as people, so when we are nice and polite, they have to realize that we are, in fact, human.

I think many people are afraid of gay people and transfolk because people tend to be afraid of what is different. It's a very simple reason. It's a shame that there isn't a simple solution to the problem of fear.

One of the most terrible things that has ever happened to me was recently, when a black girl in one of my classes yelled anti-gay epithets and threats at me. I was especially hurt because she must know what it's like to be discriminated against for being different. She must have been so badly hurt by prejudice that she feels she has to inflict it upon other people. That's a pretty sad thing. I've become much more sensitive to prejudice against other groups of people. If I hear a racial slur, I will immediately say something because it's wrong. I know how it feels to be discriminated against, and I don't think anyone should have to deal with prejudice.

Close-minded upbringings can be hard to overcome. The greatest part about living in my family is our open-mindedness. I've been around so many unconventional people and families that I've seen aspects of life that other people only hear about on talk shows. Even though we may not be your typical family, we are a very happy one. I think that going through all of this has made me a more understanding and accepting person when it comes to all kinds of different situations. True, there are many lifestyles that I see and say to myself, "Whoa, that's a little off the wall." But then I stop to think. Isn't my family a little off the wall? Aren't I a little off the wall? So I won't condemn other people just because I don't agree with or understand their lifestyles.

I want to tell other gay and transgender people not to hide who they are from their kids. We know when something is being hidden from us and we know that when something is hidden it is because it's bad and shameful. Talk to your kids. Let them know what is happening. Help them understand.

Center front: *Dominique*; standing at rear: *Laurie and Chris, with their foster family*

THE
KULESA / CASTONGUAY
FAMILY

CHRISTINE KULESA & LAURIE CASTONGUAY
DOMINIQUE EATMON (17)
AND EXTENDED FOSTER FAMILY

CHRISTINE
(Foster Parent)

I had never planned on becoming a foster parent. I gave birth to a daughter and a son, and several years later one of my daughter's friends needed a home. The Department of Social Services approved me to take Michelle, and later on I took in Michelle's sister, Dawn, and her brother, Brian. They've been here ever since, and I have become a certified foster parent.

We have rules in our household like any other household. The kids have curfews and strict bedtimes, and we all sit down together to eat dinner every night.

LAURIE
(Baker, House Cleaner)

I met Christine two years ago, and we started dating. At that time, she didn't have as many foster children. I tend to work a lot so I'm not home as much as Christine is. Sometimes I come home to a surprise. Chris tells me, "Oh, we have a new child staying with us." That's pretty much how our family has grown.

"Mostly teenagers live in this family. There are fourteen of us, and I have two lesbian foster mothers, six cats, and one dog. I see no difference between our family and any other family. We fuss and fight. We laugh. We sit down and eat together. We have chores. It's just a family."

— DOMINIQUE EATMON

If one kid leaves, shortly afterwards there's always a phone call asking us to take in another. And we always say "Yes."

Our kids are like the kids in any family. Not everyone agrees all the time, but for the most part, they all get along. And when push comes to shove, they stick by each other.

DOMINIQUE
(Student)

I grew up in Detroit with my biological mom and two younger sisters. When I was little, Shira was my favorite cartoon character. I was six, and I had a strong crush on her. When I got to sixth grade, I had a crush on a female teacher of mine, and I thought, "Something's different here."

I didn't realize the true meaning of my sexual identity until I was thirteen and had my first relationship with another girl. I felt comfortable with her, and I think she helped me figure out who I was because at the time I was also going out with guys. I didn't know what "lesbian" or "gay" meant. I had no idea. I just knew I liked females. I didn't even know I had a lesbian aunt until I was fifteen, and I figured it out on my own.

When I officially came out to my biological mother, I was thirteen. It was hell. My mother read a letter of mine that was written to me by the girl I was going out with. She asked me if it was true, and my first thought was to deny it. I wasn't ready to deal with her reaction, but for some reason I said it was true.

I had dated boys up to that point, so it was a shock to my mother to find out that I was a lesbian. She just sat there at the dining-room table and stared at me. She didn't say a word. For three months, there was no communication between us. There was nothing. She cut my allowance off, and I wasn't allowed to go anywhere for the rest of that summer. So, on October 23 of that year, I tried to commit suicide. I was tired and wanted to die, but for some reason I lived. My sister found me on the floor and called 911.

I wanted to die because my mother totally denied me and condemned me because of her religious beliefs. I had no one to turn to. I didn't know how to approach anyone in my school with this situation, so, in my opinion, I was lost. Suicide was the only exit I could imagine then.

I would tell other kids that if you are in a situation like mine where you can't trust your parents, then find someone you can trust and confide in—a teacher or a counselor or someone. Trying to commit suicide is not going to help your situation.

Seven days after I tried to commit suicide, I went to live with my father. He molested me, claiming that he was trying to cure me of homosexuality. Those were his exact words. Luckily, I was able to call the police, and my father was arrested. After that, I was sent to my first foster home. I felt like I had no parents anymore. My foster mother told me, "I don't condone homosexuality." The only support I had was from my friends at school—they were right there beside me.

Now I have lesbian foster parents. My foster mother, Christine, listens to each kid in the house. I've never had a person that I look up to like a parent who has been so supportive of me. When I need her shoulder to cry on, she's there. She's open, and she's out there, which is why she's a role model for me. I'm really out and straightforward and direct, too. Some people can deal with it, and others can't.

Mostly teenagers live in this family. There are fourteen of us, and I have two lesbian foster mothers, six cats, and one dog. I see no difference between our family and any other family. We fuss and fight. We laugh. We sit down and eat together. We have chores. It's just a family.

I enjoy living here. It's nice to be in a home where I can be out without hiding. It's nice to have the support of your family, especially my two foster mothers. It's nice to point them out at the Gay Pride march. It's just nice to have the support of two parents whom I respect.

I have become an activist. I went to the planning conference for the Governor's Commission on Gay Youth in Massachusetts. I've also joined a gay and lesbian speaker's bureau, and I speak at schools. Sometimes I hear negative comments, but I still like doing it. Some people say that when I speak I sound like a preacher, which is fine. I talk against homophobia. I educate faculty at different schools and talk about how they can create gay/straight alliances in their schools.

I like having gay, lesbian, bisexual, and straight student groups at schools because it's good for youth to have a safe place to come together, speak out, and joke around without worrying about any harm being done to them. It's also good to have the understanding of straight allies. It helps me to know that they aren't homophobic, and that they have the courage to learn and understand more.

Dominique

Amy, Miriam, and Erick

THE
LAVANDIER

FAMILY

MIRIAM LAVANDIER

ERICK LAVANDIER (11)

AMY LAVANDIER (9)

MIRIAM
(English Professor, Activist, Poet)

As a Catholic, I was taught that it was not okay to be close to women. When I started to have feelings for women at puberty, I repressed them by praying and saying the rosary to get them out of my mind. I grew up trying to push those feelings away, and it was a constant struggle.

I was born and raised in New York City. When I was twenty-one, I moved to Santiago in the Dominican Republic. I entered a religious sect, where I was pressured to get married. When I was twenty-seven, I married a man and we came back to New York City. Shortly after, we had Erick and Amy. Six years later, we got divorced for many reasons. Besides the fact that we didn't get along, I was coming to terms with my sexual orientation.

I owe a lot to my very best friend who told me, "You need to explore these feelings for women and see if this is really what your life is all about." She wasn't even gay; she was a straight woman.

"Most of the students in the college where I teach are Hispanic. After they get to know me, and they see that I'm a wholesome, normal human being, I come out to them. Then they say, 'Oh wow. How could that be? It's impossible!' 'No,' I say. 'It is possible. It's true. I have a girlfriend, and I have my children and a very good, healthy family.' That's my way of fighting homophobia in my community. My students also say, 'You look like a normal person.' I tell them, 'Lesbians are normal people. The one and only difference is that we love women instead of men.' "

— *MIRIAM LAVANDIER*

She gave me the emotional support to be able to finally confront my sexuality. I had never spoken to anyone before in my entire life about being attracted to women.

I've been in a relationship with a wonderful Latina woman for two years. The problem is that she's in the closet because she doesn't want to upset her elderly parents by telling them that she's gay. They're very traditional, conservative, and very Catholic. She's afraid that she would lose their respect and be rejected by them. She lives with her niece and her family, and I live with my mother and my two children.

I don't remember specifically how my mother found out that I was a lesbian, but I do remember that she put the Bible on my bed every day for weeks after that. She cried and prayed for me for several years. My father passed away before finding out that I was a lesbian. Usually in my culture when an elderly parent's partner passes away, the surviving parent comes to live with a daughter. Even though I'm her only daughter, my mother didn't move in with me because she didn't think she would be safe. She thought that gay people are strange, weird drug addicts or robbers. Years later, she realized she was making a mistake, and she's been living with me for the past two years. My mother still prays for me and lectures me and lets me know that she disapproves. I have to keep telling her, "Mom, no matter how much you lecture me, it's not going to work. This is something that took me years to come to terms with, and I'm not ever going to go back."

Amy and Erick were two and four years old when I started having relationships with women. As they grew up, they went to the Gay Pride parade every single year. Their father tells me that he would rather that I not take the kids to any gay events. But I do, of course, because I don't want them growing up thinking that their mother is doing anything wrong, or that they have a cursed family. I want them to know that there are people who accept us, and that there are many other kids with families like ours. The kids see thousands of gay people at these events and they don't think they are weird or different or strange.

I think their father talks to the kids about me being a lesbian in very negative terms. There was even a time when gay people made Erick nervous. I mentioned the names of some of our good friends to Erick, and I said, "Do you think so-and-so is weird?" "No. She's fun." "Do you think this other person is bad or strange or negative?" "No, she's really nice too." "Well, do you think Daddy's right when he says that gay people are bad?" And Erick said, "I think Daddy is crazy to think that."

Amy once asked me, "What is a lesbian? What does that mean?" I said, "A lesbian is a woman who falls in love with another woman. Most women fall in love with a man, but some of us love other women. That's how I am." Periodically, Amy asks me, "Do I have to grow up to be like you?" I always tell her that she doesn't, that she can grow up to love whomever she wants. It doesn't matter. The important thing is that I love her. I'm her mother, and I'm always going to be there for her.

Erick doesn't ask me directly about being a lesbian but I know he's always listening whenever Amy asks. He's very, very bright. He listens a lot, and he knows how to extract ideas from what's happening. Erick's teacher in second grade was gay and died from AIDS, and his classmates somehow found out that I was a lesbian. A lot of them were telling Erick things like, "Ewwww, that's disgusting." And he would say, "What's the big deal?" He didn't see it as a problem, and he just blew it off. So they blew it off too.

My kids are not growing up homophobic because I have never hidden being lesbian from them. There are gay and lesbian parents out there who hide their sexuality from their kids because they are afraid. That's bad for their children; it's bad for society; and it's bad for them.

In the Hispanic community, there's a lot of verbal and physical violence against gays and lesbians. People are thrown out of their families. Most Hispanics are Catholic, and they are raised to think that gay people are very bad in every sense. That's why there's rampant homophobia in the Hispanic community. Rampant. The priests are constantly saying bad things about us. They say, "Keep away from those people. They're bad. They're sinners. They're damned, and they're all going to hell." And people do listen to what the priests say.

Most of the students in the college where I teach are Hispanic. After they get to know me, and they see that I'm a wholesome, normal human being, I come out to them. Then they say, "Oh wow. How could that be? It's impossible!" "No," I say. "It is possible. It's true. I have a girlfriend, and I have my children and a very good, healthy family." That's my way of fighting homophobia in my community.

My students also say, "You look like a normal person." I tell them, "Lesbians are normal people. The one and only difference is that we love women instead of men." Some students say, "But you don't dress like a lesbian." And I say, "Well, lesbians actually dress the same way you do." They also ask me, "Do you want to be a man?" "No," I tell them, "I don't want to be a man. I'm a woman, and I'm very happy being a woman. I love being a woman so much that I love another woman, too."

I try to help my students understand that being a lesbian is not a bad thing, because that's what they think. They think that it's weird. I tell them, "You see that I'm not a drug addict. I'm not an alcoholic. I'm a professional. You see that I'm a caring person. Gay people are just people. There are good ones and bad ones, just as there are good and bad people among straight people. You shouldn't think that gay people are bad just because they're gay." My students also say things like, "You have children so you can't be gay." I tell them, "I was divorced, and I'm raising my children. I love having children, and I don't think there's anything wrong with that. My kids know that I'm gay, and they don't have a problem with it either."

ERICK
(Sixth-Grade Student)

I think a family is nice people who care about you.

We have three dogs and one cat. First, I got a little tiny puppy, and we called her "Cutie" because she was so cute. Now she's four years old. My second cousin moved into an apartment, and she can't keep her two dogs, so my mom is taking care of them. I take Cutie out. Amy takes Goldy out. And my mom walks the big dog. I still have my first cat named Yankee. He's gray, black, and white.

Kids at school always used to ask me, "Is it true that your mom is a lesbian?" I didn't tell them that she's a lesbian. My little sister Amy told them. So I said to the kids, "Please, quit bothering me." They don't tease me anymore. They still ask, but they don't tease.

I want to be a toy maker or an inventor when I grow up.

AMY
(Fourth-Grade Student)

All I know is that I love my mom, and I really like my mom's girlfriend. I keep bugging her because I want her to marry my mom. That's all.

Ellen, Natan, and Donna

174

THE
MAIMES / LACROIX
FAMILY

DONNA MAIMES & ELLEN LACROIX
NATAN MAIMES (15)

DONNA
(Business Manager)

Our family is made up of our son, Natan, our eighteen-year-old daughter, Ora, who is traveling in Europe this year before starting college, and Ellen. I've lived with Ellen for about twelve years. We always debate about exactly how long we've been together.

Ellen and I both agree that it's important for Natan to have control about who knows what his family is like. It's not up to me as his mother to advertise his personal life to people I don't even know. Ultimately the decision to be out belongs to Natan.

In the rules of conduct at the local public schools, if a student makes a negative comment about sexual orientation or race, he or she can be expelled. Negative comments about gay people are made all the time, but they aren't taken seriously by the teachers.

ELLEN
(Lawyer)

I never wanted to give birth, but I think somewhere in the back of my mind, I was always interested in parenting. When Donna and I first got together, one of the things that made it easier for me was that she allowed me equal access to the children in our parenting responsibilities. This was a great gift.

Donna's ex-husband sued her for custody of Natan and Ora after he had a religious conversion. We won the case because the laws in California say that the sexuality of a parent isn't relevant to whether they are a better parent or not.

When paperwork would come home from school, we'd cross out "father" and I'd write in "guardian." I never felt like I was Natan and Ora's mother or their "other mother." I don't think of our family as having two moms. Donna's the mother, and I'm her partner and the children's guardian. We're that kind of a family.

We've been harassed. We've had our house broken into. We've had anti-gay hate words and swastikas painted on our doors. We've talked to the mayor, the principal, and the superintendent of schools. They have expressed a sort of sympathy that sounds false and condescending. I would have felt more comfortable if they had just said, "We can't change any of this. You're on your own."

I think Natan is too modest to tell you this, but he has developed an ability to get along with all different sorts of people. His teachers say that too. I'm really proud of him. He's a remarkable kid.

NATAN
(Eleventh-Grade Student)

I don't really need to explain my family structure because most of my friends already know. People just presume, I guess. Nobody has ever directly asked me. In the seventh and eighth grade, I was harassed by other kids who would say stupid things about my mom, mostly. I just ignored them. I think they stopped because they grew up more. Maybe.

There's a lot of homophobia in the high school, I guess. People use the word "faggot" a lot, but it's not directed against homosexuals. It's basically used as a general insult. One teacher called someone in her classroom a "faggot," and my friend said something to her. The teacher said, "Oh, I didn't mean it that way. I just meant it as a general insult." There's not that much straightforward, out-and-out homophobia. It's usually a more subtle thing.

One thing I think is wrong with elementary schools is that they don't normally do anything about gay and lesbian families in kindergarten and first grade. It seems that everything is based on the totally straight family. "Tell us what you did with your mom and dad?" the teachers ask. I think they should change the curriculum.

Most kids think what their parents tell them to think. I've been exposed to more ideas, so that I can think for myself instead of just listening to what other people say. I think I've learned something from being in this family.

Yvette and Donie

THE
MIXON
FAMILY

YVETTE MIXON
DONIE MIXON (8)

YVETTE
(Entrepreneur)

I'm thirty-one, and my son, Donie, and I live with my mother. I grew up in Crown Heights in Brooklyn, and I've lived here all my life. Growing up, I was a "baby dyke," very sports oriented, and very rough. As a kid, I could not really relate to being a girl. I identified with boys far more than I did with girls. I just couldn't relate to girls on an emotional level. I couldn't even talk to them.

Being gay was just not expressed verbally among African American kids when I was coming up. It was expressed through movement, through the way you interacted. You were a tomboy, and you'd hang out with all the guys, but you could never talk about being a lesbian. That's how it was back then. I don't know how they're doing it today. Kids today are more advanced.

My first exposure to gays and lesbians was when I played sports on a neighborhood team. The kids on the elementary school teams didn't have a clue about being lesbian or gay. The junior high team members had a clue, but they were not expressing it. But the senior high team members were out.

When I got to high school, I began to say to myself, "I think I'll experiment with

> "My son, Donie, was born when I was twenty-two, and I just burst out of the closet. When I came out, life became grand. It was a sort of freedom. A whole new world!"
>
> — YVETTE MIXON

179

having a boyfriend," and all through high school, I dated guys. The guys I went out with were my friends. I played sports with them. It was a sisterly-brotherly kind of love. I didn't know how to come out at that point.

My desire to be a mother was the strongest when I went to college. I didn't have a clue that lesbians who wanted to be parents had options like artificial insemination. So when I met this nice guy, I said to myself, "Wow. He is going to be the father of my child." After I was with child, I said, "Okay. How am I going to manage now? I know. I'll go home to Mom." That's when I moved back to Brooklyn, and I've been here ever since. My son, Donie, was born when I was twenty-two, and I just burst out of the closet. When I came out, life became grand. It was a sort of freedom. A whole new world!

When I came out to my mom, I didn't come right out. I kind of thought she would just notice on her own. She did notice. Mom said, "There's something different about you. You're always hanging out with girls. What's going on?" "Oh," I said, trying to brush it off. "Please pass the tea. Those are just my girlfriends." She said, "Girlfriends?" "Yeah, my girlfriends. By the way, I'm a lesbian." She said, "Okay." Then she asked, "How are you going to raise a child and be a lesbian?" I explained it to her the best that I could. I said, "I know who I am, but I also want to express my maternal instincts." I left it for her to work out for herself. Now, my mom sees me raising Donie, and she knows that I'm doing a very good job as a parent. Lately, I've gotten heavily into holistic health. I'm always saying to Mom, "Don't eat that. Don't do this." So that's where we're at now.

When I came out to my childhood friends from Brooklyn, they had the same thing to tell me. All the people that I grew up with had the same story. All the girls I played sports with. My very best friend. My buddy that I grew up with from the neighborhood. A lot of the guys that I played sports with. Everyone came out! Twenty or more of my old friends! When I came out to my very best friend, she said, "Oh, you know my girl-friend so-and-so? That's my lover." I said, "Oh my God, this is so cool." And we just took it from there. It was awesome.

I didn't know any other lesbians who had kids when Donie was a baby. I didn't know where I fit in the community. I thought, "There's got to be someone else out there." So I had to seek out other people I could identify with. I found them. Most of the women I've dated have had children. But I wish I could meet other butch women who are single moms.

DONIE
(Fourth-Grade Student)

"Lesbian" means a lady who loves another lady. My mom won basketball trophies and she said she could beat me, but she can't really beat me at basketball! I like my mom because she's nice. She takes me lots of places. We go bike-riding, and we talk a lot. When I grow up, I want to be a lawyer in court.

Mary Ann, Zack, Ruth, and Luke

THE
NUGENT/KUZMANIC
FAMILY

MARY ANN NUGENT & RUTH L. KUZMANIC

ZACHARY KUZMANIC (6)

LUCAS KUZMANIC (4)

MARY ANN
(Teacher)

I look back on the last fifteen years with such wonder. There have been so many hurdles and accomplishments and tears and laughter. When Ruth and I met, we were instantly attracted to each other. She was twenty-three and I was twenty-five. We were young, hip lesbian feminists. We were proud and in love and continued to grow in pride and love all through our graduate school years and as we began to teach. Five years into our relationship, we started wanting a family. The clincher was when Ruth's niece was born. We saw how wonderful it was to have a baby around.

We set a two-year goal and started gathering information. I laugh when I think back on that time. If heterosexuals spent even half the time lesbians do researching having babies, this world would be a very different place. Two years later we stumbled upon an old friend who told us of a clinic that inseminated lesbians and single women. We felt this information had been dropped into our hands by some higher power. That power continued to guide us.

We called the clinic and were told that there was a six-month waiting list. However, we told them that we could only do three months worth of inseminations because Ruth was a teacher and the baby needed to be born in the summer. Back then, we thought we

> *"We thought most of the discrimination would come from the heterosexual world and what we found was just the opposite. Many of our lesbian sisters didn't want to be involved with the male gender even if it came in a four-year-old package."*
>
> — MARY ANN NUGENT

could control the timing of everything! They moved us to the top of the list and, unbelievably, Ruth got pregnant on the first try.

Little did we know then what an impact this decision would have on us and everyone we knew. We bought all the latest "carry-a-baby" gear because we thought this new addition was going to simply be an extra "carry-on." Our best friends still tease us about that. We got a baby backpack, a bike trailer, a baby jogger, and a portable crib. We were ready. Our friends in the lesbian community were so excited to become aunts, all hoping, of course, to be able to take part in raising a future feminist.

Then it was time to tell our families. Ruth's parents were very confused about the process, yet very excited about the outcome. Her siblings were tolerant to a degree, as the issue of her being a lesbian had always been tough for them for various reasons. My parents had expressed a great deal of pain and suffering when I came out a few years earlier, so this news sent them right over the edge. My dad ignored me and our news, and to this day, my mom still cries when I speak to her. This issue is still unresolved and painful for my mother and me. My siblings were fine when they first heard we were going to have a child, but they have, so far, been uninvolved in the growth and development of our kids.

I was teaching physical education at an elementary school in a town known for its right-wing Christian morality. It was easy for me to decide whether to come out to a group of right-wing folks or to lie to them. I lied. So much for educating them; that would have to come later. I told people I was adopting a child and they wanted to believe me and so they did.

Zach was born May 7, 1991, and his birth was the single most amazing event I had ever experienced. I finished out the school year and we had a truly wonderful summer with our new baby. For the first three months Zach really was portable. We were still able to go camping and jogging with him. At four months the baby sleep book we purchased said that consistency, scheduling, and making sure he slept in a crib in his own home were the measures necessary to get a child to sleep. They were right. It worked. But just as school was starting up again, we were glued to our baby's crib. He would only be awake for four hours maximum and during those hours it felt cruel to tie him into a backpack or a car seat, so we stayed at home. We also didn't feel comfortable leaving him with a baby sitter, so no more lesbian dances or coffee houses or galas. Our friends grew tired of us saying "no" to outings and hearing Zach stories instead. We went to the annual womyn's music festival, which proved to be a hot, exhausting, awful experience with a toddler. Friends meant well and said they would help out, but one-year-old kids want their moms and not their aunts.

We definitely wanted a sibling for Zach, and two years later, on May 10, 1993, Luke was born. The typical sibling rivalry started immediately. Zach proceeded to try to smother Luke with his favorite blanket. As they grew, Zach found both a punching bag as well as a best friend in Luke.

As our sons got older, Ruth and I felt more and more alone. When Zach was four, he was no longer looked upon as a cute little child. He was a boy after all. This meant he was labeled a "man" in the lesbian culture. It was ironic because we thought most of the discrimination would come from the heterosexual world and what we found was just the opposite. Many of our lesbian sisters didn't want to be involved with the male gender even if it came in a four-year-old package. Our last visit to the womyn's music festival put the nail in the coffin. We were afraid for Zach and what the women would say to him and we felt no connection there anymore. The pro-woman message had a very strong underlying anti-male message. How could we feel comfortable with this as our support group? We were raising male children after all. We felt very much like a subculture of a subculture of a subculture.

Our one constant was a lesbian moms' group which we had been a part of since before Zach's birth. That group of twenty women had metamorphosed to a group of three families with children. They proved to be our lighthouse during a pretty foggy time.

Zach was enrolled in a local Montessori school that had a very open-minded clientele. We got involved with the fixing-up of the school and we met more families and became friends with some of the heterosexual couples. One of the straight moms told us that her daughter said she wished she had two moms like Zach did. She thought that having one mom was cool but having two would be awesome. When another child asked why Zach and Luke had two moms, his mother replied that they were just lucky. Finally, we were educating others.

When it was time for Zach to start first grade in a public school, we were very nervous. By then Ruth and I were completely out to our families and at our jobs so we believed the

Mary Ann, Luke, and Zach

schools should be aware of us too. We felt it was important to present ourselves as a family. Whether or not they agreed with us was irrelevant. We were proud of our boys and our family and we wanted our boys to feel that pride. We wrote a letter to the principal explaining Zach's personality and learning styles, as well as his alternative family situation. The principal was very understanding and explained that at his school they valued diversity. He also placed Zach with a wonderful first-grade teacher. Early in the school year, this teacher purchased a book about two hens who decide to raise a baby chick together. She read the story aloud to her class. After hearing this story Zach stood up and yelled, "Hey, I have two moms, too."

RUTH
(Teacher)

Seven years ago we were still not out at our jobs and quite a bit more cautious. We found day care from a mom of one of Mary Ann's students. Mary Ann didn't want to be outed to all her parents at her school so she said she was the adoptive mom and I was a friend. We were so naive because we sent packets of breast milk for this baby and hoped the day-care provider wouldn't catch on. What were we thinking? We did eventually come out to her and it was fine. The more heterosexuals we came out to who accepted us, the more confident we became.

During my pregnancy I was teaching health education at a high school in a local town we like to call "Yuppyville." I wasn't out there, but one day after school, the principal walked in and asked to speak to me. He proceeded to tell me that they wanted me to stop teaching health classes and work as a gym teacher instead. He questioned my ability to be a role-model and was concerned about the influence my pregnancy could have on the students. After all, I was teaching AIDS awareness, and the only way to be free of this disease according to him was to be in a monogamous relationship and to practice abstinence before marriage. I simply replied, "You are assuming that I'm not in a monogamous relationship and that I conceived this baby through sexual intercourse, neither of which is your business." He had no reply, and I was permitted to continue teaching health education.

Our boys have encountered some discrimination. Two families in our old neighborhood had a problem with our sexual orientation. Unfortunately, the parents told their young boys that they could be mean to Zach. Zach was devastated by this and took it personally. We had to tell him it was because we were two moms and not a mom and a dad, and that some people didn't like that. Zach understood a bit, but it didn't help ease the pain when these two boys would ride by on their bikes and ignore him. That was one of the reasons why we moved to a new neighborhood.

Zach's best friend said he couldn't possibly have two moms because he couldn't have been born if he did. That hurt Zach's feelings. It hasn't stopped him, however, from sharing with his friends that he has two moms.

ZACHARY
(Kindergarten Student)

I like to eat cookies with my family, go to Disney World, get new computer games from my moms, and play basketball.

A family is a nice, full of fun, friendly group of people. We are friendly, joyful, and fun to be with.

LUCAS
(Preschool Student)

I like to eat pudding with my family.

Left to right, in rear: *Amber and Sevrina*; seated: *Kristin, Marty, and Doug*

THE
PHILLIPS / HATHAWAY
FAMILY

MARTIN PHILLIPS & DOUGLAS HATHAWAY

KRISTIN PHILLIPS (12)

SEVRINA PHILLIPS (7)

AMBER PHILLIPS (7)

MARTIN
(Actor, Dancer, Stained Glass Artist)

When I was nineteen, my girlfriend got pregnant and we got married. I already knew I was gay, but I wanted to help raise my baby daughter. Four years later, we had the twins and then we separated. My ex-wife had custody of the girls for about seven months, and then she agreed that I could have full custody of the children. I had been taking care of all their physical, emotional, and financial needs from the start, and I've had full custody of my three daughters since 1990. Now, my ex-wife lives far away, and she's really out of touch with the children. She hasn't even written letters to them, which has been hard for the girls.

When I took custody of my daughters, I thought about coming out but I believed that there was no way society would let me keep my children. That fear was just too much to bear. After three years of single parenting, I realized that my ability as a parent was as strong as anyone else's, and that I was doing a far better job than most two-parent households. I was not doing myself or the kids justice by hiding anymore and I was tired of being silent. I decided, "That's it, I'm coming out." And I did. First I told my mother, then my sisters, and then, at my uncle's seventieth birthday party, my entire extended family.

After I told my eldest daughter Kristin that I was gay, she said, "You spend a lot of

> "My family is very open. . . . My mother's comment when I came out to her and Dad was, 'That's wonderful,' and she gave me a big hug. My father told me that the brick work I did in front of my house looked great. That was his way of telling me that he approved of me."
>
> — MARTIN PHILLIPS

time with your friend Douglas. I think it's great, but I'm just wondering why." I told her that I was in love with him. Then she said that she was worried that Douglas might not know I was gay. I said to her, "Of course he knows that I'm gay. He's gay too. That's why we're together." And Kristin said, "Ohhhhhh." Then it all sunk in and made sense to her.

The morning we were going to our first gay and lesbian family picnic, I told the twins that Douglas and I were gay. I explained that on television they only see families with mommies and daddies, but that there are many men who want to spend their lives loving men, and women who want to spend their lives loving women. The twins didn't understand me completely, but they told me that they really liked Douglas a lot. So I said, "Daddy and Douglas are more than just friends. We spend a lot of time together. We really love each other." Amber asked, "Do you kiss Douglas?" And I said, "Yes." And then she asked me if I kiss Grandpa. I said, "I used to when I was a kid, but not really anymore. But that's not the same." Then she asked, "Do you kiss Douglas a lot?" I said, "Yeah. Douglas is my boyfriend." And she said, "Oh, okay."

During the gay and lesbian family picnic, Kristin was a little withdrawn. I asked her if she wanted to talk about anything, and she said that she didn't want to. So I said I would help her talk to me. I asked her what comes into her head when I say the word, "homosexuality." She said, "I don't know if I think it's normal." And I said, "That's fair. I like Brussels sprouts, and you don't. I think you should eat them because it's normal for me. Do you think you should?" Kristin said, "No, it's not normal for me." I explained to her that everybody has their own set of what's normal. That for me, sitting in a field listening to the birds sing is very normal. For other people, it wouldn't be. For me to live my life with a woman is not normal. For me to live my life with a man is normal. It makes me feel whole. I said, "Someday you're going to decide what's right for you." Kristin really understood, and she told me later that this discussion really helped her out.

Once when we were out at a movie, my young niece called Kristin a "homo." I explained to my niece right then and there that this word was very insulting and that I didn't ever want to hear it again. When I talked to my sister about it, she said, "Well, Marty, kids are mean. They call each other 'Barney-lover' all the time." I said, "Don't you dare consider 'Barney-lover' the same as using the word 'homo'! This word has been used against me for so long. It's what put me deep into the closet."

I've known that I was gay since I was two. I've known since I could think. You get messages at a pretty young age that being gay is not appropriate, and that these kinds of feelings will change. I tried to learn to be heterosexual by unlearning what was natural, but there's no way to do that. Being gay is part of my biology.

My family is very open. They're incredible. My mother's comment when I came out to her and Dad was, "That's wonderful," and she gave me a big hug. My father told me that the brick work I did in front of my house looked great. That was his way of telling me that he approved of me.

It was really tough being in the closet while trying to play the role of father and husband. I've found that I'm able to give my children so much more being an out gay father, than being an in-the-closet father. When I found out this summer that I'm HIV positive, it was a very hard knock. But it has almost been a good thing because it's given me more determination to fight being in the closet. I believe that more people are getting infected by HIV because they aren't out. The closet is a bad, bad place to be. And it's also bad for your kids because they're a part of it. You drag everybody into your closet with you.

We learn to play hide-and-seek at a very early age and kids pride themselves on how well they can hide. At some point, when hiding becomes our reality, not just a game, we get really good at it, but then nobody can find you. You can't even find yourself. You're lost. I don't want any kid to ever go through that. If I can put a label on my childhood, my overriding feeling was fear—the fear of being caught or that somebody was going to know my thoughts. Kids have the chance now to escape that fear, especially with more families like ours coming out.

Ours is a household where there are no secrets, where each person's opinion is valid. Every single question you have about life is a good question. This creates an atmosphere where there is no fear, and our kids get a chance to see what life is really about.

"I asked her what comes into her head when I say the word 'homosexuality.' She said, 'I don't know if I think it's normal.' And I said, 'That's fair. I like Brussels sprouts, and you don't. I think you should eat them because it's normal for me. Do you think you should?' Kristin said, 'No, it's not normal for me.' I explained to her that everybody has their own set of what's normal. That for me, sitting in a field listening to the birds sing is very normal. For other people, it wouldn't be. For me to live my life with a woman is not normal. For me to live my life with a man is normal. It makes me feel whole. I said, 'Someday you're going to decide what's right for you.' Kristin really understood and she told me later that this discussion really helped her out."

— MARTIN PHILLIPS

DOUGLAS
(Stained Glass Artist)

People are so fearful. Many folks worry that if someone tells their children that homosexuality is okay, their kids will turn out to be gay. They don't understand that being gay is not something you can learn from someone else. People are born gay. We are all conditioned to be straight in a heterosexual society and we try our hardest to be straight. Unfortunately, that effort can destroy us. If we do make it through our youth without committing suicide, then we still have to break through all the rest of the garbage.

I try to keep the load off of Martin so he can have some time. I'm not a parent to the girls, and they don't see me that way. They respect me because I'm an elder, and Martin has taught them to listen to adults. They listen well and are very well behaved. He's raised some really amazing children.

KRISTIN
(Sixth-Grade Student)

I was glad when my dad told me he was gay. It didn't exactly make a difference to me because he was still my father.

When I was little, Dad used to read me *The Wind in the Willows*. It was my favorite book. He can do the voices and stuff. He wrote songs, and now he's into making stained glass.

I don't think being gay is a bad thing. I just think it's part of life if you're born that way. None of my friends know about my dad being gay except for my best friend, Jackie. She was kind of surprised, but she didn't make fun of it or anything. I could trust her and I knew that she wouldn't tell anybody. I don't think that people who aren't gay understand what gay people go through—that they are made fun of. They feel bad. They don't need to be made fun of at school.

Lynne holding Sophie

194

THE
POLITO
FAMILY

LYNNE POLITO

SOPHIE HANNAH SCHULZ (1 MONTH)

LYNNE
(Mother)

I didn't come out even to myself until I was in my senior year in high school. I went to a conservative school, and everybody was always saying that homosexuality was so bad, so evil, so sick, and so degenerate. As early as tenth grade, I defended it. Usually when you defend something, you have to defend yourself, too. I would say, "I'm not one of them, but I don't think that it's wrong to be gay." Still, it was shocking when I realized that I was going to act on my feelings toward women. But it wasn't a complete surprise; things clicked together.

My sexuality had to be clear to my parents although we never talked about it. In fact, my parents loved my girlfriends. They played cards with them. They'd ask me, "When is Carol coming over?" My girlfriends and I would hang out, and my mother would not interrupt us. I guess she always thought that eventually I would find a man and get married. As long as she assumed that I would be heterosexual again, she let me do whatever I wanted.

I remember thinking that either you were lesbian or you weren't, with no in-between. I assumed that I would have to be a lesbian forever, even though I used to like guys.

I was sitting in oceanography class taking notes one day. Suddenly, I started to cry because I was writing in my notebook the questions, "Who are you?" and "Is this going

> "Babies don't care what gender you are. . . . They recognize who gives them the most love, who touches them, who cares for them. Sophie doesn't know that I'm bisexual, and she doesn't care. She just knows that I love her and take care of her. That's all that matters to her."
>
> — LYNNE POLITO

to change?" These questions were overwhelming to me at the time. I wondered who there was to talk to about these things, and how I was going to get through this identity crisis. I felt sad and lonely.

I thought that bisexuals were just confused. For that matter, I thought that everybody who wasn't gay was confused. But when I ended my relationship with a woman two years ago, I started a relationship with a man. This change was very painful to my girlfriend and to me, especially since she and I had spent months saying how stupid men were. But this new relationship with a man was very satisfying for me, so I had to reevaluate my feelings about men and about my sexual identity. I'm still reevaluating.

I got pregnant with a man I met in Germany. I wanted to keep the baby, and yet I didn't want to parent with anybody, including him. I wanted to be a single parent.

It's hard to describe my baby, Sophie—it's like describing a part of myself. She's a super baby. She's really sweet. Babies don't care what gender you are. They don't recognize mom or dad in the sense that "This is my mother, and this is my father." They recognize who gives them the most love, who touches them, who cares for them. Sophie doesn't know that I'm bisexual, and she doesn't care. She just knows that I love her and take care of her. That's all that matters to her.

Left to right: *Asha, Lizzie, Shirley, and Ishana*

THE
RIGA / STRAZZERO
FAMILY

SHIRLEY RIGA & LIZZIE STRAZZERO

ISHANA STRAZZERO - WILD (12)

ASHA STRAZZERO - WILD (12)

SHIRLEY
(Court Reporter, Counselor)

I've been divorced for nine years, and I have two teenage girls from my former marriage. I just married Lizzie and we live together in a house with my two daughters and with Lizzie's daughters, Asha and Ishana.

I didn't awaken to the fact that I was a lesbian until a year after my divorce. My daughters have been very much against the fact that I'm a lesbian. They found it has made their lives difficult. Their fear of hostile behavior or of being ostracized is what makes them scared. As time has passed, they've begun to warm slightly to the idea.

As long as a family is sharing love and respect for each other, it doesn't matter who the parents are. Love is essential. Respect is love's equal partner. I grew up with a mother and a father, and there was much more dysfunction in my own childhood than there is in my present blended family.

I'm happier with myself now, and I find myself more at peace inside. I'm much more pleasant to be around. I feel more alive, more truthful, more honest with myself.

"We really do have fun. It feels like there's equality in a relationship with two women. For me there's openness, emotionality, and an awareness about power and who has it and who doesn't. I think a lot of that is because we are able to be so close to our emotions."

— LIZZIE STRAZZERO

LIZZIE
(Psychotherapist)

My former partner, Zenya, and I were together for thirteen years. Our two daughters, Ishana and Asha, were adopted into a lesbian household. They came home from India in a tiny basket, with a combined weight of eight pounds. They were four weeks old and ten weeks old. When the girls were five, Zenya and I got divorced, moved out to the country, and built two houses on the same piece of land. Now I live nearby in a new home with Shirley and her daughters. Zenya and I continue to coparent the girls, and they go back and forth between our households.

There have been many advantages for my girls growing up in a lesbian community. They are close to so many adults, it's like having a very large, supportive extended family. At one of Asha's volleyball games, a lot of our lesbian friends showed up. We were all sitting up in the top bleachers, screaming and cheering for her team.

Gay and lesbian families were openly talked about in Asha and Ishana's elementary school. When Ishana was in kindergarten, she shared with the class that we'd gone to the Gay Pride march over the weekend. The teacher said, "Oh, wow, I wish I'd known about it. I would have gone." Asha talked about the parade and the rainbow balloons, and the kids got really excited about it. Not only were all these elementary schoolchildren hearing our daughters talk about having lesbian moms, but they saw both Zenya and me volunteering in the classroom on a regular basis.

The level of communication in our household is very high. We have regular family meetings to discuss issues and concerns. I remember one morning when we had woken the kids up, Asha was furious that we hadn't let them sleep late. She came upstairs and yelled at the top of her lungs, "I want a family meeting!!!!" At first there was tension, but by the end of the meeting everyone felt better because everyone had been heard. By the end of a family meeting, we're usually having a good time. We try to teach and exercise respect.

ASHA
(Seventh-Grade Student)

My friend and I were running laps in gym class. I said, "Hi, how are you doing? I saw you made the basketball team." She said, "Oh yeah, it's really fun." Then I asked her, "What's your mom's name?" She told me, and then I said, "What's your dad's name?" She said, "I don't have a dad." So I said, "Do you have two moms?" She kind of stopped for a minute, and finally she said, "Yeah." I said, "Me too." And she was like, "Really? Oh my God. Me too!" Then we just kept running and talking.

When I was younger, this new kid came to school. My best friend and I were walking down the hall, holding hands, and skipping. He said, "Hey, you lesbians. What are you doing?" I turned around, and I said, "What are you doing making fun of lesbians?" The teacher sent him to the principal's office. He never said anything bad about lesbians again.

I was in my Spanish class, and a girl who is supposedly really popular and in the cool group was saying to her friend, "Oh my God, did you hear that the teacher last year was gay? You know how sick that is?" I just said, "I don't want to hear that," and I kept on walking.

Everybody's different. There's no such thing as the perfect family. On the cover of many magazines, you'll see a mom, a dad, and their son and daughter. Brown hair, matching outfits, same color eyes. That drives me up the wall. It's a stereotypical family. In real life, everybody's family is totally different. One advantage of being in my family is that I'm able to understand differences between people. One major thing that I've learned is that all that really matters is love between people. I think that is the most important thing for people to understand.

ISHANA
(Seventh-Grade Student)

I think kids are afraid and don't know what to expect of people who are gay or lesbian. They are afraid and so they make fun of people. I was at the gym locker one day, and a girl started making fun of gays and lesbians. I just ignored it. The person she was talking to said to me later on in the day, "There's a rumor going around that your parents are gay. Is that so?" I said, "Well, are you going to make fun of me if I tell you the answer?" And she said, "No. I don't really care. People should be what they want to be." I felt happy about that.

When my mom was getting married to Shirley, one of my favorite teachers called and wished them good luck. That made me feel good. I want to be a teacher when I grow up—preschool to third grade.

Earline and Tashina

THE
ROBINSON
FAMILY

EARLINE ROBINSON

TASHINA MARIE ROBINSON (18)

EARLINE
(Musician)

I grew up in a heterosexual home in a racially mixed neighborhood as the second oldest of eight kids. When I came out to my parents, my mother said, "I couldn't tell you what to do as a child, I'll be damned if I'll start now." My father said, "Well, you've always been nuttier than a fruitcake anyway." But my father also gave me good advice: "You love whoever you want as long as they are good to you."

When I came out, my siblings were so cool. Every time they saw a gay person, they would ask them, "Do you know my sister? Her name is Earline." They would tell me about this, and I would say, "You know I'm really glad about the support, but I need to choose who I come out to. This is my life here!"

I consider my family to be my two children, Tashina and Carlos, and my partner and her children, although she and I live in separate households. Since I was a child, I never wanted to get married, but I always wanted to have three children. I'm thankful that I stopped at two.

I don't go out wearing badges and pins about being a lesbian. As a woman of color, I personally don't think I need to advertise one more thing that is unacceptable in society. There are doors that are closed to me automatically just because I'm an African American

> *"It amazes me how people flock to see the foliage because it's made up of different colors. People travel so far to see all the color, when there's all this color right here. You don't have to go anywhere. It's here—the colors of families, the different ways of people getting together."*
>
> — EARLINE ROBINSON

"I'm strong and independent. I grew up knowing who I was and how to handle myself, and I didn't have to worry about people interfering with my mom raising me. If my brother and I go out somewhere, we know how to act and how to carry ourselves."

— *TASHINA ROBINSON*

and a woman. There are already two strikes against me. My fight is not about being a lesbian. My fight is about being a woman and being a woman of color. That's my struggle. As far as the lesbianism, it's not a big deal. Being a lesbian has never been an issue in my life.

I have no clue how the black people feel in this community about me being a lesbian. Not a clue. I can hear whispers, but if people aren't going to be straightforward with me, they can go ahead and talk behind my back. If people in the black community have a problem with me being a lesbian, that's not my problem.

When I was eleven, I knew I was really attracted to women. Women felt so beautiful to me because I was always told that I was hideous, ugly, and that nobody would ever care about me. I grew up with that attitude. So, whenever I saw a female, I only saw beauty. It didn't matter what she looked like.

When I would get attracted to a woman, I would say to myself, "Earline, stop it. Just stop it. You can't think that way, it's not normal. What about your kids? How are they going to deal with this?" But another voice kept saying, "If you think you're being true to your children, and at the same time you're going out in the world pretending to be someone you're not, then you're kidding yourself." I had to accept it. I had to say that I'm an African American lesbian. What a relief!

It amazes me how people flock to see the foliage because it's made up of different colors. People travel so far to see all the color, when there's all this color right here. You don't have to go anywhere. It's here—the colors of families, the different ways of people getting together. We are so blind, and we are constantly putting blinders on our children. We are responsible for giving them all of what is here. And what's here is not just a mother, father, dog, cat, house, and 2.5 children. Why give our children crumbs when the feast is out there?

TASHINA
(Eleventh-Grade Student)

I'm strong and independent. I grew up knowing who I was and how to handle myself, and I didn't have to worry about people interfering with my mom raising me. If my brother and I go out somewhere, we know how to act and how to carry ourselves.

All my friends know my mom is a lesbian, and they don't care. I tell them, "I just wanted to let you know about my mom because if you can't accept my mom, you can't accept me." That's exactly how I deal with my boyfriends. Out of all my boyfriends, I've never had any problems with telling any of them. They just say, "That's cool."

I have quite a few girlfriends whose moms are lesbians. We just found each other over the years. Sometimes I'd go over to a friend's house and notice something in their house that was the same as in my house. Once I was sleeping over at a friend's, and the mother's friend was sleeping over too. So I asked my friend, "Is your mom a lesbian?" And she said, "Yeah. Why?" And I said, "Because my mom is a lesbian too!" We found out that our moms even knew each other. That has happened a lot of times.

Teachers need to say in their classrooms that most families don't consist of just a mom, a dad, a puppy dog, a boy, and a girl. A lot of parents are divorced by the time the kids get into elementary school. There are lots of single parents out there too. Some families have one dad or two dads. Some families have a mom and a dad; some families have one mom; some families have two moms; some families have the aunt taking care of her nephews and nieces, or grandparents taking care of grandchildren. And some parents are really old—some of my friends have parents who are almost fifty! There are so many different kinds of families. Teachers don't teach the whole story about families in schools. They're still into teaching about the old conventional families.

Adults want kids to accept everybody, but adults don't always accept everybody themselves. We should all be nice to everyone and treat everyone as equals.

Left to right: *Jason, David, Michael, Danielle, and Gene*

THE
SERKIN-POOLE
FAMILY

MICHAEL SERKIN-POOLE & DAVID SERKIN-POOLE

JASON SERKIN-POOLE (12)

DANIELLE SERKIN-POOLE (14)

GENE SERKIN-POOLE (16)

*"Life is holy. This
doesn't mean that
some life is holy.
All of it is."*

*— DAVID
SERKIN-POOLE*

MICHAEL
(At-Home Father)

On our very first date, David and I discovered that we both were open to having children but we were together eight years before actually calling an adoption agency. In 1988 we adopted Gene when he was eight years old. Three years later we adopted seven-year-old Jason and the next year we adopted nine-year-old Danielle. She is Jason's biological sister, but he didn't remember her when she first joined our family. David and I have been together for over sixteen years.

When we visited an adoption agency, they gave us a book filled with pages and pages of "special needs" kids. Then they asked us which type of kid we would accept and which type we would not accept. Not many people have to sit down and think, "What kind of child would I not be able to deal with?" You have to find out your limits, and that's what we did.

I had been a manager at a group home for developmentally disabled adults. Some of the residents would visit me on my day off, and we became friends. This experience allowed me to be open to adopting children with a variety of special needs.

When we first met our son Jason, he didn't speak at all. His caregivers thought it was because he had such a low IQ, but they were wrong. We met him at a picnic, and he walked by me carrying his hamburger and french fries. I made the American Sign Language signs for hamburger and fries,

Jason and Michael

and he looked at me as if I were crazy. But when Jason got up and went for seconds, he made the signs for hamburger and fries as he walked by me! After he had joined our family, I assumed it would take us a long time to teach him sign language, but he remembered every sign I taught him immediately! I never had to repeat a sign twice. Jason was like a sponge just waiting to learn. Nobody had ever known before how Jason felt. Nobody had ever known if he was mad or upset or had questions. It must have been incredibly frustrating for him.

All three of our children have developmental delays. Our son Gene also has fetal alcohol syndrome, attention deficit disorder, and hyperactivity. In the past Jason has had behavioral problems, but he's getting better. I'll ask him now if he remembers some of his problems. Jason tells me, "Yes, I remember." He says, "Throwing stuff away. Breaking things." But now he's smiling. He says, "No more. Finished." However, the jury's still out and we continue to work with child psychologists to help Jason deal with his "demons."

My parents were not supportive of my being gay, and this didn't change over time. We had a warmer relationship when I was first with David, but once we adopted children, my family stopped talking to me. They never expected me to have children, so it completely blew them away.

People have asked us if it's hard on the kids having gay dads. Well, it's easier to get along in our culture if you're Christian, but does that mean that we Jewish folks should raise our kids Christian? Should black people not have children because bigotry will make their lives too rough? Hogwash!

DAVID
(Cantor)

Until 1986, Michael and I led a somewhat sequestered life because of my choice to remain closeted professionally. Up until that point, I had no out gay role models in the mainstream clergy, Jewish or Christian. Fortunately, the Jewish Reform movement was becoming more and more open, and during their annual meeting in 1985, they made a formal statement declaring that they would not discriminate in their congregations on the basis of sexual orientation. Since then they've broadened this statement and they now welcome gays into their seminaries and into their pulpits as rabbis, cantors, and teachers. They even support legally binding marriage between gay couples. I had decided not to be a cantor anymore, but when a position opened up in Seattle as a cantor, I took it. I came out a few years later.

You can't raise kids if you're closeted, so I had to come out totally before we could even think about being parents. When I first came out to my relatives, there were problems mostly due to my inability to assert what was what. I just needed to say, "Hey! This is me. This is my partner. And this is my family. Here we are!"

People might assume that adopting special needs kids was the only option Michael and I had as gay men. Actually, it was our conscious choice to consider "hard-to-place" kids because there are thousands of them out there. If I could, I would like to adopt a hundred. It breaks your heart to hear some of the stories of abuse and emotional pain these kids have faced. At the time, I was working on my master's degree in psychology with a specialty in child development, so it all came together. It's not for everybody, but we thought we could do it.

One of the nice surprises for us as gay dads is that within the community of other parents who have disabled children, we have found no prejudice against us at all. I think it's because these people have already dealt with the big taboo about people not being "normal." People who get to know individuals with physical or mental disabilities often understand that there are lots of differences in the world and that they don't have to be afraid of them. They get past the barrier that implies that some people are holier than other people and some lives are more valuable than other people's lives. Life is holy. This doesn't mean that some life is holy. All of it is.

Sure, some folks are surprised when they ask us, "Where's the mom?" We simply tell them, "We're both the dads." They say, "Oh," and they may have to process it for fifteen seconds. Then they apply this understanding to families like ours and they go on. Life goes on. Someday it's not going to be a big deal at all being a gay parent. People will say, "What's the big deal? Tell me something new."

JASON (SIGNING)
(Student)

I like to play outside with Gene, Danielle, and our dog. I like to ice-skate. I like to go to temple.

DANIELLE
(Student)

I like my cat. I don't like school.

GENE
(Student)

Hanukkah was really cool this year. I got a real cool gold necklace. When I'm not wearing it, I always keep it in the white box my dads gave me.

> *"People have asked us if it's hard on the kids having gay dads. Well, it's easier to get along in our culture if you're Christian, but does that mean that we Jewish folks should raise our kids Christian? Should black people not have children because bigotry will make their lives too rough? Hogwash!"*
>
> *— MICHAEL SERKIN-POOLE*

Left to right: *Jaqué, Roberta, Nabowire, and Edwian*

THE
STOKES / DUPREÉ
FAMILY

ROBERTA STOKES & JAQUÉ DUPREÉ
EDWIAN STOKES (12)
NABOWIRE STOKES (12)

ROBERTA
(Owner of Ancestral Roots, Afrikan Natural Skin, Hair, and Body Care Salon)

I had been a lesbian all my adult life, and I felt ready to have children when I was in my thirties. I was working as a couples counselor then, so I knew about a sperm bank. I called them and explained that I was a lesbian, and that I wanted to have a family. The pregnancy was good, and having twins was not a surprise to me. Jaqué came later. We have all been a family since the children were two. It's a beautiful union.

Jaqué knew that she couldn't come into the family and simply be a friend and playmate to my children, as she had been before we became partners. The twins needed to understand that Jaqué was going to take care of them, too. They had to take discipline from her, as well as play together with her. There's child-rearing going on and we perform certain parenting tasks together, but Jaqué is not the second mother. It's been good watching their relationship change and grow over a period of years, but the children know that I'm the mother.

Growing up, I knew what was going on within me, but "lesbian" was not a popular word. I knew in junior high school exactly what I was involved in. It was really clear. I always had a girlfriend in high school.

> *"When we realize that we are first and foremost all part of the human race, and that family compositions are as diverse as cultural differences, we can then begin to better understand what evolution is all about."*
>
> — *ROBERTA STOKES*

I wasn't very forward as a young person. I went through a period of having a male friend come to parties with me and pretend to be my boyfriend. Even my friends at college wouldn't have a real dialogue with me. If they had a party, they'd just say, "Bring whomever you want to bring."

I never said to my mom, "I'm a lesbian." She knew it. My mother caught me in various situations and chose to ignore them. In fact, she protected me. If some aunt asked me if I had a boyfriend, my mom would come into the conversation and say something like, "All we ever did was get married and have babies. These days the girls don't want to do that. Roberta is traveling and going to school, so don't push her into finding a boyfriend."

I nursed my children for three years, and we have a thing about being physical with each other. My daughter, Nabowire, does it a certain way; my son, Edwian, does it a certain way. They just want to lean all over me, and it's okay. I don't think it will ever be any different. I won't let anybody make me feel strange if at sixteen, they park themselves on me. I can imagine someone saying, "Why are those teenagers sitting on your lap?" It's really all right if he or she is sitting there. We know what's going on. They could be forty and I'll be eighty, and my children can still sit on my lap. That's what we do.

When we realize that we are first and foremost all part of the human race, and that family compositions are as diverse as cultural differences, we can then begin to better understand what evolution is all about.

JAQUÉ
(Musician, Visual Artist)

I was resistant when I first realized that Roberta was interested in more than a platonic relationship with me. I needed a little more than a moment to make an emotional adjustment to this change. I'd been on the road as a musician performing at different festivals with Roberta, and I'd been a friend to her and her children for a while. I held Roberta in very high esteem. She's a spiritual dancer, earth woman, herb woman. I would describe the beginning of our relationship like a volcano—a lot of hot and fiery passion underneath that finally erupted at a music festival. I thought, "Uh oh! Full moon. Festival. What do you know." It was very magical.

I had been praying for somebody to come into my life for a long time. Someone who was very compatible, someone who was caring and sharing, someone who could give back. So, here was this gift but I didn't recognize it for a while. Over time, after all the phone calls, the conversations, and all the sharing, I realized, "Here's this gift, and you're not accepting it." Finally, I said to myself, "Yes. I deserve this. I deserve this person in my life."

One of the main reasons Roberta wanted to be with me is that she wanted to do

"We like to go on trips together. We like to have fun together and go to different places, and that's mostly what we like to do together. Our family is exciting. You never know what's around the bend."

— EDWIAN STOKES

spiritual work together. That was very important. Besides going to church every Sunday and being part of a choir, we do spiritual work together as a family in the Yoruba faith, reaching all the way back into our African heritage. We believe in honoring our ancestors as a family.

Morality and integrity are a big part of who we are while walking this path on our planet. I'm constantly talking to the children about this. I say, "There are two things in life you don't want to be. You don't want to be a liar or a thief. Any problem we have on the planet stems from those two things." It's really been important for Roberta and me to live the life in front of them as opposed to just talking about morality. So I don't lie to the children and I don't want any relationship with them to have make-believe titles. I was their friend before Roberta and I became partners, so there was no reason to change my title to "aunt" or "second mom."

Our family includes my life partner, honey, sweetheart, my love, Roberta, and her twins. Edwian and Nabowire are my

Left to right, back: *Edwian and Nabowire*; front: *Roberta and Jacqué.*

little friends whom I help to parent, raise, and am a guardian to. We also live with one of Roberta's closest friends, Asma, and her son, Akin, who have become extended family members. Since I grew up as a foster child, moving from home to home from the time I was three years old until I was emancipated at fifteen, this has been the most consistent family of my life. Nothing should be more important than family, and we function like any healthy family does.

I enjoy when our teachings over the many years are reflected by the children in ways and at times that are totally unexpected. Inside I can smile and say, "Well done. Edwian and Nabowire are getting it!"

It is very important for us as a family to deal with the truth in our lives because it will be easier for the children to understand as they grow what it is like for us to be lesbians.

Nothing outside should be more important than the family unit, whatever the family unit is, for if and when that happens, the family unit is compromised.

We are lesbians; the children live in a lesbian household. What makes children secure is knowing that you're there, that you want to be with them. I want to be with Edwian and Nabowire. We march together every year. They understand what the struggle is.

The struggle was introduced to me when I was coming up in church and we had the bus ride to Washington, D.C., and the march with Martin Luther King Jr. and the civil rights movement. With every time in history comes the responsibility of a struggle. And so Nabowire's and Edwian's coming into this world represents an issue in itself. Even though it's personal, it's political. We, as women, have the right to bring children into the world or not, as we want to. It's a political issue for us as feminists, as women, as Africans living here in the United States, and as lesbians. It's part of the homework.

When I was in elementary school, I was aware that I was different, but it wasn't until high school that I understood the word "lesbian." It was easy growing up because I didn't have to be accountable to any parent. I would hang out with musicians and play guitar and be in the folk scene. As musicians, we could be out and be artistic and eccentric with our clothing. We were sensitive people who weren't afraid of really expressing ourselves. So to speak out about lesbian issues was fine. The struggles weren't so different for me—whether they were lesbian issues, women's rights, or prison inmate rights. I was constantly on the firing line for one political issue or another. Lesbianism was, in some ways, the least of the issues I could be attacked for. But, it was there with all the many things we were struggling for.

I went to college for a while in California and in Boston. For the last fifteen years, I was part of the political music group Casselberry and DuPreé. Right now I'm taking a break from singing in that group. I'm studying again at Medgar Evers College. I want to merge together my spiritual work, my art, and my music.

NABOWIRE
(Sixth-Grade Student)

We like to go to the park sometimes. And we play basketball and baseball. We always do things that include the whole family. I play double dutch and football.

I like to ride my bike with Jaqué, especially in Prospect Park near where we live. We all like to ride our bikes as a family and go places together. Sometimes we sit down and watch a movie all together at home.

Family means the people who look out for me and treat me with love and respect. My family are the people who are in my life practically every day. These people are my mother, Jaqué, Edwian, and my mother's friend Asma and her son, Akin, who live with us.

"Don't be ashamed of who your parents are."

— NABOWIRE STOKES

My mother takes me places and she loves me. Jaqué takes me and Edwian bike-riding and she does many other fun activities with us.

I haven't been teased by anybody about my family because nobody cares if my mother is a lesbian.

Don't be ashamed of who your parents are.

EDWIAN
(Sixth-Grade Student)

I like being twins because we play together; we don't have to feel lonely. We sing and drum and take karate. We love to do African, modern, and hip-hop dance. My favorite things to do with my family are to ride my bike and go to the movies. In our family, I am the only boy.

In our family, we celebrate the African American holiday called Kwanzaa. We also celebrate the Yoruba traditions.

My family means everything to me. What I mean by that is that my family means happiness, education, fun, spending time together, and talking together. My family takes care of me and loves me. My mother makes sure I am always fed. She drives me to school. Jaqué, my mother's partner, also takes care of me. She makes sure I am fed, clothed, and that I'm going somewhere.

We like to go on trips together. We like to have fun together and go to different places, and that's mostly what we like to do together. Our family is exciting. You never know what's around the bend.

Stacey, Liza, and Amy

THE
STYLES / MACKENZIE
FAMILY

STACEY STYLES & AMY MACKENZIE
LIZA MACKENZIE STYLES (7)

STACEY
(Violin Restorer)

Amy and I got together ten years ago. The fact that we both wanted kids was definitely a factor in our feeling that we were potential partners. Fourteen months later, Amy was pregnant. During her pregnancy, my parents and my sister and her family were close by, which was really wonderful for me. We got married this year after being together for nine years.

When I came out in my twenties I thought that would be it. But having Liza is a continual process of coming out. When you have a kid, you come out every September to a whole new group of kids and parents. There are a whole new series of birthday parties where I drop Liza off and Amy picks her up, and we have to explain our family setup. And then there are the invitations from people who say, "Hi, I'm so-and-so's parent. Would you and your husband like to come to a party?"

I've found a positive force in me that I didn't know existed. You can't continually batter yourself against a brick wall. You have to soften up, become flexible, and be brave. Being a lesbian mom is a bit like white-water rafting. You keep learning to negotiate the rough parts. By being who we are, by being open and affirming about it, we change a little bit of the world.

> *"Being a lesbian mom is a bit like white-water rafting. You keep learning to negotiate the rough parts. . . . I hate the question, 'Who is the real mom?' Amy and I are both Liza's real moms."*
>
> — STACEY STYLES

Liza knows firsthand what it feels like to be different. I see her as a very compassionate kid, and part of her sensitivity comes from knowing that not everyone is the same. It may also be an advantage for Liza in terms of being able to envision alternatives for her own life. She may or may not be straight, but I hope it will be easier for her to find out who she is than it was for me to find out who I am.

I hate the question, "Who is the real mom?" Amy and I are both Liza's real moms.

AMY
(FedEx Delivery Person)

Getting married to Stacey was an astounding experience—to get up there and look out at all these people from all parts of our life smiling at us. My younger sister, a fundamentalist Christian, came to the wedding with her husband and her daughter. We had a part of our service where people could speak if they wanted, and she stood up and said she had tons of respect for us. That made me cry. Later I told her how much it meant to Stacey and me that she and her family are so loving and accepting. She said, "Well, you and Stacey make it easy because that's how you are with us."

Liza was goofing around with a seven-year-old boy, and I said to her, "Isn't it funny that in about five or six years, you may look at him with different eyes." Then Liza said, "Yeah, but maybe I won't. Maybe I'll be looking at girls that way." That's how we talk in our family. Maybe it will be boys, maybe it will be girls. Maybe it will be both.

LIZA
(Second-Grade Student)

Some kids were wondering how I was born. I told them, "Just like a regular kid." Sometimes I'd say that we found someone who would give the seed, and that's how.

I call Amy and Stacey, "Mom" and "Mom." I played something by Bach on the violin when my moms got married.

Lesbian just means that there are two women together who love each other. Some people don't like lesbians and gays, or lesbian and gay families. We're really the same as other kinds of families. There's nothing really different about anybody. It's just that everybody is different and the same.

A family is a bunch of people, or not so many, who love each other.

Greg and Mel

THE
THOMAS
FAMILY

MEL THOMAS
GREG THOMAS (31)

*"The bottom line is
that being gay is no
big deal. Be honest
and be who you are.
When you do that,
it's very easy to love
other people."*

— MEL THOMAS

MEL
(Outreach Educator, Gay Outreach Program, The Urban League)

I'm Mel Thomas, and I'm gay. I do AIDS prevention education in the African American community and lead workshops on internalized homophobia and racism. I'm also a musician.

My mother is still alive but my father passed away two years ago. They were married for sixty-four years! I've been married twice, and I have two sons, Greg and Mark, and three grandchildren. Greg and Mark are the product of my first marriage. My first wife and I split up when the boys were very young. Mark lived with his mom and Greg lived with me. As a result, Greg and I did a lot of growing up together, and we're really tight.

When I was coming up, there were two known gay men, Boo Boo and Stanley, in the African American community of my home city. They were both very effeminate and flamboyant in their dress, and their faces were loaded with makeup. They were your stereotypical gay men, and I wasn't like either of them. I used to hear myths about how gay men hated women, and I certainly did not hate women. In fact, I enjoyed being with my first wife. I heard about gay men molesting children, and I certainly had no sexual interest in children. Because these myths and stereotypes about gay men didn't fit me, I thought that I must not be gay. But, in fact, I was attracted to guys and was getting involved with them.

During the Stonewall riots in 1969, I finally saw a television documentary about a guy who said he was gay. He wasn't effeminate or flamboyant. He had on a sports jacket, shirt, and tie. He was the first gay person I had ever seen that I could identify with. It was my first cue to say, "Well, maybe after all, I am gay."

At this point, I had this strong attraction like a magnet to anything about being gay. One time I was in the grocery store and I saw the word "homo." Well, it was part of the word homogenized on a milk carton, but bells started going whirrr. I said to myself, "Mel, you really need to get hold of yourself and check this out!"

Unfortunately at that time, the main place for gays to meet other gays was the bars, and there's no use going to a bar if you're not going to drink. I used alcohol and drugs for the next thirteen years. After thirteen years of doing that, you know you've got a number of problems. I went into treatment and I've been clean and sober for close to thirteen years. I'm fifty-four now.

I was twenty-eight when I came out to most of the people in my life, but I never came out to my dad because we were never very close. There was an occasion when he and I had gone to my son Greg's graduation from Carnegie-Mellon. Out of a clear blue sky, my father asked me, "Mel, do you date women anymore?" I said, "No," and I just left it there. I also hesitated telling Greg that I was gay, not because I felt he would reject me or get angry, but because I was afraid I would disappoint him. I wondered how he was going to feel about having a gay father.

My grandmother lived with my family when I was a child and I was closest to her. It was from Gram that I got affirmations that I was okay, that I was whole. Her attitude was to be who you are, love who you are, and don't really sweat what other people think or say about you. She loved me for who I was. She may have read my beads back there long before I read them myself. Gram was the rock that stood beneath me and beside me. So when I think of some of the roughest times I've gone through, crying and cussing the storms, for the most part my feet have always been there on the ground.

If you have a partner and you want to put your arms around him, or you want to kiss and hold hands in public, you should be able to do so. They allow straight people to do it. Why can't gay folks do it?

The bottom line is that being gay is no big deal. Be honest and be who you are. When you do that, it's very easy to love other people.

GREG
(Actor)

My dad and I have always had a really great relationship. Growing up with him, I think I've gotten a privileged education. I've got a kind of Bachelor's of Gay Studies degree.

"Gay men and women are not out to destroy the heterosexual community. They're not looking to take over. They just want to have an equal portion in the world because they deserve it as people."

— GREG THOMAS

I never saw my brother, Mark, after our parents divorced. I was twenty-three when I first saw him again. He had been raised by our mom who had given him a conservative, religious upbringing. Consequently, Mark had a lack of tolerance for gay people. My dad isn't insecure about being homosexual. He walks very comfortably with it, and I feel very comfortable with it too. My brother doesn't. That's difficult for me because he doesn't accept us as we are.

I have a curiosity and a hunger for learning things. I don't reject a lot of things outright. I just don't. There's always something coming around the corner, and instead of being so concerned about what its effect is going to be on me, I'm open to exploring and seeing what it's about.

I was dealing with a lot of racial issues in high school, like being black and having white men, in particular, abuse my color. So being called a "faggot" was just a general derogatory term they used along with all the others. Because they didn't like my race, they would use anything to put me down.

By the time I went to college, it was kind of cool to be able to say, "My dad is gay." I felt okay about it. A couple of times in college, I was approached by men who were attracted to me. I always felt comfortable saying, "I'm straight, not gay."

Gay men and women are not out to destroy the heterosexual community. They're not looking to take over. They just want to have an equal portion in the world because they deserve it as people.

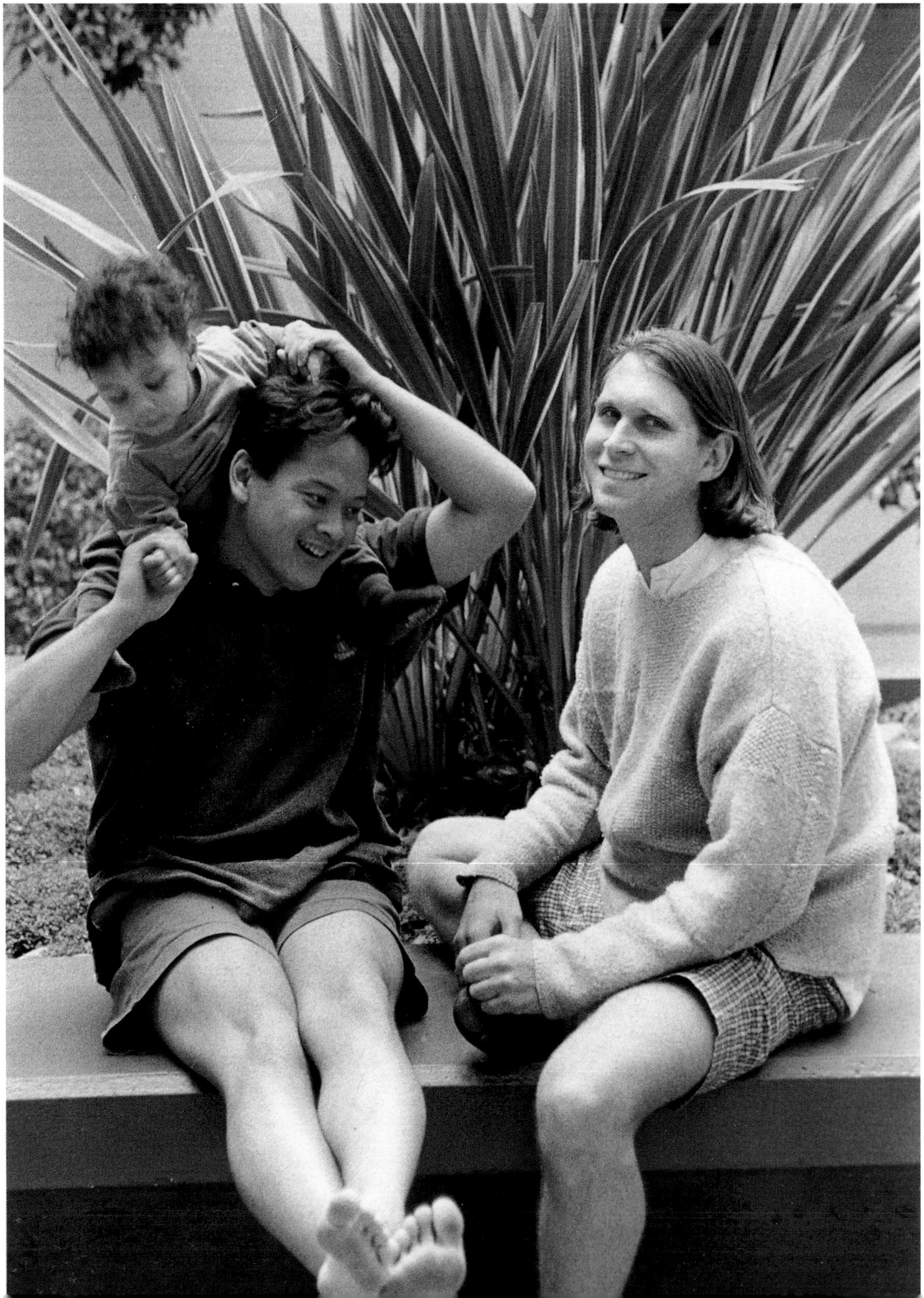

Julian, Hoa, and Perry

THE
VOSCOTT
FAMILY

PERRY VOSCOTT & HOA VOSCOTT
JULIAN VOSCOTT (20 MONTHS)

PERRY
(Househusband, Entrepreneur)

I grew up in Maine, but I went to high school in Europe for several years. During my first year abroad I fell in love with a guy, and it felt right for me.

My parents had always been extremely supportive of me and my sisters, regardless of what we did. There were never any secrets between us. When I came home from Europe during my school holidays, I felt good about being gay and I assumed my parents would be very accepting. When I told them, their response was actually quite the opposite. They were very angry at me and they felt ashamed. They thought that my being gay was somehow their fault.

I went back to Europe for five years to finish my schooling. I stayed over there all those years, primarily because of my parents' negative reaction to my coming out. Finally I said to my parents, "Are you interested in having a son or not? If you are, you're going to have to accept me for who I am. If you aren't, then you should write me off, and I will write you off because I'm not going to deal with the guilt. This is who I am, and I've accepted it. You need to accept me, too."

It took my parents eleven years to come to grips with my sexual orientation. They

"Like everyone raising infants, we don't have time to go to movies or restaurants anymore. Whether you're in a heterosexual relationship or a gay relationship, parenting is about showing up for it and giving it your all. For me and Hoa, children are the most important thing in our lives."

— *PERRY VOSCOTT*

225

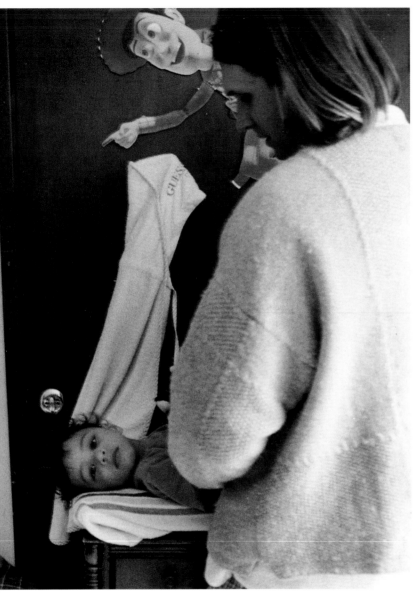

Julian and Perry

didn't fully accept my being gay until I met Hoa. He was the clincher. They adored him from the very beginning. He was a very big hit. Perhaps my parents needed to see me with someone wonderful who was meant to be my life partner.

During my six years with Hoa, my parents have been extremely supportive of our relationship and of our son, Julian. In fact, they are very doting grandparents. They moved from Maine to California about an hour north of us in order to be closer. I think they are very sorry for what they put me through, and they are trying to make up for it.

Julian's birth mother chose Hoa and me to be his adoptive parents in part because we were willing to have an open adoption. She had experienced oppression as a Latina, and she identified with the discrimination we deal with as gay men. She also had gay friends, so being gay wasn't something negative to her.

We love Julian's birth mother. She's become very much a part of our family. She lives only five minutes away, and we see her at least every two weeks. Sometimes she takes care of Julian if we want to go out. It's a nice situation.

I get very angry when people say that it is horrible for children to be brought up in a gay family and that gays are absolutely sick people. There's a lot of hatred against us and our families. It is especially horrible when a parent teaches hate to a child. Any kind of hate.

Like everyone raising infants, we don't have time to go to movies or restaurants anymore. Whether you're in a heterosexual relationship or a gay relationship, parenting is about showing up for it and giving it your all. For me and Hoa, children are the most important thing in our lives.

Julian's a sweetheart and he's always been a very easy baby. He's the star of our lives. By growing up in a gay, multiracial family, Julian will be able to understand what other marginalized people go through. He's definitely not going to be racist or homophobic.

Our society doesn't typically see men as nurturers and caretakers of children, but I'm the lucky one who gets to stay home full time with Julian. There aren't a lot of men who do this, so my support network is not huge. I've had some hard times adjusting to other people's reactions, but I've learned to face the questions at the checkout aisle such as, "Where's Mom? She must be working today," or "Is it Dad's day?" A lot of people also ask me about Julian's racial identity by saying, "What does his mom look like?"

When you get down to really simple terms, our family is much the same as any other family. Our family consists of people who love one another and want to give everything that they can to a child. Whether it's a mother and father, or a mother and a mother, or two fathers, it's love, and love makes a family.

HOA
(Environmental Engineer)

I was born in Vietnam and raised in an Asian culture that is a lot more traditional and homophobic than Western culture. I knew I was gay when I was twelve or thirteen, and I also knew that I wasn't a bad person. At the time, I was living in a very small town where I was the only Asian person besides my parents. For me, being Asian was worse than being gay. Being gay I could hide; being Asian I couldn't. I wanted to be a blue-eyed, blond, white person more than I wanted to be straight.

Perry and I met in 1991 in Maine. I was volunteering at a health food co-op and Perry was the assistant manager. I guess it was love at first sight over tofu and olive oil.

I knew that I wanted to have children, and I knew that I couldn't do it in a conventional way. But I never thought that I couldn't do it. When I met Perry, we both talked right away about our desire to have children and to be in a committed relationship. Luckily, it was very mutual. When we decided to adopt, we were open to a child of any race, so we contacted a private agency that works exclusively with minority children. As a gay couple, we obviously weren't going to pretend that we gave birth to our child. A straight couple might want a kid who looks like them, but we didn't care about having a child who was in our image.

I came out to my parents after I met Perry. I always knew I was gay, but I wanted to be in a secure relationship that I was proud of before telling them. I think they've always suspected, and they're slowly getting better about accepting my sexual orientation. But the key word is "slowly."

My parents haven't met Julian yet because they live on the East Coast, but they occasionally ask me about him. I send them photos and they have sent him gifts. I think their acknowledgment of my family with Perry and Julian is an evolving thing. I know my parents will always be in my life, and there are certain things I'll get from them and certain things I won't.

Although being in a gay family is definitely a rocky path for any child, the benefits for Julian of being in our family include openness, understanding, empathy, knowledge, and cultural diversity. We've benefited a lot since Julian came into our lives too. He's half-Latino and half-African American, and we've learned so much about his cultural heritage.

> *"We need to keep educating others and being positive role models. Everyone within our circle of life and work and play is affected by us, hopefully for the good."*
>
> — *HOA VOSCOTT*

I hope that kids from straight families will learn that families like ours are very much the same as their families. There is something special about gay families, but that specialness is neither a bad thing nor a good thing. It's just something like the color of your hair.

Some older children have asked us a lot of questions like, "Why does Julian have two daddies?" We tell them, "Julian's mommy couldn't take care of him at this time, and she asked me and Perry to be his parents. We love Julian, and we love and care for each other. We are a family just like your family."

These are new frontiers, and it's difficult. That's why we need to keep educating others and being positive role models. Everyone within our circle of life and work and play is affected by us, hopefully for the good.

Left to right: *Bobbi, Angela, Babette, and Kathy*

THE
WAINWRIGHT / KELLY
FAMILY

BABETTE WAINWRIGHT & KATHY KELLY

ANGELA WAINWRIGHT (24)

BOBBI SIMPSON (20)

BABETTE
(Psychotherapist)

When I was nineteen I knew I didn't want to be married to a man, but I wanted to have a baby. I called my mother from work and said, "I'm going to have a baby." She told me, "In Haitian culture and in our family, you marry, and then you have a baby."

I was a beautician then, and I asked a lot of my gay colleagues if they wanted to have a baby with me. One said, "I already gave at the office," because somebody had already asked him. One of my customers was a beautiful male dancer who came once a week to get his hair done. I asked him, and he said yes! We got married and sent a copy of the marriage license to my mother, so I paid my dues right there. That's how I had Angela.

I worked as a psychotherapist for twenty years, and Bobbi is a child who was sent to me for therapy when she was about nine years old. When I saw her the first time, I felt somehow that she belonged in our family. I worked with her family for a few years. At one point Bobbi was being removed from her home to be put in a foster home. I wasn't a foster parent, but I couldn't let her go just anywhere. I wanted that child to be with me, period. And that's how Bobbi came into our family. She is our child.

In Haiti we didn't have a word for lesbian. In that culture, you see women together kissing

"You have to judge people as individuals. You'll find some gay people who aren't so good, just like there are heterosexuals who aren't so good, but most gay people I meet are great people. They are more open-minded than the average person and they have a lot to share."

— *BOBBI SIMPSON*

231

"Many of the people I grew up with have experienced sexual abuse or alcoholism or other issues in their families. They come from dysfunctional families, so I don't fit in with them. I don't know anyone like me, where we can just hang out and simply talk about our good childhoods. My family when I was growing up was like the gay Ozzie and Harriet. Mom had dinner on the table, and her partner was into gardening and carpentry. It was really nice. I have no complaints. I hope that one day people can talk about their gay parents like most people talk about their mother and father."

— ANGELA WAINWRIGHT

and hugging. It's hard to discern who is a lesbian and who isn't.

All my life, I wasn't a sweet, girly child, and my parents had no choice but to take me as I was. The only problem I ever had with my family about being a lesbian was when I was with a woman who wasn't good to my child. My mother wrote to me and said, "You tell this woman of yours to go back home to her mother. I don't want her in your life." I'm very strong in my head, but I let my parents tell me what to do. I ended my relationship with that woman.

After I first met my present partner, Kathy, we saw each other at parties for quite a while. Four years ago, she mustered the courage to tell me, "You know, I like you." That's how Kathy and I got together. When Kathy met the children, she felt like they were her children. She worries more about Bobbi sometimes than I do.

KATHY
(Dentist)

I didn't identify myself as a gay person until I was in my late twenties. Before that, I always expected I would be a married person with children of my own. Children have always been important in my life, especially my nieces and nephew and the children of some of my friends.

One of the things that drew me to Babette was her involvement with children. I like the way her culture defines family very broadly. When she talks about a sister or a cousin, it may be someone who is not a relative at all as defined in American terms.

I see myself now as part of an extended family that includes my mother and sister, who have always supported me in all I've done, Babette and our kids, and my close friends and their children.

I think that gay people in our society have to make their own definitions of family, especially since so many of us face rejection from traditional families.

ANGELA
(Receptionist)

When I was in eighth grade in the early 1980s, there was a support group at my school for children of gay parents. I knew who the children of lesbians were because their moms were all friends of my mother, so I was shocked to see that lots of these children didn't show up for this group.

One girl I knew came to the support group once and never came again. I said to her, "This group is so cool. Why don't you come back?" She said, "My mother isn't really gay." I thought that was pretty sad. I was really proud of my mom being a lesbian, but I realized then that it wasn't something I should be bragging about. Now I don't tell a lot of people. I wait until I have known them for years. My best friend found out that my mother is gay after knowing me for almost six years. She was upset that I hadn't told her sooner.

Many of the people I grew up with have experienced sexual abuse or alcoholism or other issues in their families. They come from dysfunctional families, so I don't fit in with them. I don't know anyone like me, where we can just hang out and simply talk about our good childhoods.

My family when I was growing up was like the gay Ozzie and Harriet. Mom had dinner on the table, and her partner was into gardening and carpentry. It was really nice. I have no complaints. I hope that one day people can talk about their gay parents like most people talk about their mother and father.

BOBBI
(Telemarketer)

I went to stay with Babette when I was around twelve, and she was the best thing that ever could have happened to me. We just bonded on a spiritual level, and it felt like she knew me better than my mother did. The love I had for Babette was profound and I had the utmost respect for her.

For years, I had no idea that Babette was gay. I think I was probably the last person to find out. When a girl told me, I was really offended. Then Babette told me it was true. It was just a huge shock for me. It was like, okay, now that I know she's gay, do I dismiss her and kick her out of my life? Or do I accept this, knowing I haven't met anyone else in my life who measures up to Babette?

You have to judge people as individuals. You'll find some gay people who aren't so good, just like there are heterosexuals who aren't so good, but most gay people I meet are great people. They are more open-minded than the average person and they have a lot to share.

Not too long ago, I started thinking that perhaps I'm gay. I know that I am now, but I haven't had any lesbian relationships yet. I just know in my heart that I am attracted to women, and I'm glad.

Left to right: *Lisa, Ashley, Jim, Ken, and Annie*

THE
WATSON / HUTCHINS
FAMILY

KENNETH WATSON & JAMES HUTCHINS

LISA WATSON

ASHLEY WATSON (10)

ANNIE WATSON (4)

KEN
(Police Sergeant)

I'm a patrol supervisor in a police department in a small Massachusetts town with a large lesbian and gay population. I'm responsible for the officers on the street. I give directions to them as needed and I respond to the more serious calls. On occasion, I speak at various functions in my capacity as the police department's gay and lesbian liaison officer. In addition, I'm responsible for documenting any reported hate crimes. I make myself available to any officer who has questions or concerns that may involve a gay-related issue. I am also available to any member of the gay and lesbian community who has an issue with the department. I'm currently in the midst of setting up a training program on domestic violence issues in the gay and lesbian community.

Lisa and I got married in 1981, and six weeks later I told her that I was gay. Despite this, she decided that she wanted to make the marriage work. We had two children and stayed together for twelve years, but it was inevitable that at some point in time I was going to move on. I met Jim on January 23, 1992, and that was it. Lisa and I divorced after twelve years of marriage. The kids live with Lisa during the week, and on Friday afternoons they come and stay with Jim and me until Sunday.

"Kids in my old school teased me because they didn't know the full definition of 'gay.' I don't really blame them, but I hope someday that kids will understand what 'gay' really means."

— ASHLEY WATSON

Ken and Annie

When Lisa and I decided to divorce, we told our oldest daughter, Ashley, that we didn't love each other as husband and wife, but that we loved each other as friends. Ashley knew other people who had divorced with lots of fighting, but for us it wasn't like that. In fact, it was hard for Ashley to understand why we were divorcing because we were so friendly.

It's kind of fun to watch people like my parents or Lisa's parents who get to know somebody before they know that they're gay. They really like and respect this person. Then, all of a sudden, they find out that the person they like so much is gay. It's such a shock to them. They realize that all their ideas about gay people are wrong, and hopefully they won't make these same judgments in the future.

I think it's important that people know that being a gay parent is no different than being a parent in a traditional family. We have the same feeling of love for our children, the same feeling of sadness when our children have problems, and the same feeling of pride when our children do well.

Even though Massachusetts mandates that schools try to institute some dialogue about homosexuality, there are parents who say, "I don't want them talking about it in school." What is that saying to gay kids? What message is that giving? Thirteen- and fourteen-year-old gay youths are scared to death thinking about what their family and friends are going to say to them if they find out that they're gay. They feel like complete outcasts. This was the situation I was in. It's terrible to be given the message that it's not okay to talk about being gay. It was scary for me and it's scary for these young people.

Teenagers who think they are gay should reach out to some group or to a gay person to get advice. One kid I knew told his parents, and they totally blew up at him. He tried to kill himself. Fortunately, a gay officer talked to him and said, "Look, it's not the end of the world. I'm gay." Because of that connection, things turned out all right. Unless you know that your parents are open and able to talk about it, I'd say to get support before telling them.

LOVE MAKES A FAMILY

JIM
(Health Aide, Nursing Student)

I live with a man who I know is right for me, and I also get to have a family. Someday, Ken and I may adopt more kids together.

Ken, Lisa, and I feel that our family life is an advantage for Ashley and Annie because they will grow up knowing and loving people who are gay.

While I'm in nursing school, I work part time at a nursing home as a health aide. Sometimes Ashley comes with me. She loves it up there, and the residents there love having her visit too.

LISA
(Massage Therapy Student)

My father has always been a narrow-minded bigot. He uses words like "faggot" freely without thinking about it. Before my dad knew that Ken is gay, I'd ask him general questions like, "If you were friends with someone for a long time, and you found out that your friend was gay, would you end the friendship?" My dad said that he would end the friendship. Dad considered Ken one of his best friends—Ken and my dad were small-town cops together, and Ken was like a son to him. When Ken came out, my father was suddenly confronted with the fact that his beloved son-in-law was gay. At fifty-six years of age, my dad had to rethink his assumptions and attitudes about gay people.

Ken is the best father in the whole world—he's always had great rapport with kids. Even after I found out that he was gay, there was never a question in my mind that Ken should have kids. I wanted kids and I can't imagine anybody I'd rather have had kids with. Jim is also the best coparent I could have imagined. The kids love him. If anything ever happened to me, they'd be well raised. They would have two great influences in their lives. I'm very grateful that Ken used such wisdom choosing Jim as his partner—almost as much wisdom as he used choosing me the first time!

Recently, Ken, Jim, the kids, and I all went on a vacation together. I felt very comfortable, but I was concerned that Ken might have bullied Jim into going on vacation with me. I asked Jim, but he said that he was real comfortable with it. It was really neat to share the kids all together. People say to me, "Well, it's not normal." But what is normal nowadays? Unless you live in the middle of the Bible Belt, my family is perfectly normal.

It offends me that there are people who are fighting to prevent their children from having access to information about sexual orientation. Who's to say that the people who are shouting the loudest aren't going to wind up with a gay child someday?

"I think it's important that people know that being a gay parent is no different than being a parent in a traditional family. We have the same feeling of love for our children, the same feeling of sadness when our children have problems, and the same feeling of pride when our children do well."

— KEN WATSON

I hope my children grow up to be open-minded and accepting of everybody. I don't want judgmental kids. I don't care whether somebody is gay or of a different color or a different religion or has a handicap; I just don't want my kids judging anyone for those reasons. I want them to only care about who people are inside.

ASHLEY
(Fifth-Grade Student)

It didn't really occur to me at first that my dad and Jim were gay, because I didn't know what that meant. One day we were in the car, and Dad told me all about it. Because I didn't know there was anything considered to be wrong with being gay, I told my friend. She told some other classmates, and they told everyone else.

Kids in my old school teased me because they didn't know the full definition of "gay." I don't really blame them, but I hope someday that kids will understand what "gay" really means.

Growing up in a gay family is the same as growing up in a straight family. I should know because I've lived in both kinds of families. My parents divorced when I was eight, and I understood what being gay was when I was nine and my dad came out. My dad's new partner, Jim, became just like a stepfather to me and Annie. She and I go back and forth between my mom's house and my dad and Jim's house.

People used to assume that Jim was married to my mother as we often spend time all together. Recently a new friend asked me how Jim was related to me. I said, "He's my stepfather." In a very natural way, my friend asked, "Is Jim together with your mom or your dad?" It felt great.

I told one of my best friends what "gay" means. She didn't know much about it and she used to think gay people were stupid. I told her that my dad is gay, and she was like, "Oh cool, then 'gay' isn't stupid." Now she likes gays. She has always been there for me. She's a great friend.

I don't usually bother to mention that my dad is gay now that I'm in a new school. I don't like being teased, and I don't like having to explain the definition of gay to everybody. Also, some parents just don't like to hear about it. Recently, I had a dream that we were in school, and the kids were asked what they thought of gays. Then we talked about what being gay is really about. At the end of my dream, the kids looked at being gay in a whole different way.

We have experienced what it's like to be seen as different by some people. Some folks see gay people as monstrous and horrible, but gay people are no different from straight people except that they love people of the same gender.

I think gay is just another kind of love. There's nothing wrong with it. It's not something to hate. You love who you love.

If you love someone, you should express your love however you want including being able to get married whether you are gay or straight. I hope that gay and lesbian people will soon have all the rights and respect that straight people have. I don't want people to judge me and my sister because of our family.

I love to go to the nursing home with Jim. I play games with the people who live there. I help them get out of bed. I run errands and bring them lunch. There's one sweet woman who is ninety-seven years old, and she can see, she can hear, and she can walk. One day when I was leaving her room, I overheard her say to her roommate, "What a sweet child."

My ninety-seven-year-old friend in the nursing home asked me, "What does your father do?" and I said, "He's a gay police officer." She said, "Oh, I read about him in the local newspaper." "That's my dad," I said. "I'm proud of him."

Left to right: *Chris, Durwood, Michelle, and Leonard*

THE
WINCHESTER / GAFFORD
FAMILY

LEONARD WINCHESTER & DURWOOD GAFFORD

CHRIS WINCHESTER (13)

MICHELLE WINCHESTER (10)

LEONARD
(Meat Inspector, Seattle-King County Health Department)

In high school, I dated both girls and boys, but a part of me just wouldn't accept that I was attracted to men. When I went to college, I met a woman, fell in love, got married, and had two children, Christopher and Michelle. I really loved my wife, and we were together for nine years. On the surface, it seemed like everything was perfect and that I had the family I had always wanted—a father, a mother, and two kids all living together. But inside, I wasn't truly happy because I still had feelings for men.

I found the "Gay Married Men's Group," a support organization of married men like me who either had a gay relationship or wanted to have one. Some were open with their wives and some were still in the closet. I personally couldn't understand how some men could lead dual lives and allow that to become the status quo.

I never wanted to get divorced because I came from a family where I had three different stepfathers and I never knew my biological dad. I went through some real hard times thinking about what I should do. Ultimately, I realized that I needed to end the marriage and live by myself. I came to realize that I would be happier giving up the idea of staying together as a family for the children's sake. The decision to leave my marriage was a big weight off my shoulders.

> *"In our family, we don't tolerate jokes or negative statements about people of other races or other backgrounds. We don't allow the kids to do any namecalling. We know how much it can hurt."*
>
> — LEONARD WINCHESTER

When I first got divorced and began to form a committed relationship with Durwood, I shared the custody of the kids with my ex-wife. Two years after our divorce, she died suddenly. After her death, my first thoughts were to end my relationship with Durwood, go back into the closet, and raise my kids as a single dad. But after talking a lot to Durwood, I felt assured that we were both committed to the well-being of my kids. We decided to live openly as a couple and became a family together with the children.

Initially, there was some concern from my ex-wife's extended family about whether or not I would be willing to raise the children. Many of her family members didn't know about my relationship with Durwood, but they found out about it pretty quickly. When they met Durwood and got to know him, they were all supportive of my decision to raise the children with him.

One of my ex-wife's sisters wondered if I had just used her sister to have kids and a "so-called family." I explained to her that I had really loved her sister and that she had been an important part of my life, but over time my love for her had changed and I could not continue to deny the fact that I was gay.

We are still very close to my ex-mother-in-law, my children's grandmother. We just spent Thanksgiving at her house. I think my relationship with Durwood has opened a lot of eyes in all of our extended families: mine, Durwood's, and my ex-wife's.

There isn't a lot of information out there that says two men can successfully raise children, so I was particularly concerned about raising a little girl without a female role model in the home. But I knew that Michelle still had her aunts, her grandmothers, and other female friends of ours in her life.

Durwood's niece got married two summers ago and she invited our kids to be in the wedding. Michelle was the flower girl and Chris was an usher. Everybody at the wedding must have known Durwood and I were gay, but no one said anything. I was introduced as "Durwood's friend." Surprisingly, however, the Baptist pastor told me, "It looks like you two are doing a great job raising these kids."

Durwood and I didn't formally come out to the kids when they came to live with us. They just knew we were together and that we were a family. A few years ago, I explained to Chris that I was gay and I explained what "gay" means. It wasn't a big deal to him. He just said, "It's okay."

If one of Chris's friends calls and Durwood answers the phone, Chris will tell his friend, "That was Dad's friend on the phone." I don't think anyone has given Chris a hard time about us being gay, but he's in middle school now so it makes sense that he's not so open about us. When people ask Michelle where her mom is, she tells them outright, "I don't have a mom anymore. She died. But I do have two dads." She seems very comfortable with our situation.

Either people will like me or they won't. If their opinion of me is based on the fact that I'm gay, I've gotten to the point where I no longer care what they think. My family was featured in an article on the front page of the local paper, so I came out to everyone simultaneously. I have a very close working relationship with a very conservative Catholic colleague. After reading the article, he said, "I don't believe it! It's not right." I said, "Well, it's true and it is right." He said, "Why would you do that?" And I said, "It feels more natural for me to be with Durwood than it felt to be with my ex-wife." His comments didn't bother me at all.

Our house has become the center of activity in the neighborhood. My kids are so comfortable with us and our family that all their friends want to come here. Our kids often have friends sleep over or go camping with us. Their friends and their parents are quite comfortable with our family, which makes me feel good. Sometimes I think my biggest problem is how to get rid of all these kids! But it's a nice problem to have.

In our family, we don't tolerate jokes or negative statements about people of other races or other backgrounds. We don't allow the kids to do any name-calling. We know how much it can hurt.

DURWOOD
(Senior Software Engineer, Lockheed Martin Aerospace)

One of the hardest things about coming out to myself as a gay person was facing up to the fact that I probably would never have a family of my own. One of the nicest things about meeting Leonard was that he had two kids.

When the children came to live with us, we moved from a very gay-friendly neighborhood in Seattle to a more conservative neighborhood in order to have access to better schools. Our philosophy was to be very open about our family and to become very involved in our new community. I joined the homeowner's association and Leonard joined the PTA. Together we found a local church. We believe in the philosophy that if people get to know you on a personal level, they are not going to mind if you're gay. This has been true for us. We've never had any problems with discrimination from anybody here. There may be people in our neighborhood who aren't comfortable with our family, but they've been quiet about it.

I wanted to legally adopt the kids after their mother died. Leonard and I talked to a lawyer, but he explained that an adoptive father has equal rights to the kids. If Leonard and I were ever to separate, I could have fought for custody in court. Having already gone through a divorce with custody issues, Leonard did not want to give up any of his future rights to his own children. Now that we've been together for six years, I think we're closer to the point where I probably will adopt them. From a legal standpoint, I think that the adoption is important because if something were to happen to Leonard, my rights to raise the children would then be absolutely clear.

The fact that I'm not a legal parent to Chris and Michelle is the only barrier preventing me from thinking of us as a complete family. In the heat of the moment when we have our difficult times, the thought will sometimes flash in my mind, "I really don't have a right to say anything because they are Leonard's kids." While I know that Leonard doesn't think that way, the thought still comes into my mind every now and then.

Leonard tries to take each kid somewhere special during the summer on their own, either fishing or camping. I think it's good for him to have time alone with them and it's also a special time for me because I get to stay home with our other child. You really get to bond with your children during the one-on-one times.

When Leonard's ex-wife died, my parents were very supportive about us raising the kids, and they have continued to grow more and more comfortable with us as a family. We got a Christmas card this year from them that said, "To my son and his family." In the past they would have sent a more generic card to our family along with a card just for me. However, they are still not comfortable coming out to their friends and extended family members about me.

In my senior year of college, I became aware of the existence of a support organization for gays and lesbians on campus. I would go down to the student union and hang out while they were meeting, but I never got up the courage to go to one of the meetings because I was afraid. I didn't want anybody to jump to any conclusions—and I wasn't even ready to jump to the conclusion—that I was gay. In reality I think I've known I was gay since I was in second grade, but facing up to it was very difficult. After moving to Seattle, I finally came out in my late twenties.

I was teased a lot when I was a kid, but not because anyone assumed I was gay. Children can be quite cruel toward each other. When you look at the overall problems kids face, the gay issue isn't going to be that much larger than the other issues our kids will probably have to deal with.

The problems we have as a family are more typical of the problems any heterosexual family faces. I think our children have some definite advantages growing up in a gay family. Our kids are being raised to love people for who they are and not for who they love.

The mother of one of Michelle's friends once asked me, "How do you and Leonard handle open displays of affection in front of other kids?" I said, "Well, we probably handle it the way I hope you would handle it. We don't think it's appropriate for parents to make out in front of kids, no matter who they are. In fact, as a gay couple, we may be more sensitive to this issue than you might be as a heterosexual couple, and we probably wouldn't even hold hands in front of kids we don't know well. In general, any rule that applies in your household is the same here. We're no different."

This women then said, "I only asked because I don't want to have to explain to my son what it means to be gay when he is only six years old." I said to her, "Just because a kid asks a simple question, you don't have to explain the facts of life to them. You can answer their question in a simple way." I told her about the time I was in the hospital for surgery and Leonard's sister came to visit with her son. As they were all leaving, Leonard reached over and kissed me good-bye. His sister later told Leonard, "I really wish you wouldn't kiss Durwood in front of my son, because he asked me questions and I don't want to have to explain your relationship to him." I told her that she could choose to use such questions as an opening to define what being gay means, but she didn't have to. Instead, she could simply tell her son that I was sick and that Leonard felt sad and wanted to give me a kiss good-bye.

Once, I overheard Chris talking to a friend who had come over to our house. He asked who I was and Chris said, "Oh, that's my other dad." And I heard the kid say, "You've got two dads? Cool!"

CHRIS
(Middle-School Student)

I like to go camping and fishing with my dad. Awhile ago we went fishing up in Canada on a chartered boat and we caught salmon and halibut. Then we went to Alaska with my Grandma and my dad where I caught my big halibut. It was 105 pounds! We still have tons left in the freezer.

As a family we all go to see the Thunderbirds, our local hockey team.

Gay is when two people of the same sex like each other. It's just like a regular family except that you have two dads.

MICHELLE
(Fourth-Grade Student)

I went to the Indian Princess program at the YMCA with my dad. And I play soccer with my dad. I like to play goalie. We all go camping together with Dad and Durwood. I like to go fishing, but I hate eating fish. I love cats and I want to be a cat veterinarian when I grow up.

When friends ask about my family, I just say I have two dads. That's it.

Left to right: *Sarah, Lynn, Amy, and Allie*

THE
ZASHIN / JACOBSON
FAMILY

LYNN ZASHIN & AMY JACOBSON

SARAH ZASHIN-JACOBSON (12)

ALLIE ZASHIN-JACOBSON (4)

LYNN
(Family Physician)

Amy and I have been together since 1975. We chose to have Amy get pregnant for our first child, Sarah, and we chose to adopt our second child, Allie. Amy is "Mommy," and I'm "Mom."

Our families are very important to Amy and me. Acceptance by our families has been a slow but steady process that has taken work on all sides. We've had some huge, wonderful Thanksgiving gatherings at our house with both sides of the family together. Both of our children are being raised as Jews, as our religion and our cultural background are both very important to us. Another significant part of our culture is our Latin American roots, which Allie brought from her birth country, Guatemala.

I've had many occasions in my life to deal with homophobic situations and people. Now that we have become a multicultural, multiracial family, I have been on the receiving end of racist comments as well. Dealing with racism from this perspective is much newer to me. For example, for years we hired a particular woman to do our sewing. She was pinning up a dress for me, and she pointed to six-month-old Allie. She asked me, "Is her father black?" I didn't know what to say, but finally I just said, "No." The woman replied, "If he was, I couldn't have her here." I couldn't believe it. That night I told Amy what had happened, and we talked for a long time. When I went to pick up my dress, I said to the seamstress, "Do you remember when

"My parents are always there for me, and as far as I'm concerned, it doesn't matter what your family is like as long as they love you and you love them. And it doesn't matter what other people think because I know that my family is special no matter what."

— SARAH
ZASHIN-JACOBSON

you asked about Allie's father?" She answered, "Yes. I just never grew up with those kinds of people, and I'm afraid of them." I said, "There's no difference in a person because of their skin color. I'm not going to be able to come to you anymore because I can't be comfortable with a person who feels that way." I was scared out of my mind. I'm not a confrontational kind of person. That was one of our first experiences with the reality of responding to racial discrimination.

The best part of our family is that the kids have choices and permission to explore all the possibilities in life. They'll know that we will stand by them for any of their choices. That's the benefit of having a "different" family. And we are a really happy, "different" family.

AMY
(Physician's Assistant)

I have two clear remembrances of my early childhood: I wanted to be a doctor and I wanted to be a mother. I always thought of mothering in terms of adoption. I knew that there were lots of kids already in the world who needed good parents and that I would be one of those parents.

As I grew tumultuously into adolescence I had more questions than anyone could answer. As I tried to sort out the world during the sixties, my desire to be a doctor did not fade, but was overshadowed by life events. I still wanted to be a parent but the world seemed less safe than ever. My questions turned into an emerging political awareness, although I didn't begin to act until my cousin was with one of the women killed at Kent State on the day of the shooting. It could easily have been my cousin who died there. What did this all mean?

When I dropped out of college and moved to Boston, the openness of the seventies allowed me to love "whomever" and I became actively bisexual. After a year or two, I came out as a lesbian and moved into a commune in the country. I was introduced to feminism, not from books, but from other women. Eventually I returned to school, and in 1975 I met my current partner, Lynn.

Lynn was in medical school in New York City, so I moved there and was accepted into a physician's assistant program. After we both finished school, I talked with Lynn about having children, but starting a private medical practice made negotiations about when to start our family a long process. In 1985, I began to look into adoption. Unfortunately, many agencies were not open to me because I was single, which was the only way a lesbian couple could possibly adopt at that time. You had to pretend you didn't have a partner at all. After many long discussions and tears, Lynn and I decided that I should get pregnant.

Lynn and I imagined our patients and the members of our local medical community saying things like, "How did she get pregnant? I didn't know Amy was with anyone." And we wondered what Lynn would say to people when she was out shopping with a baby.

"The best part of our family is that the kids have choices and permission to explore all the possibilities in life. They'll know that we will stand by them for any of their choices. That's the benefit of having a 'different' family. And we are a really happy, 'different' family."

— *LYNN ZASHIN*

Despite our fears, we decided to go ahead. The following January our daughter, Sarah, was born. We decided to use the hospital forty-five minutes away from our home for the birth in order to insure our privacy, as Lynn was working at our local hospital.

We were outed by having a baby, and at times it felt very scary, but we hung together as a couple and as individual parents. When I decided to return to work, the process of finding family day care was not easy. There were very few lesbian couples with children in our community back then, and many day-care providers' mouths dropped open when I told them that my partner was a woman.

When Sarah was two, she went to group day care. I felt that the staff didn't have a clue as to how to deal with our family and the questions that the other kids might ask about us. So before Sarah started at the center, I explained to the staff exactly what Lynn and I were saying to Sarah about our family. I wanted the staff to be consistent when they answered questions and to respond in an age-appropriate manner. Sarah had not even started going to school there, and already I felt so exposed and vulnerable.

When Sarah went to public elementary school, I had a meeting with her principal to discuss our needs as a lesbian family. I wanted him to know from the start that we would hold him accountable should teasing or name-calling come up. He was actually quite receptive and that groundwork has paid off over the years. Every year, I feel like a protective mother bear paving a safe path for my daughters.

It doesn't matter whether kids are calling someone "fatty," or "four eyes," or "fag." All kinds of name-calling must be dealt with. We need to talk to kids about tolerance for any difference—whether someone is in a wheelchair, or a family has two moms, or someone has red hair, or whatever.

When we tried to join the local temple as a family, there was a problem. There was no membership category for same-gender couples and their children as a "family." The membership chairman told me that the board of directors had to vote on this issue. After making numerous phone calls to garner the support I knew existed within the membership, I finally called the president and said, crying, "You mean to tell me that I'm a Jew and my partner is a Jew and we cannot be a family in this synagogue. It's not like we're in a mixed marriage. We just want our kids to go to Hebrew school and get bat-mitzvahed." Of all the struggles I had gone through as a lesbian and as a parent, this was the most painful. I'm happy to say that with the rabbi's firm support, the vote passed and we did receive a family membership at the temple. We feel very comfortable there now.

When we decided to add another child to our family, the recent changes in adoption laws made it possible for Lynn and me to adopt. Together, we discussed having a multiracial family and decided to go ahead. Sarah was thrilled about having a sibling. In 1993, we all went to Guatemala with Lynn's mother to bring Allie home.

> *"It doesn't matter whether kids are calling someone 'fatty,' or 'four eyes,' or 'fag.' All kinds of name-calling must be dealt with. We need to talk to kids about tolerance for any difference—whether someone is in a wheelchair, or a family has two moms, or someone has red hair, or whatever."*
>
> — AMY JACOBSON

I've felt the racism of our community much more than the homophobia when I'm with my family in public places like the supermarket. I get really angry and frustrated at times. I think the deepest feeling is pain. I have channeled that pain into working within the public school system around issues of bias. I don't know what else to do other than to work to educate both kids and adults.

I find the issue of racism even more painful than homophobia. I think homosexuality challenges people at a moral, religious core. When people react negatively to gay people, I am able to develop some compassion for them and I use education to deal with their attitudes. But when people judge people just by the color of their skin, I don't have any compassion.

SARAH
(Sixth-Grade Student)

When I get asked about my family, I sometimes say, "You don't need to know," and sometimes I tell them. Sometimes I like to talk about my family and sometimes I don't. Most of the time I only tell my good friends because I know I can count on them not to tell anyone else. Sometimes it's not easy to tell people, but usually they won't stop asking until you tell.

Having two moms didn't really matter up until about third grade. Then it mattered. The kids started to grow up and growing up means they start making fun of other people. Sixth grade has been really hard. Kids are almost always making fun of other people.

Growing up with two moms is not always easy. There are times when people will make fun of gays and lesbians. Although it isn't being directed at me, it still feels like it is. Like when some kid says to another kid, "Eww, you're gay." Or, "Eww, you're a lesbian." Kids can be really mean.

Recently, my parents were going to talk to my class at school. After talking with both my moms, we decided that only one of them should come so that I could have control over who knows about my parents.

I like to do lots of things with my moms. My favorite things are to do family projects, bake, go to plays, go to my piano recitals, bike, swim, go out to dinner, and go camping. I especially like going on trips with my family, like when we went to Disney World. The time with my family was really special. There was no one there who knew my family, so I didn't have to worry.

Having two moms means a lot to me. It's hard, but it's my family, and I like it the way it is. It's hard having two moms because I'm afraid that people will tease me. But there are a lot of good things about having two moms. I like having two moms because I like having a family of all girls. It's really nice. And they are easier to talk to about private stuff.

My parents are always there for me, and as far as I'm concerned, it doesn't matter what your family is like as long as they love you and you love them. And it doesn't matter what other people think because I know that my family is special no matter what.

April Martin

Left to right: *Emily, Jess, Susan, and April*

Gay, lesbian, bisexual, and transgender people have always been parents. Broad estimates place the number of such parents in the United States at somewhere between 3 and 8 million. Historically, they have often been pushed out of their families and barred from contact with their children. Many who continued to raise their children have lived in hiding and secrecy—denying or marginalizing their same-sex partnerships, allowing the world to presume they were heterosexual. Getting away with it was sometimes the best one could hope for.

What dramatic change the last few decades have seen! Gay, lesbian, bisexual, and transgender parents have become aware: Of ourselves. Of each other. Of our collective voice. Of our rich potential for parenting openly and proudly. Of the true definition of family. Of the majesty of love as it is revealed in the families we create.

We have become visible, known. We have increased in numbers through adoption, donor insemination, and surrogacy. And we have discovered that we have something to teach the world.

We are living proof that family roles and responsibilities need not be based on gender, but can instead be creatively molded to suit the individual and collective needs of the family members themselves. We are proof that children thrive in an atmosphere of honesty and respect for difference, in which the adults are true to themselves, in which self-expression is respected and encouraged, and in which an understanding of humanity transcends the prejudices of the day.

As it turns out, the basic presumptions our institutions have made about what sorts of families are good for children have simply been wrong. They assumed that two was an optimal number of parents, that there should be one male and one female, that they should be biological creators of the children, and that they should be heterosexual. The legal system, the educational system, the mental health profession, and certainly the insurance industry, to name a few such institutions, have reflected these assumptions.

In comparison, other kinds of families have been portrayed as less than optimal constructions. Families formed by adoption have been seen as families that couldn't have their own children. Parents raising children they did not create biologically have been described as not the child's real parents. The same-gender life partner of a biological parent has been described as not a parent at all, but merely a parent's "friend." And gays and lesbians have been slandered as the vilest and darkest danger to children. The prevailing belief has been that mom-and-dad families were the only good places for children to grow up.

The families of gay, lesbian, bisexual, and transgender parents are witness to a different reality. Our children, it turns out, have no trouble understanding that biology and parental care giving are not necessarily related. They have no problem understanding that there are people who make children, and the parents who raise children—and there may or may not be some overlap. They experience nonbiological parents as indistinguishable from biological parents in their willingness to play catch, help with homework, teach right from wrong, make them a sandwich, or sing them to sleep.

We are also living testimony to the fact that there is nothing sacred about the number two for parenting. In fact, as long as the parents work together as a respectful and cooperative team, three, four, or even more parents, or for that matter, one parent with a backup team of honorary aunts and uncles and grandparents, enhance the richness of a child's experience.

Nor does it matter whether parents are male, female, or people whose gender identities are more complex. Neither is the parents' sexual orientation a relevant variable in whether a child is healthy and secure.

Several dozen research studies have been done to date, and more are in the works. Without exception, every scientifically valid study has found that when examining children's emotional, social, intellectual, gender role, and sexual orientation development, it is impossible to tell which children came from mom-and-dad biological families and which came from a whole range of other constellations. All the notions about needing strong males and nurturing females, or needing heterosexually married parents appear to stem from the fact that these were the only families considered.

Evidence from gay, lesbian, bisexual, and transgender-parented families suggests that we need to shift completely the emphasis in our ideas about child rearing. We must discard notions that attribute undue importance to family constellation, and instead recognize that love, resources, and commitment are the relevant variables. A parenting family is that grouping of people, bound together by affection and dedication, with a commitment to love, take care of, educate, and be responsible for a child. Ask our children.

As our world grows increasingly complex, we are all concerned for the next generation and are seeking ways to reduce the violence of our society and to articulate morality and ethics. Some traditionalists warn that we must preserve a certain image of family (regardless of whether the image is accurate) in order to restore a peace and order that society is nostalgically presumed to have had. The families of gay, lesbian, bisexual, and transgender parents, by contrast, warn against being fooled by superficial images and cookie-cutter criteria. When evaluating a family, one should look instead at the maturity of the parents, their humanity, their constancy, their willingness to learn from their mistakes, their ability to let their actions be guided by both their hearts and their better judgment, their playfulness, and their capacity to find goodness across a range of diversity.

The photographs and interviews in this book are portraits of families that transcend traditionalist thinking. These are not sentimental "Hallmark" images of people looking their best for the camera. What you find here are living, working, struggling families, just as they are. Different from one another in many ways—economic, racial, ethnic, regional, family structure and life experience—they offer a collective cry of joy for the principles of family spirit that unite them.

NATIONAL ORGANIZATIONS

American Civil Liberties Union (ACLU) National Gay and Lesbian Rights Project, 132 West 43rd Street, New York, NY 10036. Phone: (212) 944-9800, ext. 545.

American Federation of Teachers—The National Gay and Lesbian Caucus. AFT/NGLC tries to influence local affiliates to become more aware of lesbian and gay issues in schools. P.O. Box 19856, Cincinnati, OH 45219.

American Psychological Association, Committee on Lesbian and Gay Concerns, 750 First Street, N.E., Washington, DC 20002-4241. Phone: (202) 336-6052.

The Bridges Project of the American Friends Service Committee facilitates communication among gay youth service providers through its newsletter and other activities. The Bridges Project, c/o AFSC, 1501 Cherry Street, Philadelphia, PA 19102. Phone: (215) 241-7133.

Friends of Project 10, Inc. The original gay/straight student alliance founded by educator Virginia Uribe. Project 10, 7850 Melrose Avenue, Los Angeles, CA 90046. Phone: (818) 577-4553.

Gay and Lesbian Alliance against Defamation (GLAAD). GLAAD's mission is to promote fair, accurate, and inclusive media representation of lesbians, gay men, bisexuals, and transgender people in the media. GLAAD, 1360 Mission Street, Suite 200, San Francisco, CA 94103. Phone: (415) 861-2244.

The Gay and Lesbian Parents Coalition International (GLPCI) offers support for gay parents and also for children of gay parents through its subgroup, Children of Gays and Lesbians Every-where (COLAGE). GLPCI has an annual national conference, a regular newsletter, and sponsors "Family Week" in Provincetown, Massachusetts, during August. GLPCI, P.O. Box 50360, Washington, DC 20091. Phone: (202) 583-8029.

The Gay, Lesbian, and Straight Educators' Network (GLSEN). GLSEN is a national organization directed by Kevin Jennings that brings together gay and straight teachers in order to combat homophobia in their schools and support gay teachers. GLSEN, 121 W. 27th Street, Suite 804, New York, NY 10001. Phone: (212) 727-0135.

The Hetrick-Martin Institute is a New York-based social service agency and has long been the leader in providing services for gay youth. It also publishes *You Are Not Alone: The National Lesbian, Gay, and Bisexual Youth Directory,* a state-by-state listing of organizations serving gay youth. The Hetrick-Martin Institute, 2 Astor Place, New York, NY 10003. Phone: (212) 674-7133.

The Human Rights Campaign (HRC). The Human Rights Campaign, the largest national lesbian and gay political organization, envisions an America where lesbian and gay people are ensured of their basic equal rights and safety. HRC has more than 250,000 members, both gay and non-gay. HRC maintains the largest full-time lobbying team in the nation devoted to issues of fairness for lesbian and gay Americans. HRC's National Coming Out Project promotes the values of honesty and openness about being lesbian, gay or bisexual on campus, in the workplace and at home. HRC, 1101 14th ST. N.W., Washington, DC. 20005. Phone (202) 628-4160.

The National Black Lesbian and Gay Leadership Forum (NBLGLF) is the only national organization that advocates for the nation's 2.5 million black lesbians, gays, bisexuals, and transgender people. Founded in 1988, the organization has thousands of members nationwide and around the world. NBLGLF, 1436 U Street, N.W., Suite 200, Washington, DC 20009. Phone (202) 483-6786.

National Gay and Lesbian Task Force (NGLTF) is a very active and helpful political organization which also sponsors an excellent national conference yearly. NGLTF, 2320 17th Street N.W., Washington, DC 20009-2702. Phone: (202) 332-6483.

Parents and Friends of Lesbians and Gays (PFLAG) offers support to family members and friends of gay people throughout the nation. It sponsors regional conferences and an annual national conference. PFLAG's national office has a listing of local chapters. PFLAG, P.O. Box 27605, Washington, DC 20038. Phone: (202) 638-4200.

BOOK LIST
Children's Books (Grades K-6)

Abramchik, L. *Is Your Family Like Mine?* New York: Open Heart, Open Mind Publishing, 1993.

Alden, Joan. *A Boy's Best Friend.* Boston: Alyson Publications, 1993.

DePaola, Tomie. *Oliver Button Is a Sissy.* San Diego: Harcourt Brace Jovanovich, 1979.

Elwin, Rosamund, and Michele Paulse. *Asha's Mums.* Toronto: Women's Press, 1990.

Greenberg, Keith E. *Zack's Story: Growing Up with Same-Sex Parents.* Minneapolis: Lerner Publications, 1996.

Heron, Ann, and Meredith Maran. *How Would You Feel if Your Dad Was Gay?* Boston: Alyson Publications, 1991.

Jenness, Aylette. *Families: A Celebration of Diversity, Commitment and Love.* New York: Houghton Mifflin, 1990.

Jordan, Marykate. *Losing Uncle Tim.* Morton Grove, IL: Albert Whitman & Co., 1993.

Kennedy, Joseph. *Lucy Goes to the Country.* Los Angeles: Alywn Books, 1998.

Leaf, Munro. *The Story of Ferdinand.* New York: Puffin Books, 1936.

Newman, Leslea. *Gloria Goes to Gay Pride.* Boston: Alyson Publications, 1991.

———. *Heather Has Two Mommies.* Boston: Alyson Publications, 1991.

Shannon, Margaret. *Elvira.* New York: Ticknor & Fields, 1993.

Valentine, Johnny. *The Day They Put a Tax on Rainbows.* Boston: Alyson Publications, 1992.

———. *The Duke Who Outlawed Jelly Beans and Other Stories.* Boston: Alyson Publications, 1991.

———. *One Dad, Two Dads, Brown Dads, Blue Dads.* Boston: Alyson Publications, 1995.

———. *Two Moms, the Zark, and Me.* Boston: Alyson Publications, 1993.

Wickens, Elaine. *Anna Day and the O-Ring.* Boston: Alyson Publications, 1994.

Wiener, Lori S. *Be a Friend: Children Who Live with HIV Speak.* Morton Grove, IL: Albert Whitman & Co., 1994.

Willhoite, Michael. *Daddy's Roommate.* Boston: Alyson Publications, 1990.

———. *Families: A Coloring Book.* Boston: Alyson Publications, 1991.

———. *Uncle What-Is-It Is Coming to Visit!* Boston: Alyson Publications, 1993.

Books for Young Adults

Alyson, Sasha, ed. *Young, Gay and Proud!* Boston: Alyson Publications, 1981.

Bass, Ellen, and Kate Kaufman. *Free Your Mind: The Book for Gay, Lesbian, and Bisexual Youth and Their Allies.* New York: HarperPerennial, 1996.

Bauer, Marion Dane, ed. *Am I Blue? Coming Out from the Silence.* New York: HarperCollins, 1994.

Bell, Ruth. *Changing Bodies, Changing Lives: A Book for Teens on Sex and Relationships.* New York: Vintage Books, 1988.

Borhek, Mary V. *Coming Out to Parents: A Two-Way Survival Guide for Lesbians and Gay Men and Their Parents.* Cleveland, OH: Pilgrim Press, 1983.

Chandler, Kurt. *Passages of Pride: True Stories of Lesbian and Gay Teenagers.* Boston: Alyson Publications, 1997.

Chandler, Kurt, and Mitchell Ivers, eds. *Passages of Pride: Lesbian and Gay Youth Come of Age.* New York: Random House, 1995.

Curtis, Wayne. *Revelations: A Collection of Gay Male Coming Out Stories.* Boston: Alyson Publications, 1988.

Eichberg, Rob. *Coming Out: An Act of Love.* New York: Dutton, 1990.

Fricke, Aaron. *Reflections of a Rock Lobster: A Story about Growing Up Gay.* Boston: Alyson Publications, 1981.

Garden, Nancy. *Annie on My Mind.* New York: Farrar, Strauss & Giroux, 1982.

Grima, Tony, ed. *Not the Only One: Lesbian and Gay Fiction for Teens.* Boston: Alyson Publications, 1995.

Hanckel, Frances. *A Way of Love, A Way of Life: Young Person's Introduction to What It Means to Be Gay.* New York: Lothrop Lee & Shepard, 1979.

Heger, Heinz. *The Men with the Pink Triangle.* Boston: Alyson Publications, 1980.

Heron, Ann, ed. *One Teenager in Ten: Testimony by Gay and Lesbian Youth.* Boston: Alyson Publications, 1995.

———. *Two Teenagers in Twenty: Writings by Gay and Lesbian Youth.* Boston: Alyson Publications, 1994.

Holbrook, Sabra. *Fighting Back: The Struggle for Gay Rights.* New York: Lodestar, 1987.

Holmes, Sarah. *Testimonies: A Collection of Coming Out Stories.* Boston: Alyson Publications, 1989.

Hutchins, Loraine, and Lani Kaahumanu, eds. *Bi Any Other Name: Bisexual People Speak Out.* Boston: Alyson Publications, 1991.

Marcus, Eric. *Is It a Choice? Answers to 300 of the Most Frequently Asked Questions about Gays and Lesbians.* San Francisco: HarperSanFrancisco, 1993.

Mastoon, Adam. *The Shared Heart: Portraits and Stories Celebrating Lesbian, Gay, and Bisexual Young People.* New York: Lothrop Lee & Shepard, 1997.

Miller, Deborah A. *Coping When a Parent Is Gay.* New York: Rosen Publishing Group, 1993.

Plant, Richard. *The Pink Triangle: The Nazi War against Homosexuals.* New York: Henry Holt, 1986.

Robson, Ruthann, and Martin B. Duberman. *Gay Men, Lesbians, and the Law (Issues in Lesbian and Gay Life).* Broomall, PA: Chelsea House Publishers, 1996.

Sherrill, Jan-Mitchell, and Craig A. Hardesty. *The Gay, Lesbian, and Bisexual Students' Guide to Colleges, Universities, and Graduate Schools.* New York: New York University Press, 1994.

Singer, Bennett L., ed. *Growing Up Gay: A Literary Anthology.* New York: New Press, 1994

Springer, Nancy. *Looking for Jamie Bridger.* New York: Dial Books for Young Readers, 1995.

Velasquez, Gloria. *Tommy Stands Alone.* Houston, TX: Arte Publico Press, 1995.

BOOKS ABOUT LESBIAN, GAY, BISEXUAL, AND TRANSGENDER PARENTS

Ali, Turan, Tom Robinson, and Catherine Hopper. *We Are Family: Testimonies of Lesbian and Gay Parents.* Herndon, VA: Cassell Academic, 1996.

Barret, Robert L., and Bryan E. Robinson. *Gay Fathers.* Lexington, MA: Lexington Books, 1990.

Bozett, Frederick W., ed. *Gay and Lesbian Parents.* New York: Praeger Publications, 1987.

Clunis, D. Merilee, and Dorsey G. Green. *The Lesbian Parenting*

Book: A Guide to Creating Families and Raising Children. Seattle, WA: Seal Press, 1995.

Mackey, Richard A., Bernard A. O'Brien, Eileen F. Mackey. *Gay and Lesbian Couples: Voices from Lasting Relationships.* Westport, CT: Greenwood Publishing Group, 1997.

MacPike, Loralee. *There's Something I've Been Meaning to Tell You.* Tallahassee: Naiad Press, 1989.

Martin, April. *The Lesbian and Gay Parenting Handbook: Creating and Raising Our Families.* New York: HarperCollins, 1993.

Morgan, Kenneth B. *Getting Simon: Two Gay Doctors' Journey to Fatherhood.* New York: Bramble Books, 1995.

Pies, Cheri. *Considering Parenthood: A Handbook for Lesbians.* San Francisco: Spinsters Books, 1985.

Pollack, Jill S. *Lesbian and Gay Families: Redefining Parenting in America.* New York: Franklin Watts, 1995.

Pollack, Sandra, and Jeanne Vaughn. *Politics of the Heart: A Lesbian Parenting Anthology.* Ithaca, NY: Firebrand Books, 1987.

Rafkin, Louise, ed. *Different Mothers: Sons and Daughters of Lesbians Talk about Their Lives.* Pittsburgh: Cleis Press, 1990.

Rizzo, Cindy, and Jo Schneiderman, eds. *All the Ways Home: Parenting and Children in the Lesbian and Gay Community, a Collection of Short Fiction.* Norwich, VT: New Victoria Press, 1995.

Saffron, Lisa. *What about the Children? Sons and Daughters of Lesbian and Gay Parents Talk about Their Lives.* Herndon, VA: Cassell Academic, 1997.

Tasker, Fiona L., and Susan Golombok. *Growing Up in a Lesbian Family: Effects on Child Development.* New York: Guilford Press, 1997.

Weston, Kath. *Families We Choose: Lesbians, Gays, and Kinship (Between Men—Between Women).* New York: Columbia University Press, 1997.

GENERAL READING LIST

Aarons, Leroy. *Prayers for Bobby: A Mother's Coming to Terms with the Suicide of Her Gay Son.* San Francisco: HarperSanFrancisco, 1995.

Allison, Dorothy. *Skin: Talking about Sex, Class, and Literature.* Ithaca, NY: Firebrand Books, 1994.

———. *Two or Three Things I Know for Sure.* New York: Plume, 1996.

Back, Gloria Guss. *Are You Still My Mother? Are You Still My Family?* New York: Warner Books, 1985.

Beck, Evelyn Torton, ed. *Nice Jewish Girls: A Lesbian Anthology.* Trumansburg, NY: The Crossing Press, 1982.

Bell, A., and M. Weinberg. *Sexual Preference: Its Development in Men and Women.* New York: Simon & Schuster, 1981.

Benkov, Laura. *Reinventing the Family: The Emerging Story of Lesbian and Gay Parents.* New York: Crown Publishing, 1994.

Berzon, Betty. *Positively Gay.* New York: Celestial Arts, 1992.

———. *Setting Them Straight: You Can Do Something about Bigotry and Homophobia in Your Life.* New York: Plume, 1996.

Błasius, Mark, and Shane Phelan, eds. *We Are Everywhere: A Historical Sourcebook in Gay and Lesbian Politics.* New York: Routledge Press, 1997.

Blumenfeld, Warren J. *Homophobia: How We All Pay the Price.* Boston: Beacon Press, 1993.

Blumenfeld, Warren J., and Diane Raymond. *Looking at Lesbian and Gay Life.* Boston: Beacon Press, 1993.

Bornstein, Kate. *Gender Outlaw: On Men, Women, and the Rest of Us.* New York: Vintage Books, 1995.

———. *My Gender Workbook: How to Become a Real Man, a Real Woman, the Real You or Something Else Entirely.* New York: Routledge Press, 1998.

Boston Women's Health Collective. *The New Our Bodies, Ourselves: A Book by and for Women.* New York: Simon & Schuster, 1984.

Boswell, John. *Christianity, Social Tolerance, and Homosexuality: Gay People in Western Europe from the Beginning of the Christian Era to the Fourteenth Century.* Chicago: University of Chicago Press. 1980.

Brelin, Christa, Michael J. Tyrkus, and Michael Bronski. *Outstanding Lives: Profiles of Lesbians and Gay Men.* Detroit: Visible Ink Press, 1997.

Brown, Rita Mae. *Rubyfruit Jungle.* New York: Bantam, 1987.

Burke, Phyllis. *Family Values: Two Moms and Their Son.* New York: Random House, 1993.

———. *Gender Shock: Exploding the Myths of Male and Female.* New York: Anchor, 1996.

Clark, Donald. *Loving Someone Gay.* New York: Celestial Arts, 1997.

Clausen, Jan, and Martin B. Duberman. *Beyond Gay or Straight: Understanding Sexual Orientation.* Broomall, PA: Chelsea House Publications, 1996.

Coe, Roy M. *A Sense of Pride: The Story of Gay Games II.* San Francisco: Pride Publications, 1986.

Cohn, Meryl. *Do What I Say: Ms. Behavior's Guide to Gay and Lesbian Etiquette.* New York: Houghton Mifflin, 1995.

Corley, Rip. *The Final Closet: The Gay Parents' Guide for Coming Out to Their Children,* Miami: Editech Press, 1990.

Dew, Robb F. *The Family Heart: A Memoir of When Our Son Came Out.* New York: Ballantine, 1994.

Duberman, Martin. *About Time: Exploring the Gay Past.* Burtonsville, MD: Meridian Books, 1991.

———. *Queer Representations: Reading Lives, Reading Cultures.* New York: New York University Press, 1997.

———. *A Queer World: The Center for Lesbian and Gay Studies Reader.* New York: New York University Press, 1997.

———, ed. *Hidden from History: Reclaiming the Gay and Lesbian Past.* New York: Penguin 1990.

Fairchild, Betty, and Nancy Hayward. *Now That You Know: What Every Parent Should Know about Their Gay and Lesbian Children.* New York: Harcourt Brace Jovanovich, 1998.

Feinberg, Leslie. *Stone Butch Blues.* Ithaca, NY: Firebrand Books, 1993.

———. *Transgender Warriors: Making History from Joan of Arc to RuPaul.* Boston: Beacon Press, 1997.

Galindo, Rudy, and Eric Marcus. *Icebreaker: The Autobiography of Rudy Galindo.* New York: Pocket Books, 1997.

Geller, Thomas, ed. *Bisexuality: A Reader and Source Book.* Ojai, CA: Times Change Press, 1990.

Gettings, John. *Couples: A Photographic Documentary of Gay and Lesbian Relationships.* Hanover, NH: University Press of New England, 1996.

Goss, Robert, and Amy A. S. Strongheart, eds. *Our Families, Our Values: Snapshots of Queer Kinship.* Binghamton, NY: Harrington Park Press, 1997.

Griffin, Pat. *Strong Women, Deep Closets: Lesbians and Homophobia in Sports.* Champaign, IL: Human Kinetics Publications, 1998.

Harbeck, Karen, ed. *Coming Out of the Classroom Closet: Gay and Lesbian Students, Teachers, and Curricula.* Binghamton, NY: Harrington Park Press, 1992.

Jennings, Kevin, ed. *Becoming Visible: A Reader in Gay and Lesbian History for High School and College Students.* Boston: Alyson Publications, 1994.

———. *One Teacher in 10: Gay and Lesbian Educators Tell Their Stories.* Boston: Alyson Publications, 1994.

Jones, Bill T., and Peggy Gillespie. *Last Night on Earth.* New York: Pantheon, 1997.

Kaeser, Gigi, photographer, and Peggy Gillespie, ed. *Of Many Colors: Portraits of Multiracial Families.* Amherst: University of Massachusetts Press, 1997.

Kahn, Arthur D. *The Many Faces of Gay Activists Who Are Changing the Nation.* New York: Praeger Publications, 1997.

Kissen, Rita M. *The Last Closet: The Real Lives of Lesbian and Gay Teachers.* Portsmouth, NH: Heinemann Press, 1996.

Laird, Joan, and Robert Jay Green, eds. *Lesbians and Gays in Couples and Families: A Handbook for Therapists.* San Francisco: Jossey-Bass, 1996.

Lipkin, Arthur. *Understanding Homosexuality/Changing Schools: A Text for Teachers, Counselors, and Administrators.* Boulder: Westview Press, 1998.

Louganis, Greg and Eric Marcus. *Breaking the Surface*. New York: Plume, 1996.

Miller, Isabel. *Patience and Sarah*. New York: Fawcett Books, 1990.

Monette, Paul. *Becoming a Man: Half a Life Story*. New York: Harcourt Brace Jovanovich, 1992.

Pratt, Minnie Bruce. *Crime against Nature: The Lamont Poetry Selection for 1989*. Ithaca, NY: Firebrand, 1990.

———. *Rebellion: Essays 1980-91*. Ithaca, NY: Firebrand, 1991.

———. *S/He*. Ithaca, NY: Firebrand, 1995.

Slater, Suzanne. *Lesbian Family Life Cycle*. New York: The Free Press, 1995.

Sutton, Roger. *Hearing Us Out: Voices from the Gay and Lesbian Community*, New York: Little, Brown and Co., 1994.

Swallow, Jean, and Geoff Manasse. *Making Love Visible: In Celebration of Gay and Lesbian Families*. Freedom, CA: The Crossing Press, 1995.

Woog, Dan. *Jocks: True Stories of America's Gay Male Athletes*. Boston: Alyson Publications, 1998.

———. *School's Out: The Impact of Gay and Lesbian Issues on America's Schools*. Boston: Alyson Publications, 1995.

VIDEOS

"Before Stonewall: The Making of a Gay and Lesbian Community" is an Emmy Award winning documentary of gay life in the United States before 1969. Available in video stores, or from the Cinema Guild, 1697 Broadway, Suite 506, New York, NY 10019. Phone: (212) 246-5522.

"Both My Moms' Names Are Judy" is a ten-minute video about elementary school students who are the children of lesbian and gay parents. This wonderful video is suitable for viewing by children of all ages and is also a good teacher-training tool. LGPA, 6705 California Street #1, San Francisco, CA 94121. Phone: (415) 522-8773.

"Common Threads: Stories from the Quilt" won the 1990 Academy Award for best documentary. This film tells the human and political history of the AIDS epidemic through stories behind the panels of the Names Project Quilt. Available in some video stores or by calling (415) 863-1966.

"Gay Youth" is considered one of the best videos about lesbian and gay teens. It includes very poignant stories of two adolescents: one who committed suicide, the other who was openly gay in high school. It comes with a classroom guide. Wolfe Video, P.O. Box 64, New Almaden, CA 95042. Phone: (800) 438-9653.

"Hate, Homophobia and Schools" is a video available from Northeastern Wisconsin In-School Telecommunications. NEWIST, Room IS 1040, 2420 Nicolet Drive, University of Wisconsin, Green Bay, WI 54311. Phone: (800) 633-7445.

"It's Elementary: Talking about Gay Issues in School" is a video made by Academy Award–winning filmmakers Debra Chasnoff and Helen Cohen. This ground-breaking video documents in a moving and powerful way how gay issues are taught in elementary and middle-school classrooms. Mainly used for teacher training, this video is also suitable for viewing by children and young adults. Women's Educational Media, 2180 Bryant Street, Suite 203, San Francisco, CA 94110. Phone: (415) 641-4616. Fax: (415) 641-4632.

"Setting the Record Straight" is an excellent and informative video produced by the Gay, Lesbian, Straight Educators' Network (GLSEN). GLSEN, 121 W. 27th Street, Suite 804, New York, NY 10001. Phone: (212) 727-0135.

"Sexual Orientation: Reading between the Labels" is an excellent video that presents basic information about homosexuality by defining words like "homosexual," "sexual orientation," and "coming out." An accompanying guide includes lessons for students developed by Northeastern Wisconsin In-School Telecommunications. NEWIST, Room IS 1040, 2420 Nicolet Drive, University of Wisconsin, Green Bay, WI 54311. Phone: (800) 633-7445.

"Teaching Respect for All" is a video produced by the Gay, Lesbian, Straight Educators' Network (GLSEN). It is designed to help

adults understand why schools need to address anti-gay bias. GLSEN, 121 W. 27th Street, Suite 804, New York, NY 10001. Phone: (212) 727-0135.

"The Times of Harvey Milk" is a powerful and moving documentary which recounts the political aspirations and assassination of the first openly gay city supervisor of San Francisco. Available in most video stores; highly recommended.

"Tongues Untied" is a controversial film with adult content directed by Emmy Award–winning filmmaker Marlon Gibbs. This film documents life among black gays and depicts the homophobia and racism they face. This film became the center of controversy in 1991 when public television stations refused to air it as part of the P.O.V. series. Zebra'z, P.O. Box 157710, San Antonio, TX 78212. Phone: (800) 788-4729.

"The Truth about Alex," an HBO special, is the story of a teenager who discovers his best friend is gay. There is a fifty-minute version with pauses for classroom discussion and a half-hour version. Phoenix Films and Video, 2349 Chaffee Drive, St. Louis, MO 63146. Phone: (800) 777-8100.

"What If I'm Gay? A Search for Understanding" is a CBS-TV School Break Special which focuses on the coming-out story of a teenage boy. Phoenix Films and Video, 2349 Chaffee Drive, St. Louis, MO 63146. Phone: (800) 777-8100.

OTHER RESOURCES
Curriculum Guides, Bibliographies, Posters

A Bibliography: Lesbian, Gay and Bisexual Issues in Education. Compiled by educator Tracy Phariss. GLSEN-Colorado, P.O. Box 280346, Lakewood, CO 80228. Phone: (303) 936-6562.

Confronting Homophobia: Gays and Lesbians and the Media. This issue of *FAIR/Extra!* 6, no. 4 (June 1993) was published by Fairness & Accuracy in Reporting, a media watch group. It examines how gays are portrayed in the media. FAIR, 130 West 25th Street, New York, NY 10003. Phone: (800) 847-3993.

Education Issues Information Packet: Addressing Sexual Orientation and Developing Support Systems in Schools. This packet is put out by the National Youth Advocacy Coalition Bridges Project, 1711 Connecticut Avenue, NW, Suite 206, Washington, DC 20009. Phone: (202) 319-7596.

Famous Lesbian, Gay, and Bisexual People in History. Poster of 57 historical figures and 7 historical events; includes a bibliography of resources. GLAAD, 1360 Mission Street, Suite 200, San Francisco, CA 94103. Phone: (415) 861-2244.

Gay/Straight Alliances: A Student Guide. Safe Schools Program for Gay and Lesbian Students. Massachusetts Department of Education, 350 Main Street, Malden, MA 02148-5023. Phone: (617) 388-3300.

Making Schools Safe for Gay and Lesbian Youth: Breaking the Silence in Schools and in Families, Education Report, The Governor's Commission on Gay and Lesbian Youth, State House, Room 111, Boston, MA 02133. Phone: (617) 727-9173.

Project 10 Handbook, Addressing Lesbian and Gay Issues in Our Schools. Virginia Uribe, c/o Friends of Project 10, Inc., 7850 Melrose Avenue, Los Angeles, CA 90046. Phone: (818) 577-4553.

Speaking Out: A Manual for Gay, Lesbian, and Bisexual Public Speakers, by noted author Warren J. Blumenfeld. Public Education Services, c/o GLBSB, P.O. Box 2232, Boston, MA 02107.

The Stonewall Riots and the History of Gays and Lesbians in the United States, by educator, author, and scholar Arthur Lipkin. Lipkin also has excellent curriculum materials on various subjects related to gay and lesbian studies for schools (K-12). Harvard Gay and Lesbian School Issues Project, Harvard Graduate School of Education, 210 Longfellow Hall, Cambridge, MA 02138. Phone: (617) 495-3441.

Additional Educational Resources, including school materials, staff development resources, and theoretical materials, can be found in the GLSEN Blackboard Newsletter. To receive this newsletter/catalogue, contact GLSEN Publications Department, 121 W. 27th Street, Suite 804, New York, NY 10001. Phone: (212) 727-0135.

BOOK CATALOGUES

Alyson Publications, Inc. Alyson is one of the largest publishers of books by and about gay, lesbian, bisexual, and transgender people and their families. It has two catalogues, one for adults and one for children, listing 500 titles. Alyson Publications, 6922 Hollywood Blvd., Suite 1000, Los Angeles, CA 90028. Phone: (213) 871-1225.

Anti-Defamation League Catalogue. The A WORLD OF DIFFERENCE Institute is a comprehensive, international anti-bias education and diversity training program of the ADL. The institute's goals are to combat prejudice and discrimination of all kinds and to promote the valuing of diversity. ADL is one of the largest publishers of human relations materials in the United States. ADL National Headquarters, 823 U.N. Plaza, New York, NY 10017. Phone: (212) 885-7700.

Chinaberry Book Catalogue. An extraordinarily thorough and creatively annotated catalogue of books and tapes for all ages of children and adults on all topics, including multiracial families, child development, and diversity. Phone: (800) 776-2242. Fax: (619) 670-5203.

Everyone's Kids' Books. An excellent catalogue of nonfiction and fiction books for children and adults on gender, adoption, race, gay and lesbian issues, as well as diverse children's literature. Everyone's Kids' Books, 23 Elliot Street, Brattleboro, VT 05301. Phone: (802) 254-8160.

Great Owl Book Catalogue and Bookstore. An excellent free catalogue for children's books with diversity themes. Great Owl, 33 Watchung Plaza, Montclair, NJ 07042. Phone: (800) 299-3181.

Karol Media. For more than twenty years, a nationwide distributor of educational and special interest videos, CD-ROMS, and other resource materials for the educational community. A catalogue of more than 3,000 titles is available. Karol Media, P.O. Box 7600, Wilkes-Barre, PA 18773-7600. Phone: (800) 884-0555.

Lambda Book Report: A Review of Contemporary Gay and Lesbian Literature. Published by Lambda Literary Foundation, P.O. Box 73910, Washington, DC 20056. Phone: (202) 462-7924.

The Olive Press. An excellent catalogue of multicultural books and teaching resources. Olive Press, 5727 Dunmore, West Bloomfield, MI 48322. Phone: (248) 855-6063.

Pact Press Magazine and *Pact Booksource Reference Guide.* The magazine reviews books about diversity on a quarterly basis. The reference guide is published once a year. Pact Press, 3450 Sacramento Street, Suite 239, San Francisco, CA 94118. Phone: (415) 221-6957.

Tapestry Books. A thorough guide to a wide range of books for children, especially about adoption themes. Tapestry Books, P.O. Box 359, Ringoes, NJ 08551. Phone: (800) 765-2367.

Thrift Books. A catalogue specializing in children's books about adoption and multicultural themes, with all titles sold at a discount. Thrift Books, 9 Foxboro Circle, Madison, WI 53717. Phone: (608) 833-5238.

LOVE MAKES A FAMILY

Lesbian, Gay, Bisexual, and Transgender People and Their Families

A Photo-Text Exhibit

Children viewing the "Love Makes a Family" exhibit, Hawthorne School, Madison, Wisconsin.

Love Makes a Family: Lesbian, Gay, Bisexual, and Transgender People and Their Families is a traveling photo-text exhibit distributed by Family Diversity Projects, Inc. By educating people of all ages to celebrate and appreciate diversity, this exhibit contributes to making the world a safer place for all families.

Love Makes a Family has traveled nationwide since 1995 to public and private schools, universities, houses of worship, workplaces, corporate headquarters, public libraries, community centers, conferences, pride events, galleries, and museums. You can bring this powerful exhibit to your community too. The exhibit comes with two versions of the text. One is appropriate for elementary school students (K-6); the other is suitable for older students and adults.

Family Diversity Projects, Inc. (FDP) is a nonprofit organization founded by interviewer-editor Peggy Gillespie and photographer Gigi Kaeser. FDP distributes multiple copies of four exhibits: *Love Makes a Family: Lesbian, Gay, Bisexual, and Transgender People and Their Families*; *Of Many Colors: Portraits of Multiracial Families*; *Nothing To Hide: Mental Illness in the Family*; and *In Our Family: Portraits of All Kinds of Families*.

To get information about how to bring any of these exhibits to your community, please contact:

Peggy Gillespie,
Family Diversity Projects
P.O. Box 1209
Amherst, MA 01004-1209
Phone: 413-256-0502 (9A.M.-5P.M. EST)
E-mail: famphoto@aol.com.
Website: http://www.familydiv.org

Gigi Kaeser and Peggy Gillespie are co-directors of Family Diversity Projects, Inc., in Amherst, Massachusetts. They collaborated on a previous book, *Of Many Colors: Portraits of Multiracial Families* (University of Massachusetts Press, 1997). Kaeser's photographs have been featured in numerous publications, and Gillespie is author with choreographer Bill T. Jones of *Last Night on Earth*. Minnie Bruce Pratt is author of *S/HE*. Kath Weston is author of *Families We Choose: Lesbians, Gays, Kinship*. April Martin is author of *The Lesbian and Gay Parenting Handbook*.